BOOK 3 – FIXED INCOME PORTFOLIO MANAGEMENT, FIXED INCOME DERIVATIVES, AND EQUITY PORTFOLIO MANAGEMENT

SCHWESERNOTES™ 2011 CFA LEVEL 3 BOOK 3: FIXED INCOME PORTFOLIO
MANAGEMENT, FIXED INCOME DERIVATIVES, AND EQUITY PORTFOLIO
MANAGEMENT

©2010 Kaplan, Inc. All rights reserved.

Published in 2010 by Kaplan Schweser.

Printed in the United States of America.

ISBN: 978-1-4277-2729-9 / 1-4277-2729-5

PPN: 3200-0076

READINGS AND LEARNING OUTCOME STATEMENTS

READINGS

The following material is a review of the Fixed Income Portfolio Management, Fixed Income Derivatives, and Equity Portfolio Management principles designed to address the learning outcome statements set forth by CFA Institute.

LEARNING OUTCOME STATEMENTS (LOS)

The CFA Institute learning outcome statements are listed below. These are repeated in each topic review. However, the order may have been changed in order to get a better fit with the flow of the review.

STUDY SESSION 9

The topical coverage corresponds with the following CFA Institute assigned reading:

28. **Fixed-Income Portfolio Management—Part I**
    The candidate should be able to:
    a. <u>compare</u> and <u>contrast</u>, with respect to investment objectives, the use of liabilities as a benchmark and the use of a bond index as a benchmark. (page 9)
    b. <u>compare</u> and <u>contrast</u> pure bond indexing, enhanced indexing, and active investing with respect to the objectives, techniques, advantages, and disadvantages of each. (page 10)
    c. <u>discuss</u> the criteria for selecting a benchmark bond index and <u>justify</u> the selection of a specific index when given a description of an investor's risk aversion, income needs, and liabilities. (page 13)
    d. <u>review</u> and <u>justify</u> the techniques, such as duration matching and the use of key rate durations, by which an enhanced indexer may seek to align the risk exposures of the portfolio with those of the benchmark bond index. (page 15)
    e. <u>contrast</u> and <u>illustrate</u> the use of total return analysis and scenario analysis to assess the risk and return characteristics of a proposed trade. (page 18)
    f. <u>design</u> a bond immunization strategy to ensure funding of a predetermined liability and <u>evaluate</u> the strategy under various interest rate scenarios. (page 20)
    g. <u>demonstrate</u> the process of rebalancing a portfolio to reestablish a desired dollar duration. (page 28)
    h. <u>explain</u> the importance of spread duration. (page 30)
    i. <u>discuss</u> the extensions that have been made to classical immunization theory, including the introduction of contingent immunization. (page 32)
    j. <u>explain</u> the risks associated with managing a portfolio against a liability structure, including interest rate risk, contingent claim risk, and cap risk. (page 36)
    k. <u>compare</u> and <u>contrast</u> immunization strategies for a single liability, multiple liabilities, and general cash flows. (page 36)
    l. <u>compare</u> and <u>contrast</u> risk minimization with return maximization in immunized portfolios. (page 39)
    m. <u>demonstrate</u> the use of cash flow matching to fund a fixed set of future liabilities and <u>contrast</u> the advantages and disadvantages of cash flow matching to those of immunization strategies. (page 40)

The topical coverage corresponds with the following CFA Institute assigned reading:

29. **Relative-Value Methodologies for Global Credit Bond Portfolio Management**
    The candidate should be able to:
    a. <u>explain</u> classic relative-value analysis, based on top-down and bottom-up approaches to credit bond portfolio management. (page 55)
    b. <u>discuss</u> the implications of cyclical supply and demand changes in the primary corporate bond market and the impact of secular changes in the market's dominant product structures. (page 56)

c. summarize the influence of investors' short- and long-term liquidity needs on portfolio management decisions. (page 57)

d. discuss common rationales for secondary market trading, including yield-spread pickup trades, credit-upside trades, credit-defense trades, new issue swaps, sector-rotation trades, yield curve-adjustment trades, structure trades, and cash flow reinvestment. (page 57)

e. discuss and evaluate corporate bond portfolio strategies that are based on relative value, including total return analysis, primary market analysis, liquidity and trading analysis, secondary trading rationales and trading constraints, spread analysis, structure analysis, credit curve analysis, credit analysis, and asset allocation/sector analysis. (page 59)

STUDY SESSION 10

The topical coverage corresponds with the following CFA Institute assigned reading:

30. Fixed-Income Portfolio Management—Part II

The candidate should be able to:

a. evaluate the effect of leverage on portfolio duration and investment returns. (page 68)

b. discuss the use of repurchase agreements (repos) to finance bond purchases and the factors that affect the repo rate. (page 71)

c. critique the use of standard deviation, target semivariance, shortfall risk, and value at risk as measures of fixed-income portfolio risk. (page 73)

d. demonstrate the advantages of using futures instead of cash market instruments to alter portfolio risk. (page 76)

e. construct and evaluate an immunization strategy based on interest rate futures. (page 77)

f. explain the use of interest rate swaps and options to alter portfolio cash flows and exposure to interest rate risk. (page 82)

g. compare and contrast default risk, credit spread risk, and downgrade risk and demonstrate the use of credit derivative instruments to address each risk in the context of a fixed-income portfolio. (page 83)

h. explain the potential sources of excess return for an international bond portfolio. (page 86)

i. evaluate 1) the change in value for a foreign bond when domestic interest rates change and 2) the bond's contribution to duration in a domestic portfolio, given the duration of the foreign bond and the country beta. (page 88)

j. recommend and justify whether to hedge or not hedge currency risk in an international bond investment. (page 90)

k. illustrate how breakeven spread analysis can be used to evaluate the risk in seeking yield advantages across international bond markets. (page 96)

l. discuss the advantages and risks of investing in emerging market debt. (page 97)

m. discuss the criteria for selecting a fixed-income manager. (page 98)

The topical coverage corresponds with the following CFA Institute assigned reading:
31. **Hedging Mortgage Securities to Capture Relative Value**
The candidate should be able to:
a. <u>demonstrate</u> how a mortgage security's negative convexity will affect the performance of a hedge. (page 114)
b. <u>explain</u> the risks associated with investing in mortgage securities and discuss whether these risks can be effectively hedged. (page 115)
c. <u>contrast</u> an individual mortgage security to a Treasury security with respect to the importance of yield-curve risk. (page 116)
d. <u>compare</u> and <u>contrast</u> duration-based approaches with interest rate sensitivity approaches to hedging mortgage securities. (page 117)

STUDY SESSION 11

The topical coverage corresponds with the following CFA Institute assigned reading:
32. **Equity Portfolio Management**
The candidate should be able to:
a. <u>discuss</u> the role of equities in the overall portfolio. (page 128)
b. <u>discuss</u> the rationales for passive, active, and semiactive (enhanced index) equity investment approaches and <u>distinguish</u> among those approaches with respect to expected active return and tracking risk. (page 129)
c. <u>recommend</u> an equity investment approach when given an investor's investment policy statement and beliefs concerning market efficiency. (page 130)
d. <u>distinguish</u> among the predominant weighting schemes used in the construction of major equity share indices and evaluate the biases of each. (page 131)
e. <u>compare</u> and <u>contrast</u> alternative methods for establishing passive exposure to an equity market, including indexed separate or pooled accounts, index mutual funds, exchange-traded funds, equity index futures, and equity total return swaps. (page 133)
f. <u>compare</u> and <u>contrast</u> full replication, stratified sampling, and optimization as approaches to constructing an indexed portfolio and <u>recommend</u> an approach when given a description of the investment vehicle and the index to be tracked. (page 135)
g. <u>explain</u> and <u>justify</u> the use of equity investment-style classifications and discuss the difficulties in applying style definitions consistently. (page 137)
h. <u>explain</u> the rationales and primary concerns of value investors and growth investors and <u>discuss</u> the key risks of each investment style. (page 137)
i. <u>compare</u> and <u>contrast</u> techniques for identifying investment styles and <u>characterize</u> the style of an investor when given a description of the investor's security selection method, details on the investor's security holdings, or the results of a returns-based style analysis. (page 139)
j. <u>compare</u> and <u>contrast</u> the methodologies used to construct equity style indices. (page 146)
k. <u>interpret</u> the results of an equity style box analysis and <u>discuss</u> the consequences of style drift. (page 147)
l. <u>explain</u> the use of stock screens based on socially responsible investing criteria and <u>discuss</u> their potential effect on a portfolio's style characteristics. (page 148)
m. <u>compare</u> and <u>contrast</u> long-short versus long-only investment strategies, including their risks and potential alphas, and <u>explain</u> why greater pricing inefficiency may exist on the short side of the market. (page 148)

©2010 Kaplan, Inc.

n. explain how a market-neutral portfolio can be "equitized" to gain equity market exposure and compare and contrast equitized market-neutral portfolios with short-extension portfolios. (page 150)

o. compare and contrast the sell disciplines of active investors. (page 152)

p. contrast derivatives-based versus stock-based enhanced indexing strategies and justify enhanced indexing on the basis of risk control and the information ratio. (page 153)

q. discuss and justify, in a risk-return framework, the optimal portfolio allocations to a group of investment managers. (page 155)

r. explain the core-satellite approach to portfolio construction and discuss the advantages and disadvantages of adding a completeness fund to control overall risk exposures. (page 156)

s. distinguish among the components of total active return ("true" active return and "misfit" active return) and their associated risk measures and explain their relevance for evaluating a portfolio of managers. (page 159)

t. explain alpha and beta separation as an approach to active management and demonstrate the use of portable alpha. (page 161)

u. review the process of identifying, selecting, and contracting with equity managers, including the development of a universe of suitable candidates based on both qualitative and quantitative factors, the composition of equity manager questionnaires, and the analysis of fee structures. (page 162)

v. contrast the top-down and bottom-up approaches to equity research. (page 164)

STUDY SESSION 12

The topical coverage corresponds with the following CFA Institute assigned reading:

33. Corporate Governance

The candidate should be able to:

a. explain the ways in which management may act that are not in the best interest of the firm's owners (moral hazard) and illustrate how dysfunctional corporate governance can lead to moral hazard. (page 180)

b. evaluate explicit and implicit incentives that can align management's interests with those of the firm's shareholders. (page 182)

c. explain the shortcomings of boards of directors as monitors of management and state and discuss prescriptions for improving board oversight. (page 184)

d. discuss why active monitoring by investors requires control, the various mechanisms by which control is exercised, and the limitations of active monitoring. (page 187)

e. critique the effectiveness of debt as a corporate governance mechanism. (page 189)

f. explain the social responsibilities of the corporation in a "stakeholder society" and evaluate the advantages and disadvantages of a corporate governance structure based on stakeholder rather than shareholder interests. (page 190)

g. discuss the Cadbury Report recommendations for best practice in maintaining an effective board of directors whose interests are aligned with those of shareholders. (page 192)

The topical coverage corresponds with the following CFA Institute assigned reading:

34. International Equity Benchmarks

The candidate should be able to:

a. <u>discuss</u> the need for float adjustment in the construction of international equity benchmarks. (page 203)

b. <u>discuss</u> the trade-offs involved in constructing international indices, including 1) breadth versus investability, 2) liquidity and crossing opportunities versus index reconstitution effects, 3) precise float adjustment versus transactions costs from rebalancing, and 4) objectivity and transparency versus judgment. (page 204)

c. <u>discuss</u> the effect that a country's classification as either a developed or an emerging market can have on market indices and on investment in the country's capital markets. (page 205)

The topical coverage corresponds with the following CFA Institute assigned reading:

35. Emerging Markets Finance

The candidate should be able to:

a. <u>discuss</u> the process of financial liberalization and <u>explain</u> the expected impact on pricing and expected returns as a segmented market evolves into an integrated market. (page 210)

b. <u>explain</u> the benefits that may accrue to an emerging market economy as a result of financial liberalization. (page 212)

c. <u>discuss</u> the major issues confronting emerging market investors, including excess correlations during times of crisis (contagion), corporate governance, price discovery, and liquidity. (page 214)

The following is a review of the Management of Passive and Active Fixed-Income Portfolios principles designed to address the learning outcome statements set forth by CFA Institute®. This topic is also covered in:

FIXED-INCOME PORTFOLIO MANAGEMENT—PART I[1]

EXAM FOCUS

Be sure you can discuss the construction or selection of a benchmark for an actively managed portfolio as well as the different considerations when managing a portfolio to outperform a benchmark compared to managing a portfolio to fund a liability structure. Immunization has been a long-time favorite of CFA Institute, and immunization strategies, including contingent immunization, may show up on the exam. In particular, be able to discuss contingent immunization, including its calculation, and describe and compare classical immunization to cash flow matching.

BOND PORTFOLIO BENCHMARKS

LOS 28.a: Compare and contrast, with respect to investment objectives, the use of liabilities as a benchmark and the use of a bond index as a benchmark.

Using a Bond Index as a Benchmark

Bond fund managers (e.g., bond mutual funds) are commonly compared to a benchmark that is selected or constructed to closely resemble the managed portfolio. Assume, for example, a bond fund manager specializes in one sector of the bond market. Instead of simply accepting the return generated by the manager, investors want to be able to determine whether the manager consistently earns sufficient returns to justify management expenses. In this case, a custom benchmark is constructed so that any difference in return is due to strategies employed by the manager, not structural differences between the portfolio and the benchmark.

Another manager might be compared to a well-diversified bond index. If the manager mostly agrees with market forecasts and values, she will follow a *passive* management approach. She constructs a portfolio that mimics the index along several dimensions of risk, and the return on the portfolio should track the return on the index fairly closely.

If the manager believes she has a superior ability to forecast interest rates and/or identify under-valued individual bonds or entire sectors, she follows an *active* management approach. She will construct the portfolio to resemble the index in many ways but, through various active management strategies, she hopes to consistently *outperform* the index. Active bond portfolio management strategies are discussed throughout this topic review.

---

1. Much of the terminology utilized throughout this topic review is industry convention as presented in Reading 28 of the 2011 CFA Level 3 curriculum.

Using Liabilities as a Benchmark

The investment objective when managing a bond portfolio against a single liability or set of liabilities is rather straightforward; the manager must manage the portfolio to maintain sufficient portfolio value to meet the liabilities.

BOND INDEXING STRATEGIES

LOS 28.b: <u>Compare</u> and <u>contrast</u> pure bond indexing, enhanced indexing, and active investing with respect to the objectives, techniques, advantages, and disadvantages of each.

As you may surmise from this LOS, there are many different strategies that can be followed when managing a bond portfolio. For example, the manager can assume a completely passive approach and not have to forecast anything. In other words, the manager who feels he has no reason to disagree with market forecasts has no reason to assume he can outperform an indexing strategy through active management. On the other hand, a manager who is confident in his forecasting abilities and has reason to believe market forecasts are incorrect can generate significant return through active management.

The differences between the various active management approaches are mostly matters of degree. That is, bond portfolio management strategies form more or less a continuum from an almost do-nothing approach (i.e., pure bond indexing) to a do-almost-anything approach (i.e., full-blown active management) as demonstrated graphically in Figure 1.

Figure 1: Increasing Degrees of Active Bond Portfolio Management

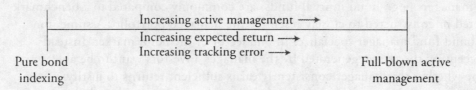

In Figure 1, you will notice the increase of three characteristics as you move from pure bond indexing to full-blown active management. The first, *increasing active management*, can be defined as the gradual relaxation of restrictions on the manager's actions to allow him to exploit his superior forecasting/valuation abilities. With pure bond indexing, the manager is restricted to constructing a portfolio with all the securities in the index and in the same weights as the index. This means the portfolio will have exactly the same risk exposures as the index. As you move from left to right, the restrictions on the manager's actions are relaxed and the portfolio risk factor exposures differ more and more from those of the index.

The next characteristic, *increasing expected return*, refers to the increase in portfolio expected return from actions taken by the manager. Unless the manager has some superior ability that enables him to identify profitable situations, he should stick with pure bond indexing or at least match primary risk factors.

The third, *increasing tracking error*, refers to the degree to which the portfolio return tracks that of the index. With pure bond indexing, even though management fees and transactions are incurred, the reduced return on the portfolio will closely track the return on the index. As you move to the right, the composition and factor exposures of the portfolio differ more and more from the index. Each enhancement is intended to increase the portfolio return, but is not guaranteed to do so. Thus, the amount by which the portfolio return exceeds the index return can be quite variable from period to period and even negative. The difference between the portfolio and index returns (i.e., the portfolio excess return) is referred to as **alpha**. The standard deviation of alpha across several periods is referred to as **tracking error**, thus it is the *variability* of the portfolio excess return that increases as you move towards full-blown active management. This increased variability translates into increased uncertainty.

The five classifications of bond portfolio management can be described as: (1) *pure bond indexing*, (2) *enhanced indexing by matching primary risk factors*, (3) *enhanced indexing by small risk factor mismatches*, (4) *active management by larger risk factor mismatches*, and (5) *full-blown active management*.

> **For the Exam:** These five classifications of bond portfolio management strategies are presented by H. Gifford Fong and Larry D. Guin.[1] On the exam, you will most likely not be asked to determine the category into which a certain type of portfolio management falls, as they are almost impossible to divide into distinct strategies. That is, bond portfolio management strategies are more of a continuum rather than finite points along a curve. This is demonstrated by words such as *small*, *large*, and *major* that are very subjective or even the term *mismatch*. Just how much difference is considered a mismatch? The thrust of this LOS is for you to understand the various tactics that can be taken rather than be able to discern each from the others and be able to categorize management strategies.

1. *Managing Investment Portfolios: A Dynamic Process*, Third Edition, John L. Maginn, Donald L. Tuttle, Jerald E. Pinto, and Dennis W. McLeavey, editors.

Pure Bond Indexing

This is the easiest strategy to describe as well as understand. In a pure bond indexing strategy, the manager replicates every dimension of the index. Every bond in the index is purchased and its weight in the portfolio is determined by its weight in the index. Due to varying bond liquidities and availabilities, this strategy, though easy to describe, is difficult and costly to implement.

Enhanced Indexing by Matching Primary Risk Factors

Due to the number of different bond issues in the typical bond index as well as the inefficiencies and costs associated with pure bond indexing, that strategy is rarely implemented. Instead, managers will enhance the portfolio return by utilizing a sampling approach to replicate the index's primary risk factors while holding only a percentage of the bonds in the index. Sampling reduces the costs associated with constructing the portfolio, and matching the risk factors means the portfolio is exposed to the same risk factors as the index. This means the portfolio will track the index closely, and since lower transactions costs are incurred, this strategy will outperform a pure bond indexing strategy.

Enhanced Indexing by Small Risk Factor Mismatches

This is the first level of indexing that is designed to earn about the same return as the index. While maintaining the exposure to large risk factors, such as duration, the manager slightly tilts the portfolio towards other, smaller risk factors by pursuing relative value strategies (e.g., identifying undervalued sectors) or identifying other return-enhancing opportunities. The small tilts are only intended to compensate for administrative costs.

Active Management by Larger Risk Factor Mismatches

The only difference between this strategy and enhanced indexing by small risk factor mismatches (the preceding strategy) is the degree of the mismatches. In other words, the manager pursues more significant quality and value strategies (e.g., overweight quality sectors expected to outperform, identify undervalued securities). In addition, the manager might alter the duration of the portfolio somewhat. The intent is earning sufficient return to cover administrative as well as increased transactions costs without increasing the portfolio's risk exposure beyond an acceptable level.

Full-Blown Active Management

Full-blown active management is a no-holds-barred strategy. The manager actively pursues tilting, relative value, and duration strategies.

 Professor's Note: As used here, tilting *refers to overweighting some risk factor while (usually) reducing exposure to another. For example, the manager might feel one bond sector (e.g., CMBS) will perform well over the coming period and increase its weight in the portfolio while reducing the weight of another sector expected to under-perform. Relative value strategies can entail identifying undervalued securities or entire sectors.*

For the Exam: You will see in later study sessions that by using a derivatives overlay, the manager can tilt the portfolio toward or away from risk factors without changing the composition of the portfolio.

Figure 2 is a summary of the advantages and disadvantages of the bond portfolio strategies discussed. Note that in each case, relative phrases (e.g., lower, increased) refer to the cell immediately above the one in which the phrase is written. For example *less costly to implement,* under advantages for enhanced indexing by matching primary risk factors, refers to lower costs than those associated with pure bond indexing.

Figure 2: Advantages and Disadvantages of Bond Portfolio Management Strategies

Strategy	Advantages	Disadvantages
Pure bond indexing (PBI)	• Tracks the index (zero or very low tracking error) • Same risk factor exposures as the index • Low advisory and administrative fees	• Costly and difficult to implement • Lower expected return than the index
Enhanced indexing by matching primary risk factors (sampling)	• Less costly to implement • Increased expected return • Maintains exposure to the index's primary risk factors	• Increased management fees • Reduced ability to track the index (i.e., increased tracking error) • Lower expected return than the index
Enhanced indexing by small risk factor mismatches	• Same duration as index • Increased expected return • Reduced manager restrictions	• Increased risk • Increased tracking error • Increased management fees
Active management by larger risk factor mismatches	• Increased expected return • Reduced manager restrictions • Ability to tune the portfolio duration	• Increased risk • Increased tracking error • Increased management fees
Full-blown active management	• Increased expected return • Few if any manager restrictions • No limits on duration	• Increased risk • Increased tracking error • Increased management fees

Professor's Note: The decision to move down the list from pure bond indexing toward full-blown active management is dependent upon the optimal combination of the client's objectives and constraints and the manager's abilities to provide profitable active management.

SELECTING A BENCHMARK BOND INDEX

LOS 28.c: Discuss the criteria for selecting a benchmark bond index and justify the selection of a specific index when given a description of an investor's risk aversion, income needs, and liabilities.

Out-performing a bond index on a consistent basis is difficult at best, especially when risk and *net* return are considered. The primary benefits to using an indexing approach include diversification and low costs. The typical broad bond market index contains thousands of issues with widely varying maturities, coupon rates, and bond sector coverage. Therefore, as mentioned previously, a bond portfolio manager should move from a pure indexing position to more active management only when the client's objectives and constraints permit and the manager's abilities justify it.

Regardless of the strategy employed, the manager should be judged against a benchmark, and the benchmark should match the characteristics of the portfolio. Among others, there are four primary considerations when selecting a benchmark: (1) *market value risk*, (2) *income risk*, (3) *credit risk*, and (4) *liability framework risk*.

Market value risk. The market values of long maturity (i.e., long duration) portfolios are more sensitive to changes in yield than the market values of shorter maturity portfolios. From a market value perspective, therefore, the greater the investor's risk aversion, the shorter the appropriate maturity of the portfolio and the selected benchmark.

Income risk. If the client is dependent upon cash flows from the portfolio, those cash flows should be consistent and low-risk. Since long-term interest rates are generally less variable than short-term rates, long-term bonds offer the investor a longer and more certain income stream. The longer the maturity of the portfolio and benchmark, therefore, the lower the income risk.. Investors desiring a stable, long-term cash flow should invest in longer-term bonds and utilize long-term benchmarks.

Credit risk. The credit risk (i.e., default risk) of the benchmark should closely match that of the portfolio, which is determined according to the portfolio's position in the client's overall portfolio of assets.

Liability framework risk. This risk, which is faced when managing a portfolio to meet liabilities, should always be *minimized*. It concerns mismatches in the firm's asset and liability structures. For example, a firm trying to meet long-term liabilities (e.g., insurance companies, pension funds) should utilize long-term assets in its asset portfolios. If the liabilities are shorter term, the assets should also be shorter term.

> **For the Exam:** Here are four points to remember for the exam:
>
> 1. *Market value risk* varies directly with maturity. The greater the risk aversion, the lower the acceptable market risk, and the shorter the appropriate maturity of the portfolio and benchmark.
>
> 2. *Income risk* varies indirectly with maturity. The more dependent the client is upon a reliable income stream, the longer the appropriate maturity of the portfolio and benchmark.
>
> 3. *Credit risk*. The credit risk of the benchmark should closely match the credit risk of the portfolio.
>
> 4. *Liability framework risk* is applicable only to portfolios managed to meet a liability structure and should always be minimized.

ALIGNING RISK EXPOSURES

LOS 28.d: <u>Review</u> and <u>justify</u> the techniques, such as duration matching and the use of key rate durations, by which an enhanced indexer may seek to align the risk exposures of the portfolio with those of the benchmark bond index.

For a valid comparison of the portfolio return to the benchmark return, the benchmark must have the same *risk profile* as the managed portfolio. The portfolio and benchmark risk profiles can be measured along several dimensions, such as duration, key rate duration, duration contributions, spread durations, sector weights, distribution of cash flows, and diversification. Each of the primary factors affecting the risk profile is discussed below, but we first address the sampling processes that can be utilized to guarantee that the portfolio and benchmark are *comparable*.

The pure bond indexing strategy, as discussed earlier, entails purchasing every bond in the index. As the portfolio is typically much smaller than the benchmark, the manager uses each security's weight in the benchmark to determine the amount to purchase. The drawbacks to such a strategy center on the associated costs and inefficiencies. To avoid the costs associated with purchasing every bond in the index yet maintain the same risk exposures, the manager will usually hold a sample of the bonds in the index.

One sampling technique often utilized is **stratified sampling** (a.k.a. *cell-matching*). The manager first separates the bonds in the index into cells in a matrix according to risk factors, such as sector, quality rating, duration, callability, et cetera. Next, the manager measures the total value of the bonds in each of the cells and determines each cell's weight in the index. Finally, the manager selects a sample of bonds from each cell and purchases them in an amount that produces the same weight in the portfolio as that cell's weight in the index. By doing this, the manager is assured that the nature and extent of the portfolio's risk exposures are close to those of the benchmark.

Through stratified sampling, the portfolio contains only a sample of the bonds in the index. Constructing a portfolio with risk exposures identical to the benchmark, however, does not require the composition of the portfolio (i.e., the bonds held) to be representative of the index. The primary concern is exposure to risk factors. That is, a portfolio can be constructed with exactly the same risk factor exposures as the benchmark but with different securities. This is done by utilizing a **multifactor model**, but to use a multifactor model the manager must determine the risk profile of the benchmark. Risk profiling the index requires measuring the index's exposure to factors including duration, key rate duration, cash flow distribution, sector and quality weights, and duration contribution, et cetera.

> *Professor's Note: Parallel yield curve shifts are those rare events where interest rates of all maturities move by the same amount, either up or down. More common are yield curve twists, which involve unequal changes in interest rates of different maturities or movements in some rates with no accompanying movements in others. In other words, a twist entails a change in the overall shape of the yield curve.*

Duration. Effective duration (a.k.a. option-adjusted or adjusted duration), which is used to estimate the change in the value of a portfolio given a small *parallel shift* in the yield curve, is probably the most obvious risk factor to be measured. Due to the linear nature of duration, which makes it underestimate the increase and overestimate the decrease in the value of the portfolio, **convexity** must also be considered.

Key rate duration. Where effective duration measures the portfolio's sensitivity to parallel shifts in the yield curve, key rate duration measures the portfolio's sensitivity to *twists* in the yield curve. It is fairly easy to weight a portfolio so that its duration is the same as the index, but that does not insure it matches the index's key rate durations (i.e., that it will have the same sensitivities to yield curve twists as the index). Mismatches occur when the portfolio and benchmark contain different combinations of bonds with varying maturities and key rate durations but the same overall effective duration.

Present value distribution of cash flows. In addition to duration and key rate duration, the manager might also consider matching the present value distribution (PVD) of cash flows of the index. PVD measures the *proportion* of the index's total duration attributable to cash flows (both coupons and redemptions) falling within selected time periods. For example, if the index contains bonds with maturities up to ten years, the manager could measure the cash flows in each 6-month period over the entire ten years.

The manager first determines the present value of the cash flows from the benchmark index that fall in every 6-month period. He then divides each present value by the present value of total cash flows from the benchmark to determine the percentage of the index's total market value attributable to cash flows falling in each period. We'll consider those the *weights* of each period.

Since the cash flows in each 6-month period can be considered zero-coupon bonds, their duration is the end of the period. For example, the very first 6-month time period has a duration of 0.5. The next time period has a duration of 1.0; the next 1.5, and so forth.

The manager multiplies the duration of each period by its weight to arrive at the *duration contribution* for that period. The duration contribution for the period is divided by the index duration (i.e., the sum of all the periods' duration contributions) and the process is continued for all the time periods. The resulting pattern across the time periods is the index's PVD. If the manager duplicates the index PVD, the portfolio and the index will have the same sensitivities to both shifts and twists in the yield curve.

Assume a 5-year maturity and 6-month periods as in Figure 3:

Figure 3: Hypothetical Cash Flow Weights: 6-Month Periods for Five Years

1 yr.	2 yrs.	3 yrs.	4 yrs.	5 yrs.

5%   6%   8%   10%   10%   11%   11%   15%   13%   11%

In Figure 3, the weight of the first 6-month period is 5% (5% of the index cash flows fall in the first 6-month period), 6% in the second period, 8% in the third, and so forth. (Remember, the weight for each period is the present value of that period's total cash flows divided by the total market value of the index.) Multiplying each weight by its respective duration yields each period's *duration contribution*. For example, the contribution of the first 6-month period is calculated as $0.05(0.5) = 0.025$. The contribution of the second period is $0.06(1.0) = 0.06$, and so forth. The analyst then divides each period's duration contribution by the index duration, and the pattern across the total maturity of the index is the index's PVD. Using linear programming or some other technique, the manager constructs a portfolio to match the PVD of the index.

> **For the Exam:** PVD effectively describes how the total duration of the index (i.e., benchmark) is *distributed* across its total maturity. Be sure you can discuss how PVD is used to match the portfolio and benchmark risk characteristics. If the manager can mimic the PVD of the index, his portfolio will have the same sensitivities to interest rate changes as the index. You should not have to perform related calculations, but be sure you can discuss the process.

Sector and quality percent. The manager matches the weights of sectors and qualities in the index.

Sector duration contributions. The manager matches the proportion of the index duration that is contributed by each *sector* in the index.

Quality spread duration contribution. The manager matches the proportion of the index duration that is contributed by each *quality* in the index, where quality refers to categories of bonds by rating.

Sector/coupon/maturity cell weights. Convexity is difficult to measure for callable bonds. To mimic the *callability* of bonds in the index (i.e., the sensitivity of their prices to interest rate changes), the manager is better off matching their sector, coupon, and maturity weights in the index.

Issuer exposure. The final risk factor considered is issuer exposure, which is a measure of the index's *event exposure*. In mimicking the index, the manager should use a sufficient number of securities in the portfolio so that the event risk attributable to any individual issuer is minimized.

Figure 4 contains a summary of the risk exposures for *non-MBS* bonds.[2] Note that MBS primary risk exposures include sector, prepayment, and convexity risk.

---

2. Figure 4 is based on Exhibit 3 in the 2011 Level 3 CFA curriculum, Vol. 4, p. 15.

Figure 4: Bond Risk Exposures: Non-MBS

Risk	"Primary" Risk Factors				
	Interest Rate	Yield Curve		Spread	Credit	Optionality
What is Measured	Exposure to yield curve shifts	Exposure to yield curve twists		Exposure to spread changes	Exposure to credit changes	Exposure to call or put
Measure Used	Duration	PVD	Key rate durations	Spread duration	Duration contribution by credit rating	Delta

For the Exam: This material on bond portfolio risk factors is quite likely to show up on the exam in essay form. You might be asked to recommend and describe several of the factors. Alternatively, you might be asked to agree or disagree with statements made by an analyst and explain your decision. One example would be an analyst who declares that matching effective durations is sufficient to align the market risk exposures (interest rate risk) of the portfolio and the index used as a benchmark. You would *disagree* and state that key rate durations must be considered. In addition, to ensure that the portfolio has the same sensitivities to both twists and parallel shifts in the yield curve, the manager should match the PVD of the index.

SCENARIO ANALYSIS

LOS 28.e: <u>Contrast</u> and <u>illustrate</u> the use of total return analysis and scenario analysis to assess the risk and return characteristics of a proposed trade.

For the Exam: In this case, the command word *illustrate* could imply the need to perform supporting calculations on the exam.

Rather than focus exclusively on the portfolio's expected total return, **scenario analysis** allows a portfolio manager to assess portfolio total return under a varying set of assumptions (different scenarios). Possible scenarios would include simultaneous assumptions regarding interest rates and spreads at the end of the investment horizon as well as reinvestment rates over the investment horizon.

Regulators frequently require some institutions to conduct scenario analysis based on institution-specific assumptions. Bank regulators, for example, often require depository institutions to conduct a special case of scenario analysis called *sensitivity analysis*. Unlike scenario analysis, which considers simultaneous changes in several variables (complete, different scenarios), sensitivity analysis measures the effect of changes in only one variable—the others are held constant. For instance, regulators often require institutions to test the total return sensitivity of their portfolios to an instantaneous parallel shift in the yield curve.

Potential Performance of a Trade

Estimating expected total return under a single set of assumptions only provides a point estimate of the investment's expected return (i.e., a single number). Combining total return analysis with scenario analysis allows the analyst to assess not only the return but also its volatility (distribution) under different scenarios.

Example: Scenario analysis

Consider a 7-year, 10% semiannual, $100 par corporate bond. The bond is priced to yield 9% ($105.11), and it is assumed that coupons can be reinvested at 7% over the 1-year investment horizon.

The yield curve is expected to remain flat at its current level. However, the issue's credit spread is expected to change, but by an unknown amount. Thus, the manager has opted to use total return analysis in a scenario analysis framework to assess the range of potential outcomes and has generated the information in the figure below.

Total Return Sensitivity to Horizon Yield: One-Year Horizon

Horizon Yield*(%)	Horizon Price	Bond Equivalent Yield (%)	Effective Annual Return (%)
11	$95.69	0.717	0.718
10	100.00	4.77	4.82
9	**104.56**	**8.96**	**9.16**
8	109.39	13.31	13.76
7	114.50	17.82	18.62
6	119.91	22.50	23.77
5	125.64	27.35	29.22

*Required return on the bond in one year.

Sample calculation, assuming 9% horizon yield (bold in the table):

1. **Horizon price (in one year the bond will have a 6-year maturity):**
   N = 6 × 2 = 12; FV = 100; I/Y = 9/2 = 4.5%; PMT = 5; CPT → PV = 104.56

2. **Semiannual return:**
   horizon value of reinvested coupons = $5 + $5\left(1 + \dfrac{0.07}{2}\right) = \$10.175$

   total horizon value = 104.56 + 10.175 = $114.735
   PV = –105.11; FV = 114.735; N = 2; CPT → I/Y = 4.478%

3. **BEY** = 4.478% × 2 = 8.96%

4. **EAR** = $(1.04478)^2 - 1 = 9.16\%$

Calculation assuming an 11% horizon yield:

1. Horizon value = horizon price + reinvested coupons = 95.69 + 10.175 = 105.865

2. Semiannual return = PV = –105.11; FV = 105.865; N = 2; CPT $\rightarrow$ I/Y = 0.3585%

3. BEY = 0.3585% × 2 = 0.717%

4. EAR = $(1.003585)^2 - 1 = 0.718\%$

Each row in the table represents a different scenario (possible horizon yield). The last two columns in the table display the bond-equivalent yield and effective annual return, which result under each of the possible scenarios. As shown, as the horizon yield decreases from 11% to 5%, the bond-equivalent yield increases from 0.72% to 27.35%, and the effective annual return increases from 0.72% to 29.22%.

Scenario analysis provides the tools for the manager to do a better job in quantifying the impact of a change in the horizon yield assumption on the expected total return of the bond. A more complete scenario/total return analysis could include the simultaneous impacts of nonparallel shifts in the yield curve, different reinvestment rates, et cetera.

Assessing the performance of a benchmark index over the planning horizon is done in the same way as for the managed portfolio. When you *compare* their performances, the primary reasons for different performance, other than the manager's active bets, are duration and convexity. For example, the convexities (rate of change in duration) for the benchmark and portfolio may be different due to security selection, and the manager may deliberately change the portfolio convexity and/or duration (relative to the benchmark) in anticipation of twists or shifts in the yield curve.

CLASSICAL IMMUNIZATION

LOS 28.f: <u>Design</u> a bond immunization strategy to ensure funding of a predetermined liability and <u>evaluate</u> the strategy under various interest rate scenarios.

Immunization is a strategy used to minimize interest rate risk, and it can be employed to fund either single or multiple liabilities. Interest rate risk has two components: price risk and reinvestment rate risk. *Price risk,* also referred to as market value risk, refers to the decrease (increase) in bond prices as interest rates rise (fall). *Reinvestment rate risk* refers to the increase (decrease) in reinvestment income as interest rates rise (fall).

It is important to note that price risk and reinvestment rate risk cause opposite effects. That is, as interest rates increase, prices fall but reinvestment rates rise. As interest rates decrease, prices rise but reinvestment rates fall.

Suppose you have a liability that must be paid at the end of five years, and you would like to form a bond portfolio that will fully fund it. However, you are concerned about the effect that interest rate risk will have on the ending value of your portfolio. Which bonds should you buy? You should buy bonds that result in the effects of price risk and reinvestment risk exactly offsetting each other. This is what is known as classical immunization.

Reinvestment rate risk makes matching the maturity of a coupon bond to the maturity of a future liability an inadequate means of assuring that the liability is paid. Since future reinvestment rates are unknown, the total future value of a bond portfolio's coupon payments plus reinvested income is uncertain.

Classical Single-Period Immunization

Classical immunization is the process of structuring a bond portfolio that balances any change in the value of the portfolio with the return from the reinvestment of the coupon and principal payments received throughout the investment period. The goal of classical immunization is to form a portfolio so that:

- If interest rates increase, the gain in reinvestment income ≥ loss in portfolio value.
- If interest rates decrease, the gain in portfolio value ≥ loss in reinvestment income.

To accomplish this goal, we use effective duration. If you construct a portfolio with an effective duration equal to your liability horizon, the interest rate risk of the portfolio will be eliminated. In other words, price risk will exactly offset reinvestment rate risk.

> *Professor's Note: The value of a portfolio constructed to fund an obligation is only immunized for an immediate, 1-time parallel shift in the yield curve (i.e., interest rates change one time, by the same amount, and in the same direction for all maturities). The importance of this assumption will become apparent as you progress through this topic review.*

Immunization of a Single Obligation

To effectively immunize a single liability:

1. *Select* a bond (or bond portfolio) with an effective duration equal to the duration of the liability.

2. *Set* the present value of the bond (or bond portfolio) equal to the present value of the liability.

For example, suppose you have a $100 million liability with a duration of 8.0 and a present value of $56,070,223. Your strategy should be to select a bond (or bond portfolio) with a duration of 8.0 and a present value of $56,070,223.

> *Professor's Note: Similar to a zero-coupon bond, the duration of an obligation requiring a single payment is the time until it must be paid. Similar to a coupon bond, the duration of a pension obligation (i.e., a series of required payments) is less than the time until the last payment.*

Theoretically, this should ensure that the value of your bond portfolio will equal $100 million in eight years, even if there is a small 1-time instantaneous parallel shift in yields. Any gain or loss in reinvestment income will be offset by an equal gain or loss in the value of the portfolio.

What does it mean if the duration of the portfolio is not equal to the duration of the liability?

- If portfolio duration is less than liability duration, the portfolio is exposed to reinvestment risk. If interest rates are decreasing, the *losses* from reinvested coupon and principal payments would more than offset any gains from appreciation in the value of outstanding bonds. Under this scenario, the cash flows generated from assets would be insufficient to meet the targeted obligation.
- If portfolio duration is greater than liability duration, the portfolio is exposed to price risk. If interest rates are increasing, this would indicate that the *losses* from the market value of outstanding bonds would more than offset any gains from the additional revenue being generated on reinvested principal and coupon payments. Under this scenario, the cash flows generated from assets would be insufficient to meet the targeted obligation.

Adjustments to the Immunized Portfolio

Without rebalancing, classical immunization only works for a 1-time instantaneous change in interest rates. In reality, interest rates fluctuate frequently, changing the duration of the portfolio and necessitating a change in the immunization strategy. Furthermore, the mere passage of time causes the duration of both the portfolio and its target liabilities to change, although not usually at the same rate.

Remember, portfolios cease to be immunized for a single liability when:

- Interest rates fluctuate more than once.
- Time passes.

Thus, immunization is not a buy-and-hold strategy. To keep a portfolio immunized, it must be rebalanced periodically. Rebalancing is necessary to maintain equality between the duration of the immunized portfolio and the decreasing duration of the liability. Rebalancing frequency is a cost-benefit trade-off. Transaction costs associated with rebalancing must be weighed against the possible extent to which the terminal value of the portfolio may fall short of its target liability.

Bond Characteristics to Consider

In practice, it is important to consider several characteristics of the individual bonds that are used to construct an immunized portfolio. Bond characteristics that must be considered with immunization include:

- *Credit rating*. In immunizing a portfolio, it is implicitly assumed that none of the bonds will default.
- *Embedded options*. For bonds with embedded options, it may be difficult to estimate duration because cash flows are difficult to forecast.
- *Liquidity*. If a portfolio is to be rebalanced, it will be necessary to sell some of the bonds. Thus, liquidity is an important concern.

Optimization procedures are often used to build immunized portfolios. These procedures consider the many variations that typically exist within the universe of available bonds.

Immunization Against Nonparallel Shifts

An important assumption of classical immunization theory is that any changes in the yield curve are parallel. This means that if interest rates change, they change by the same amount and in the same direction for all bond maturities. The problem is that in reality, parallel shifts rarely occur. Thus, equating the duration of the portfolio with the duration of the liability does not guarantee immunization.

Immunization risk can be thought of as a measure of the relative extent to which the terminal value of an immunized portfolio falls short of its target value as a result of arbitrary (nonparallel) changes in interest rates.

Since there are many bond portfolios that can be constructed to immunize a given liability, you should select the one that minimizes immunization risk.

How do you do this? As it turns out, immunized portfolios with cash flows that are concentrated around the investment horizon have the lowest immunization risk. As the dispersion of the cash flows increases, so does the immunization risk. Sound familiar?

In general, the portfolio that has the *lowest reinvestment risk* is the portfolio that will do the best job of immunization:

- An immunized portfolio consisting entirely of zero-coupon bonds that mature at the investment horizon will have zero immunization risk because there is zero reinvestment risk.
- If cash flows are concentrated around the horizon (e.g., bullets with maturities near the liability date), reinvestment risk and immunization risk will be low.
- If there is a high dispersion of cash flows about the horizon date (as in a barbell strategy), reinvestment risk and immunization risk will be high.

WARM-UP: DURATION AS A MEASURE OF BOND PORTFOLIO RISK

For the Exam: This material on duration, dollar duration, and duration contribution is provided solely as a review of the basics required for a complete understanding of the material in LOS 28.g.

The major factor that drives bond price movements (and returns) is changing interest rates, and duration is used to measure individual bond and portfolio exposure to changes in interest rates. Duration is often considered a more useful measure of bond risk than standard deviation derived from historical returns, because the number of estimates needed to calculate standard deviation increases dramatically as the number of bonds in the portfolio increases, and historical data may not be readily available or reliable. Estimating duration, on the other hand, is quite straightforward and uses easily obtainable price, required return, and expected cash flow information.

WARM-UP: DURATION AS A MEASURE OF BOND PORTFOLIO RISK (CONT.)

Effective Duration

A portfolio's effective duration is the *weighted average* of the individual effective durations of the bonds in the portfolio:

$$D_p = \sum_{i=1}^{n} w_i D_i = w_1 D_1 + w_2 D_2 + w_3 D_3 + ... + w_n D_n$$

where:
D_p = the effective duration of the portfolio
w_i = the weight of bond i in the portfolio
D_i = the effective duration of bond i

Example: Calculating portfolio effective duration

Brandon Mason's portfolio consists of the bonds shown in the following figure.

Bond Portfolio of Brandon Mason

Bond	Market Value ($ million)	Effective Duration
A	$37	4.5
B	$42	6.0
C	$21	7.8
Portfolio	$100	?

Calculate the effective duration of Mason's portfolio and **interpret** the significance of this measure.

Answer:

The duration of Mason's portfolio is:

$$D_p = w_A D_A + w_B D_B + w_C D_C$$

$$D_p = \frac{37}{100} 4.5 + \frac{42}{100} 6.0 + \frac{21}{100} 7.8 = 5.8$$

A duration of 5.8 indicates that the market value of the portfolio will change by approximately 5.8% for every 1.0 percentage point (100 bps) change in interest rates.

WARM-UP: DURATION AS A MEASURE OF BOND PORTFOLIO RISK (CONT.)

Professor's Note: Recall that duration assumes linear changes in price (i.e., the change in price for a 100 bp increase in rates has the same absolute value as the change from a 100 bp decrease in rates). Convexity, which approximates the amount of "curve" in the price-yield curve, is added to the calculation to improve the estimate of the price change.

The effective duration for a bond index is computed in the same way as that for a bond portfolio. In this case, however, we can use the average effective duration of the sectors rather than the durations of the individual bonds in the sectors, which would be far more tedious:

$$D_{Index} = \sum_{i=1}^{n} w_i D_i = w_1 D_1 + w_2 D_2 + w_3 D_3 + ... + w_n D_n$$

where:
D_{Index} = the effective duration of the index
w_i = the weight of sector i in the index
D_i = the effective duration of sector i

If the duration of the portfolio is less than (greater than) that of the index, the portfolio is less sensitive (more sensitive) to a parallel shift in interest rates.

DURATION CONTRIBUTION

Effective Duration

Managers sometimes rely on a bond or sector's market-value weight in their portfolio as a measure of the exposure to that bond or sector. An alternative way to measure exposure is to measure the contribution of a sector or bond to the overall portfolio duration. Specifically, the contribution of an individual bond or sector to the duration of the portfolio is the weight of the bond or sector in the portfolio multiplied by its duration.

contribution of bond or sector i to the portfolio duration $= w_i D_i$

where:
w_i = the weight of bond or sector i in the portfolio

$$= \frac{\text{market value of bond or sector i in the portfolio}}{\text{total portfolio value}}$$

D_i = the effective duration of bond or sector i

Example: Duration contribution

Assume you have a 10-year corporate bond in an actively managed portfolio. The bond has a market value of $5 million and a duration of 4.7, and the portfolio has a total value of $20 million. **Calculate** the contribution of the corporate bond to the overall *duration* of the portfolio.

WARM-UP: DURATION AS A MEASURE OF BOND PORTFOLIO RISK (CONT.)

> **Answer:**
>
> The contribution of the corporate bond to the duration of the actively managed portfolio is:
>
> contribution to portfolio duration = ($5 million / $20 million) × 4.7 = 1.175

Professor's Note: The duration contribution measured in this example is the "amount" of duration the bond or sector contributes to the portfolio. For example, if the above portfolio has a duration of 6.0, the bond contributes 1.175 of that, or about 20% of the portfolio duration.

Dollar Duration

The exposure can also be measured in terms of a *dollar* exposure, for which the *dollar duration* of the bond issue or sector is used instead of duration. The dollar duration of a bond can be calculated as:

$$DD = -(\text{modified or effective duration})(0.01)(\text{price})$$

Professor's Note: The equation for dollar duration has a negative sign, because fixed income values move opposite to the change in interest rates. For example, if the change is positive (i.e., $+\Delta y$), the resulting price change is negative. If the change in rates is negative (i.e., $-\Delta y$) the price change is positive.

> **Example: Dollar duration**
>
> Consider a bond that is trading at 95 with a duration of 7.0. **Calculate** the change in value for a 100, 50, and 1 basis point change in interest rates. Note that since we are interested only in the *amount* of the change in value, in either direction, we can ignore the negative sign that is usually in front of the dollar duration equation.
>
> **Answer:**
>
> The dollar duration (i.e., change in value for a *100 basis point* move in rates) is (7)(0.01)($95) = $6.65.
>
> The change in value of this bond for a *50 basis point* move is (7)(0.005)($95) = $3.325.
>
> The change in value of this bond for a *1 basis point* move is (7)(0.0001)($95) = $0.0665.

WARM-UP: DURATION AS A MEASURE OF BOND PORTFOLIO RISK (CONT.)

 Professor's Note: You may have noticed that dollar duration (just like effective and modified duration) is linear. That is, the 50 bp change in value is half the 100 bp change in value, and the 1 bp change in value is 1/50 the 50 bp change in value. Also, the use of modified or effective duration, whichever is given on the exam, would be acceptable.

Portfolio Dollar Duration

The dollar duration of a portfolio can be defined in the same way as the dollar duration for an individual bond (i.e., the change in dollar value for a 100 bps change in interest rates). However, unlike the duration of the portfolio, which is a weighted average of the individual bond durations, the *dollar duration* of the portfolio is the *sum* of the individual dollar durations:

$$DD_P = \sum_{i=1}^{n} DD_i = DD_1 + DD_2 + DD_3 + ... + DD$$

where:
DD_P = the dollar duration of the portfolio
DD_i = the dollar duration of bond or sector i

Example: Contribution to portfolio dollar duration

Assume you have a 10-year corporate bond in an actively managed portfolio. The bond has a market value of $5 million and a duration of 4.7. The portfolio has a total value of $20 million and a duration of 6.8. **Calculate** the contribution of the corporate bond to the *dollar duration* of the portfolio.

Answer:

The dollar duration of the portfolio and bond (assuming a 100 bp change) is:

$$DD \ = (P)(D)(\Delta y)$$

$$DD_P = (\$20 \text{ million})(6.8)(0.01) = \$1,360,000$$

$$DD_B = (\$5 \text{ million})(4.7)(0.01) = \$235,000$$

The bond contributes $235,000 to the portfolio dollar duration of $1.36 million or about 17.3% of the portfolio dollar duration.

ADJUSTING DOLLAR DURATION

LOS 28.g: Demonstrate the process of rebalancing a portfolio to reestablish a desired dollar duration.

For the Exam: The LOS asks you to *demonstrate* rebalancing a portfolio to a desired dollar duration, so you could be asked to perform the related calculations on the exam.

Dollar duration, just like any other duration measure, changes as interest rates change or simply as time passes. Therefore, the portfolio manager must occasionally adjust the portfolio's dollar duration. There are two primary steps:

1. Calculate the new dollar duration of the portfolio.

2. Calculate the **rebalancing ratio** and use it to determine the required percentage change (i.e., cash needed) in the value of the portfolio.

Adjusting the dollar duration with this process is best demonstrated with an example.

Example: Reestablishing the Portfolio Dollar Duration

A portfolio with a dollar duration of $162,658 consists of four bonds with the indicated weights, durations, and dollar durations:

	Market Value	×	Duration	× 0.01 =	Dollar Duration
Bond 1	$1,000,000		5.0		$50,000
Bond 2	1,350,000		4.5		60,750
Bond 3	965,000		3.0		28,950
Bond 4	883,000		2.6		22,958
Portfolio	$4,198,000				$162,658

One year later, the yield curve has shifted upward with the following results:

	Market Value	×	Duration	× 0.01 =	Dollar Duration
Bond 1	$958,500		4.1		$39,299
Bond 2	1,100,000		3.6		39,600
Bond 3	725,000		2.2		15,950
Bond 4	683,000		1.8		12,294
Portfolio	$3,466,500				$107,143

$$\text{rebalancing ratio} = \frac{\text{old DD}}{\text{new DD}} = \frac{162{,}658}{107{,}143} = 1.52$$

To readjust back to the original dollar duration as well as maintain *the current proportions* of each bond in the portfolio, we subtract 1.0 from the rebalancing ratio to arrive at the necessary increase in the value of each bond in the portfolio and, thus, the total increase in the portfolio value (i.e., required additional cash):

$$1.52 - 1 = 0.52;\ 0.52 \times \$3,466,500 = \$1,802,580$$

The increases (in dollars) required for the individual bonds in the portfolio are:

Bond 1: $958,500   × 0.52 = $498,420
Bond 2: $1,100,000   × 0.52 = $572,000
Bond 3: $725,000   × 0.52 = $377,000
Bond 4: $683,000   × 0.52 = $355,160
                                 $1,802,580

To return the portfolio back to its original dollar duration, the manager could add cash and purchase the bonds in the amounts indicated. Alternatively, the manager could select one of the bonds to use as a *controlling position*. Since the dollar duration has fallen dramatically and Bond 1 has the longest duration, the manager could use less additional cash by increasing only the holding in Bond 1 (i.e., using Bond 1 as the controlling position):

desired increase in DD = $162,658 − $107,143 = $55,515

increase in Bond 1: new DD of Bond 1 = $39,299 + $55,515 = $94,814

$$\text{required new value of Bond 1} = \frac{\$94,814}{\$39,299} \times \$958,500 = \$2,312,507$$

Thus, instead of investing $1,802,580 in all the bonds, the manager could purchase another $1,354,007 (= $2,312,507 − $958,500) of Bond 1 and return the portfolio dollar duration back to its original level.

	Market Value	×	Duration	× 0.01 =	Dollar Duration
Bond 1	$2,312,507		4.1		$94,813
Bond 2	1,100,000		3.6		39,600
Bond 3	725,000		2.2		15,950
Bond 4	683,000		1.8		12,294
Portfolio	$4,820,507				$162,657

(Note: The slight difference in total dollar duration is due to rounding.)

SPREAD DURATION

LOS 28.h: Explain the importance of spread duration.

Duration measures the sensitivity of a bond to a 1-time parallel shift in the yield curve. *Spread duration* measures the sensitivity of non-Treasury issues to a change in their spread above Treasuries of the same maturity. (Remember that the amount of the spread is a function of perceived risk as well as market risk aversion.)

Although yield spread and spread duration can be defined and measured for individual bonds, they are typically used for entire classifications of bonds, where classification is by rating and/or sector. Calculating the spread duration for a sector allows the manager to both forecast the future performance of the sector and select superior bonds to represent each sector in the portfolio.

For example, the manager might forecast a widening of the spread for one sector of bonds and a narrowing of the spread for a second. The manager would want to reduce the weight of the first sector to minimize the impact of the increase in interest rates (falling prices). He would want to increase the weight of the second sector to maximize the impact of falling rates (rising prices). The manager may then focus on selecting superior bonds within each sector.

There are three spread duration measures used for fixed-rate bonds:

1. *Nominal spread* is the spread between the nominal yield on a non-Treasury bond and a Treasury of the same maturity. When spread duration is based on the nominal spread, it represents the approximate percentage price change for a 100 basis point change in the nominal spread.

2. *Zero-volatility spread* (or *static spread*) is the spread that must be added to the Treasury spot rate curve to force equality between the present value of a bond's cash flows (discounted at the Treasury spot rates plus the static spread) and the market price of the bond plus accrued interest. Computing spread duration using the zero-volatility spread measures the percentage change in price given a 1-time, 100 basis point change in the zero-volatility spread.

3. *Option-adjusted spread* (OAS) is determined using a binomial interest rate tree. Suffice it to say that when spread duration is based on OAS, it is the approximate percentage change in price for a 100 basis point change in the OAS.

Spread duration may be computed using any of these methods. As a result, observed discrepancies among reported values for spread duration may be a result of the different methods used.

A portfolio's spread duration is the market value-weighted average of the individual sector spread durations.

Example: Spread duration

Compute the spread duration for the following portfolio.

Spread Duration

Sector	Weight	Spread* Duration
Treasury	30	0.00
Mortgage	40	3.41
Corporate	30	5.89

* Spread defined in terms of OAS.

Answer:

spread duration = 0.30(0) + 0.40(3.41) + 0.30(5.89) = 3.13

Interpretation: If the OAS of each sector increases by 100 basis points with no change in Treasury yields, the value of the portfolio will decrease by approximately 3.13%.

Professor's Note: The names spread duration, effective duration, adjusted duration, and option-adjusted duration can all mean the same thing. Technically, spread duration is inappropriate for Treasuries, however, as spread is typically measured relative to Treasuries.

A portfolio's duration, which is a weighted average of the individual bond durations, measures the percentage change in the total value of the portfolio for a 100 bps change in the required return on the portfolio. Duration assumes a 1-time parallel shift in the yield curve, which causes the yields on all bonds to increase or decrease the same amount. Spread duration measures the percentage change in the total value of the portfolio given a parallel 100 bps change in the spread over Treasuries.

In the former (duration), the parallel shift in the yield curve could be caused by a change in inflation expectations, which causes the yields on all bonds, including Treasuries, to increase/decrease the same amount. In the latter (spread duration), the shift is in the spread only, indicating an overall increase in risk aversion (risk premium) for all bonds *in a given class.*

By weighting classes (sectors) differently in the bond portfolio, the manager exposes the portfolio to spread risk (i.e., the risk that the spread for a given class will change). Of course, the active manager typically weights the sectors in a portfolio differently from the benchmark in an effort to capture favorable changes in spreads.

EXTENSIONS TO CLASSICAL IMMUNIZATION

LOS 28.i: <u>Discuss</u> the extensions that have been made to classical immunization theory, including the introduction of contingent immunization.

Thus far we have looked at classical immunization as if there were few uncertainties. For instance, we assumed any changes in the yield curve were parallel so that we could immunize our portfolio using duration strategies. We have explored more detailed measures (e.g., the present value distribution of cash flows) to refine our use of duration, but we assumed the portfolio manager's goal was mimicking or outperforming an index. That is, the index benchmark represented the *minimum target value* for our portfolio, which is similar to the goal of immunizing a portfolio against a liability structure.

When the goal is to immunize against a liability, however, we must also consider changes in the value of the liability, which in turn could change the amount of assets needed for the immunization. We must also consider the ability to combine indexing (immunization) strategies with active portfolio management strategies. Note that since active management exposes the portfolio to additional risks, immunization strategies are also *risk-minimizing strategies*.

The bottom line is that classical immunization strategies may not be sufficient in managing a portfolio to immunize against a liability. To address the deficiencies in classical immunization, four extensions have been offered: (1) *multifunctional duration*, (2) *multiple-liability immunization*, (3) *relaxation of the minimum risk requirement, and* (4) *contingent immunization*.

The first modification or extension to classical immunization theory is the use of **multifunctional duration** (a.k.a. **key rate duration**). To incorporate multifunctional duration into our immunization strategy, the manager focuses on certain key interest rate maturities. For example, the manager's portfolio might contain mortgage-backed securities, which are exposed to prepayment risk. Unlike other fixed-income securities that increase in value when interest rates fall, MBS act like callable corporate bonds that are retired when rates fall. Thus, MBS and callable corporates do not increase in value as much as non-callables when rates fall below their coupon rates, so the portfolio's sensitivity to changes in different interest rate maturities can be unique, making the analysis of its exposures to key rates very important.

The second extension is **multiple-liability immunization**. The goal of multiple-liability immunization is ensuring that the portfolio contains sufficient liquid assets to meet all the liabilities as they come due. That is, rather than monitor the value of the portfolio as if the liability is its minimum target value at a single horizon date, there can be numerous certain or even uncertain liabilities with accompanying numerous horizon dates.

The third extension is allowing for **increased risk**, or otherwise relaxing the minimum risk requirement of classical immunization. As will be demonstrated when we discuss contingent immunization, as long as the manager does not jeopardize meeting the liability structure, he can pursue increased risk strategies that could lead to excess portfolio value (i.e., a terminal portfolio value greater than the liability).

The fourth extension is **contingent immunization**, which mixes active and passive (i.e., immunization) strategies.

Contingent Immunization

Contingent immunization is the combination of active management strategies and passive management techniques (immunization). As long as the rate of return on the portfolio exceeds a prespecified *safety net return*, the portfolio is managed actively. If the portfolio return declines to the safety net return, the immunization mode is triggered to "lock in" the safety net return. The safety net return is the minimum acceptable return as designated by the client.

Key considerations in implementing a contingent immunization strategy include:

- Determining available target returns.
- Identifying an appropriate safety net return.
- Establishing effective monitoring procedures to ensure adherence to the contingent immunization plan.

Example: Contingent immunization

You have decided to pursue a contingent immunization strategy over a 3-year time horizon. You just purchased at par $20 million worth of 9%, semiannual coupon, 15-year bonds. The current rate of return for immunized strategies is 9%, and you are willing to accept a return of 8% (this is the *safety net return*).

1. **Determine** the cushion spread.

2. **Compute** the required terminal value and the required assets needed at initial implementation.

3. **Determine** whether active management is still viable should interest rates immediately rise to 12%.

Answer:

1. The cushion spread is 1% [i.e., the difference between the current rate of return on immunized strategies (9%) and the return you are willing to accept (8%)].

2. Next we determine the required terminal value and the required assets needed at initial implementation:

   Step 1: The required terminal value using the safety net return:

   $$(\$20 \text{ million})(1.04)^6 = \$25,306,380$$

Professor's Note: The safety net return is the discount rate that equates the present values of the portfolio and the liability (or liabilities). In this case, the required terminal value is determined by using the safety net return. In other cases, the required terminal value may be a predetermined liability payment in the future, so you would determine the safety net return using that value and the current value of the portfolio.

Step 2: Assets required at implementation, assuming you can invest at an immunized rate of 9%:

$$\text{assets required} = \frac{\$25,306,380}{(1.045)^6} = \$19,432,661$$

On your financial calculator:

FV = $25,306,380; N = 6; I/Y = 4.5; PMT = 0;
CPT → PV = $19,432,661

This is the minimum level of assets needed today to achieve the required terminal value if locked in at the immunized rate. Hence, the initial *dollar safety margin* is:

$20 million – $19,432,661 = $567,339

If the immunized rate rises to 12% immediately following your initial purchase, you must determine whether the present value of your assets still exceeds the present value of your liabilities. If not, you can no longer use active management.

Step 3: **Calculate** the current value of the portfolio at the current immunization rate.

Using your financial calculator:

PMT = ($20,000,000)(0.045) = $900,000; N = 30;
I/Y = 12/2 = 6%; FV = $20,000,000;
CPT → PV = $15,870,551

The price of the bond portfolio will fall to $15,870,551 as a result of the rate increase (remember, this is a 15-year bond: N = 30 periods).

Step 4: **Calculate** the value necessary to fund the minimum target value at the current immunization rate.

required terminal value (from Step 1) = $25,306,380

$$\text{assets required } = \frac{\$25,306,380}{(1.06)^6} = \$17,839,999$$

Since the current portfolio value is less than the amount necessary to fund the minimum target value (i.e., the dollar safety margin is negative: $15,870,551 – $17,839,999 = –$1,969,448), a switch to immunization is necessary.

Monitoring the Immunization Strategy

It is sometimes easier for the portfolio manager to think of the safety margin in terms of returns rather than dollars. The frequency of rebalancing the portfolio is determined by the relationship between the safety net return and current market interest rates (and immunized rates). Once this is determined, the manager need only watch interest rates.

A very low safety net return (relative to the returns achievable in the market) means infrequent rebalancing, as the portfolio can experience a significant decrease in value before immunization is required. (It could mean, however, that the manager is devoting too many funds to the portfolio.) Setting the safety net return too close to the returns achievable in the market can mean little opportunity for active management, particularly in a period of significant interest rate volatility, as the *trigger rate* is easily hit (the rate that triggers a fully immunized strategy). Of course, this could also indicate that the manager has dedicated insufficient funds to the portfolio for active management to be viable.

Two factors can cause failure to attain the minimum target return in spite of effective monitoring procedures:

1. Adverse movements in market yields that occur too quickly for management to trigger the immunization mode soon enough (this factor occurred in our example).

2. The lack of assurance that the immunization rate will be achieved once the immunization mode is activated.

 Professor's Note: The manager must monitor (or predict) how changes in interest rates will change the durations of the bonds used in the immunization strategy. In addition, the manager must also consider the convexity of the bonds.

IMMUNIZATION RISKS

LOS 28.j: Explain the risks associated with managing a portfolio against a liability structure, including interest rate risk, contingent claim risk, and cap risk.

Three risks that the portfolio manager must be aware of relate to market interest rates and the structure of the bonds in the portfolio. They are (1) interest rate risk, (2) contingent claim risk (i.e., call or prepayment risk), and (3) cap risk.

Interest rate risk is the primary concern when managing a fixed income portfolio, whether against a liability structure or a benchmark. Since the values of most fixed-income securities move opposite to changes in interest rates, changing interest rates are a continual source of risk. As already mentioned, to help avoid interest rate risk, the manager will match the duration and convexity of the liability and the portfolio. Convexity can be difficult to measure for some fixed-income securities, especially those with *negative* convexity. This is the concern when fixed-income securities are subject to early retirement (e.g., mortgage-backed securities, callable corporate bonds).

Contingent claim risk (a.k.a. call risk or prepayment risk). Callable bonds are typically called only after interest rates have fallen. This means that the manager not only loses the higher stream of coupons that were originally incorporated into the immunization strategy, she is faced with reinvesting the principal at a reduced rate of return. Thus, contingent claim risk has significant potential to affect the immunization strategy through its effect on the value of the portfolio. To adjust for this potential, rather than simply comparing the portfolio duration to that of the liability, the manager must consider the convexity of the bonds.

Cap risk. Thus far in our discussion of immunization strategies we have not addressed the payment structure (i.e., cash flow structure) of the portfolio. That is, if any of the bonds in the portfolio have floating rates, they may be subject to *cap risk*. As used here, cap risk refers to a cap on the floating rate adjustment to the coupon on a floating rate (asset) security. If the bonds are subject to caps when interest rates rise, they might not fully adjust and thus would affect the immunization capability of the portfolio.

IMMUNIZING SINGLE LIABILITIES, MULTIPLE LIABILITIES, AND GENERAL CASH FLOWS

LOS 28.k: Compare and contrast immunization strategies for a single liability, multiple liabilities, and general cash flows.

If a manager could invest in a zero-coupon Treasury with a maturity equal to the liability horizon, he has constructed an immunization strategy with no risk. Since this is rarely the case, however, the manager must take steps to *minimize risk*.

One strategy is *minimizing reinvestment risk* (i.e., the risk associated with reinvesting portfolio cash flows). To reduce the risk associated with uncertain reinvestment rates, the manager should minimize the *distribution* of the maturities of the bonds in the portfolio around the (single) liability date. If the manager can hold bullet securities with maturities very close to the liability date, reinvestment risk is low.

Concentrating the maturities of the bonds around the liability date is known as a **bullet strategy**. Think of a strategy employing two bonds. One bond matures one year before the liability date and the other matures one year after the liability date. When the first matures, the proceeds must be reinvested for only one year. At the date of the liability, the maturity of the other is only one year off. Thus the reinvestment rate on the first will have a minimal impact on the terminal value of the portfolio and the value of the second is only minimally sensitive to interest rates.

Now consider a **barbell strategy** where the first bond matures several years before the liability date and the other several years after the liability date. The face value of the first must be reinvested when it matures, so the manager must be concerned with both the reinvestment rate and, since the new bond will have several years until maturity, all the other risk factors associated with such a bond. The second bond, since it matures several years after the liability date, is subject to significant interest rate risk.

> **For the Exam:** You could see an essay question about portfolio immunization in the morning section of the exam. This material is perfect for an essay question with a template where you have to agree with a statement or disagree and explain why you disagree. For example, an analyst could state, "As long as the portfolio manager matches the duration and convexity of the portfolio to the liability, whether he uses a barbell or bullet strategy should make no difference." You would disagree with the statement and explain that the barbell will have more reinvestment risk than the bullet strategy.

Obviously, as the maturities of the bullet strategy move away from the liability date and the maturities of the barbell move toward the liability date, the distinction between the two will begin to blur. Rather than base the strategy on subjective judgment, therefore, the manager can minimize M-Square (M^2) (a.k.a. *maturity variance*).

Maturity variance is the variance of the differences in the maturities of the bonds used in the immunization strategy and the maturity date of the liability. For example, if all the bonds have the same maturity date as the liability, M^2 is zero. As the dispersion of the maturity dates increases, M^2 increases.

> **For the Exam:** When dealing with reinvestment risk, it will help to think in terms of maturity variance rather than M^2, because of the M^2 used in Study Session 17 to measure risk-adjusted portfolio performance. On the exam, you may see maturity variance referenced as M^2. If that should be the case, however, you will be able to quickly determine which M^2 is being referenced by the context of the question.

Multiple Liabilities

The key to immunizing multiple liabilities is to decompose the portfolio payment streams in such a way that the component streams separately immunize each of the multiple liabilities. Multiple-liability immunization is possible if the following three conditions are satisfied (*assuming parallel rate shifts*):

1. Assets and liabilities have the same present values.

2. Assets and liabilities have the same aggregate durations.

3. The range of the distribution of durations of individual assets in the portfolio exceeds the distribution of liabilities. This is a necessary condition in order to be able to use cash flows generated from our assets (which will include principal payments from maturing bonds) to sufficiently meet each of our cash outflow needs.

A point of clarification for the second condition is in order. Even if a liability structure includes individual liabilities that exceed 30 years in duration (e.g., a pension fund), a multiple-liability immunization strategy can still be used effectively. The condition requires that the *weighted average* durations of the liabilities and assets are equal. Because of the additive property of duration, this strategy will work as long as the weight of the short-duration liabilities is sufficient to bring the average below 30 years.

It is important to note that satisfying these three conditions will assure immunization only against parallel rate shifts. In the case of *nonparallel rate changes*, linear programming models can be used to construct minimum-risk immunized portfolios for multiple liabilities. The procedure is to minimize a measure of immunization risk for multiple liabilities and nonparallel rate changes. The minimization procedure is subject to the constraints imposed by the conditions required for immunization under the assumption of a parallel shift along with any other relevant investment constraints.

Conditions for Cash Flow Matching

Cash flow matching is used to construct a portfolio that will fund a stream of liabilities out of portfolio returns and asset value such that the portfolio value is zero after the last liability is paid. It serves as an alternative to immunization for funding a stream of liabilities. The following points describe the process.

- Select a bond with a maturity date equal to that of the last liability payment date.
- Buy enough in par value of this bond such that its principal and final coupon fully fund the last liability.
- Using a recursive procedure (i.e., working backwards), choose another bond so that its maturity value and last coupon plus the coupon on the longer bond fully fund the second-to-last liability payment and continue until all liability payments have been addressed.

Linear programming can be used to construct the least-cost cash flow matching portfolio.

General Cash Flows

General cash flows in this case refers to using cash as part of an immunization strategy even though the cash has not yet been received. For example, expecting a cash flow in six months, the portfolio manager does not put the entire amount required for immunization into the portfolio today. Instead he looks at the expected cash flow as a zero and incorporates its payoff and duration into the immunization strategy.

Let's assume the manager expects to receive a cash flow in six months. Treating this like a zero, the duration is 0.5. To construct the portfolio to immunize a liability due in 1.5 years with a duration of 1.0, the manager could "combine" the cash to be received with an appropriate amount of bonds with durations greater than 1.0, so that the conditions for immunization are met, including a weighted average portfolio duration of 1.0.

RISK MINIMIZATION VS. RETURN MAXIMIZATION

LOS 28.l: Compare and contrast risk minimization with return maximization in immunized portfolios.

One standard condition for classical immunization is **risk minimization**. As we have discussed in several sections of this topic review, the portfolio manager has many tools to minimize exposure to risks faced when immunizing a portfolio to meet a liability. We have neglected to mention the relationship of risk minimization to the level of portfolio expected return.

Return maximization is the concept behind *contingent immunization*. Consider the manager who has the ability to lock in an immunized rate of return equal to or greater than the required safety net return. As long as that manager feels he can generate even greater returns, he should pursue active management in hopes of generating excess value.

Professor's Note: One consideration of liability immunization that has received almost no mention thus far is the amount of assets committed to the immunizing portfolio. The amount of assets required for the immunization will vary inversely with the expected return on the portfolio. For example, a manager could lock in a totally passive, risk-less immunization by purchasing Treasury zeros with the same maturity as the liability. The return on that portfolio would obviously be quite low, so the manager would effectively "pay" for the benefit of not having to monitor the portfolio by committing a large amount of assets. On the other hand, the manager could commit fewer assets by constructing an actively-managed, higher expected return portfolio.

CASH FLOW MATCHING

LOS 28.m: <u>Demonstrate</u> the use of cash flow matching to fund a fixed set of future liabilities and <u>contrast</u> the advantages and disadvantages of cash flow matching to those of immunization strategies.

Cash flow matching is used to construct a portfolio that will fund a stream of liabilities with portfolio coupons and maturity values. To construct the portfolio, the manager first selects a bond with a maturity date and value equal to the last liability. (Maturity value includes the face value and last coupon.) Once that bond has been selected, the manager reduces all earlier liabilities to reflect the other coupons received on that bond.

Another bond is then selected to match the maturity of the second to last liability with a maturity value reflecting the remaining value of that liability. The earlier coupons on the second bond are then applied against all remaining liabilities. This progression of matching the maturity value and date of a bond to each successively closer liability is continued until all the liabilities are funded.

Professor's Note: The timing of the coupons does not have to exactly match the timing of the liabilities. As long as a coupon (or any cash flow) is received on or before the liability due date, it can be applied to the liability. For example, assume the last two liabilities are separated by eight months and the manager matches a long bond with semi-annual coupons to the last liability. That means that two coupons from that bond will be applied to the last liability: the last coupon and the one received two months after the second to last liability.

Since it is unlikely that the cash flows from a bond portfolio will exactly match the liabilities, reinvestment risk is inherent in cash flow matching. As such, a minimum-risk immunization approach to funding multiple liabilities is at least equal to cash flow matching, and probably better, since it would be less expensive to fund a given stream of liabilities.

The following are the differences between cash flow matching and multiple-liability immunization:

- Cash flow matching depends upon all the cash flows of the portfolio, so expectations regarding short-term reinvestment rates are critical. For this reason, managers must use conservative reinvestment assumptions for all cash flows. This tends to increase the overall value of the required immunizing portfolio. An immunized portfolio is essentially fully invested at the duration of the remaining horizon, so only the average reinvestment rate over the entire investment horizon must be considered.
- Owing to the exact matching problem, only asset flows from a cash-flow-matched portfolio that occur prior to the liability may be used to meet the obligation. An immunized portfolio is only required to have sufficient *value* on the date of each liability because funding is achieved through portfolio rebalancing.

In spite of these drawbacks, cash flow matching is occasionally used because it is easier to understand.

Combination matching, also known as *horizon matching*, is a combination of multiple-liability immunization and cash flow matching that can be used to address the asset cash flow/liability matching problem. This strategy creates a portfolio that is *duration* matched. During the first few years, the portfolio would also be cash flow matched in order to make sure that assets were properly dispersed to meet the near-term obligations.

Combination matching offers the following *advantages* over multiple-liability immunization:

- Provides liquidity in the initial period.
- Reduces the risk associated with nonparallel shifts in the yield curve, which usually take place in the early years.

The primary *disadvantage* of combination matching is that it tends to be more expensive than multiple-liability immunization.

KEY CONCEPTS

LOS 28.a

Using a bond index as a benchmark: A manager might manage a bond fund that mimics a well-diversified bond index. The manager could follow either a passive or an active management approach. If the manager mostly agrees with market forecasts and values, they will follow a *passive* management approach. They will construct a portfolio that mimics the index along several dimensions of risk, and the return on the portfolio should track the return on the index fairly closely. In an *active* management approach, the manager constructs the portfolio to resemble the index in many ways but, through various active management strategies, hopes to consistently *outperform* the index.

Using liabilities as a benchmark: The investment objective when managing a bond portfolio against a single liability or set of liabilities is to maintain sufficient portfolio value to meet the liabilities..

LOS 28.b

Strategy	Advantages	Disadvantages
Pure bond indexing (PBI)	• Tracks the index (zero or very low tracking error) • Same risk factor exposures as the index • Low advisory and administrative fees	• Costly and difficult to implement • Lower expected return than the index
Enhanced indexing by matching primary risk factors (sampling)	• Less costly to implement • Increased expected return • Maintains exposure to the index's primary risk factors	• Increased management fees • Lowered ability to track the index (i.e., increased tracking error) • Lower expected return than the index
Enhanced indexing by small risk factor mismatches	• Same duration as index • Increased expected return • Reduced manager restrictions	• Increased risk • Increased tracking error • Increased management fees
Active management by larger risk factor mismatches	• Increased expected return • Reduced manager restrictions • Ability to tune the portfolio duration	• Increased risk • Increased tracking error • Increased management fees
Full-blown active management	• Increased expected return • Few if any manager restrictions • No limits on duration	• Increased risk • Increased tracking error • Increased management fees

LOS 28.c

A bond portfolio manager should move from a pure indexing position to more active management only when the client's objectives and constraints permit and the manager's abilities justify it.

- *Market value risk* varies directly with maturity. The greater the risk aversion, the lower the acceptable market risk, and the shorter the benchmark maturity.
- *Income risk* varies indirectly with maturity. The more dependent the client is upon a reliable income stream, the longer the maturity of the benchmark.
- *Credit risk*. The credit risk of the benchmark should closely match the credit risk of the portfolio.
- *Liability framework risk* is applicable only to portfolios managed according to a liability structure and should always be minimized.

LOS 28.d

Duration. Effective duration (a.k.a. option-adjusted or adjusted duration), which is used to estimate the change in the value of a portfolio given a small parallel shift in the yield curve, is probably the most obvious risk factor to be measured. Due to the linear nature of duration, which causes it to underestimate the increase and overestimate the decrease in the value of the portfolio, the convexity effect is also considered.

Key rate duration measures the portfolio's sensitivity to twists in the yield curve by indicating the portfolio's sensitivity to certain interest rates. Due to the nearly endless combinations of assets that will have the same duration as the index, the manager must take the time to ensure that the portfolio also matches the index's exposure to important key rates. Mismatches can occur when the portfolio and benchmark contain different combinations of bonds with varying maturities and key rate durations but the same overall effective duration.

LOS 28.e

Scenario analysis allows a portfolio manager to assess portfolio total return under a varying set of assumptions (different scenarios). Possible scenarios would include simultaneous assumptions regarding interest rates and spreads at the end of the investment horizon as well as reinvestment rates over the investment horizon.

Estimating expected **total return** under a single set of assumptions (predictions) only provides a point estimate of the investment's expected return (i.e., a single number). Combining total return analysis with scenario analysis allows the analyst to assess not only the return but also its volatility (distribution) under different scenarios.

LOS 28.f
To effectively immunize a single liability:
1. *Select* a bond (or bond portfolio) with an effective duration equal to the duration of the liability.
2. *Set* the present value of the bond (or bond portfolio) equal to the present value of the liability.

Without rebalancing, classical immunization only works for a 1-time instantaneous change in interest rates. *Immunization risk* can be thought of as a measure of the relative extent to which the terminal value of an immunized portfolio falls short of its target value as a result of arbitrary (nonparallel) changes in interest rates. In general, the portfolio that has the *lowest reinvestment risk* is the portfolio that will do the best job of immunization:

- An immunized portfolio consisting entirely of zero-coupon bonds that mature at the investment horizon will have zero immunization risk because there is zero reinvestment risk.
- If cash flows are concentrated around the horizon (as in a bullet), reinvestment risk and immunization risk will be low.
- If there is a high dispersion of cash flows about the horizon date (as in a barbell strategy), reinvestment risk and immunization risk will be high.

LOS 28.g
Δvalue = –(effective duration)(decimal change in interest rates)(price)

dollar duration = –(effective duration)(0.01)(price)

Portfolio dollar duration is the sum of the dollar durations of the individual bonds in the portfolio.

A manager must occasionally adjust the portfolio's dollar duration due to interest rate changes or the passing of time. The two steps in adjusting dollar duration are (1) calculate the new dollar duration and (2) calculate the rebalancing ratio and use it to determine the required percentage change in the value of the portfolio.

rebalancing ratio = old DD / new DD

LOS 28.h
Spread duration measures the sensitivity of non-Treasury issues to a change in their spread above Treasuries of the same maturity. Calculating the spread duration for a sector allows the manager to both forecast the future performance of the sector and select superior bonds to represent each sector in the portfolio. There are three spread duration measures used for fixed-rate bonds:
1. *Nominal spread* is the spread between the nominal yield on a non-Treasury bond and a Treasury of the same maturity.
2. *Zero-volatility spread* (or *static spread*) is the spread that must be added to the Treasury spot rate curve to force equality between the present value of a bond's cash flows and the market price of the bond plus accrued interest.
3. *Option-adjusted spread* (OAS) is determined using a binomial interest rate tree.

LOS 28.i

To address the deficiencies in classical immunization, four extensions have been offered:

- **Multifunctional duration** (a.k.a. **key rate duration**). Where the manager focuses on certain key interest rate maturities.
- **Multiple-liability immunization**. Where the portfolio contains sufficient liquid assets to meet all the liabilities as they come due.
- **Increasing risk**, or otherwise relaxing the minimum risk requirement, the manager can pursue increased risk strategies that could lead to excess portfolio value (i.e., a terminal portfolio value greater than the liability).
- **Contingent immunization** is the combination of active management strategies and passive management techniques (immunization). As long as the rate of return on the portfolio exceeds a prespecified *safety net return*, the portfolio is managed actively. If the portfolio return declines to the safety net return, the immunization mode is triggered to "lock in" the safety net return. The safety net return is the minimum acceptable return as designated by the client.

LOS 28.j

Interest rate risk: Since the values of most fixed income securities move opposite to changes in interest rates, changing interest rates are a continual source of risk. To help avoid interest rate risk, the manager will match the duration and convexity of the liability and the portfolio.

Contingent claim risk (a.k.a. **call risk** or **prepayment risk**): Callable bonds are typically called only after interest rates have fallen. This means that the manager not only loses the higher stream of coupons that were originally incorporated into the immunization strategy, but they are faced with reinvesting the principal at a reduced rate of return.

Cap risk refers to a cap on the adjustment to the coupon on a floating rate security. If the bonds are subject to caps when interest rates rise, they might not fully adjust and thus would affect the immunization capability of the portfolio.

LOS 28.k

Single Liability: One strategy is *minimizing reinvestment risk* (i.e., the risk associated with reinvesting portfolio cash flows). To reduce the risk associated with uncertain reinvestment rates, the manager should minimize the *distribution* of the maturities of the bonds in the portfolio around the (single) liability date. If the manager can hold bullet securities with maturities very close to the liability date, reinvestment risk is low.

Multiple Liabilities: The key to immunizing multiple liabilities is to decompose the portfolio payment streams in such a way that the component streams separately immunize each of the multiple liabilities. Multiple liability immunization assumes parallel rate shifts.

General cash flows in this case refers to using cash as part of an immunization strategy even though the cash has not yet been received. For example, a portfolio manager expecting a cash flow in six months does not put the entire amount required for immunization into the portfolio today. Instead he looks at the expected cash flow as a zero coupon bond and incorporates its payoff and duration into the immunization strategy.

LOS 28.l

One standard condition for classical immunization is **risk minimization**. As we have discussed in several sections of this topic review, the portfolio manager has many tools to minimize exposure to risks faced when immunizing a portfolio to meet a liability. We have neglected to mention the relationship of risk minimization to the level of portfolio expected return.

Return maximization is the concept behind *contingent immunization*. Consider the manager who has the ability to lock in an immunized rate of return equal to or greater than the required safety net return. As long as that manager feels they can generate even greater returns, they should pursue active management in hopes of generating excess value.

LOS 28.m

Cash flow matching is used to construct a portfolio that will fund a stream of liabilities with portfolio coupons and maturity values. To construct the portfolio, the manager first selects a bond with a maturity date and value equal to the last liability.

Another bond is then selected to match the maturity of the second to last liability with a maturity value reflecting the remaining value of that liability. The earlier coupons on the second bond are then applied against all remaining liabilities. This progression of matching the maturity value and date of a bond to each successively closer liability is continued until all the liabilities are funded.

- Cash flow matching depends upon all the cash flows of the portfolio, so expectations regarding short term reinvestment rates are critical.
- An immunized portfolio is essentially fully invested at the duration of the remaining horizon, so only the average reinvestment rate over the entire investment horizon must be considered.
- Only asset flows from a cash-flow-matched portfolio that occur prior to the liability may be used to meet the obligation. An immunized portfolio is only required to have sufficient *value* on the date of each liability.

CONCEPT CHECKERS

Use the following information to answer Questions 1 through 3.

Brian Reid is the portfolio manager of AA Corporate Bond Investors, Inc. His current $10 million bond position is as follows:

Bond	Market Value Weight (%)	Effective Duration
1	50	2.00
2	40	3.00
3	10	4.00

The Investment Policy Statement (IPS) allows the portfolio manager to leverage the portfolio by 20%, or $2 million.

1. What is the duration of the bond portfolio?
   A. 1.5.
   B. 2.0.
   C. 2.6.

2. What is the contribution of Bond 2 to the duration of the bond portfolio?
   A. 1.0.
   B. 1.2.
   C. 1.4.

3. Reid's bond portfolio is potentially exposed to:
   A. spread risk.
   B. default risk.
   C. both spread risk and default risk.

4. Which of the following spreads is determined using binomial interest rate trees?
   A. Nominal spread.
   B. Zero-volatility spread.
   C. Option-adjusted spread.

5. Drew Promadi and Louie Cheung are both employed by FI Associates, a bond trading firm. Promadi is a trader and Cheung is a performance analyst. After a performance tracking meeting, the two discuss alpha and tracking error. Promadi states that he doesn't think it is fair that his portfolio tracking error is being criticized, since his performance is evaluated against a custom benchmark containing Treasury bonds, which he does not hold. Promadi also argues that he should have some tracking error because he pursues an active strategy. In response, Cheung makes the following statements:

   Statement 1: I agree that over the period, your portfolio didn't contain exactly the same allocations as the benchmark, and you deliberately constructed your portfolio that way with the goal of generating positive alpha.

   Statement 2: However, the fact that you have a non-zero tracking error implies that you occasionally generate a negative alpha.

   Regarding these statements, is Cheung correct?
   A. Both statements are correct.
   B. Both statements are incorrect.
   C. One statement is correct.

6. Kirsten Radomski analyzes spread duration (based on OAS) for SAM Advisors, a fixed-income firm. One of her smaller portfolios consists of $5 million in U.S. Treasuries and $10 million of corporate bonds. If the portfolio's spread duration is 5.6, the spread duration of the corporate bonds is *closest* to:
   A. 3.75.
   B. 5.70.
   C. 8.40.

7. Given a market value of $100,000 for a bond and an effective duration of 6, **calculate** the bond's contribution to portfolio effective duration and dollar duration, if the portfolio is valued at $15 million and has a duration of 9.
   Contribution to:

	Effective duration	Dollar duration
A.	0.00450	$4,500
B.	0.04000	$6,000
C.	0.66009	$6,600

©2010 Kaplan, Inc.

8. A bond portfolio manager is contemplating the purchase of a corporate bond with the following characteristics:
    - A coupon rate of 11%, paid semiannually.
    - Four years remain until maturity.
    - The current price of the bond is 98.4321 with a yield to maturity of 11.50%.
    - The Treasury yield curve is flat at 8.0%.
    - The credit spread for the issuer is 350 basis points at all maturities.

    Calculate the total effective return on this investment, assuming a 1-year investment horizon, a coupon reinvestment rate of 6%, no change in the Treasury yield curve at the horizon date, and a 250 basis point decline in the credit spread for all maturities at the horizon date.
    A. 8.71%.
    B. 17.42%.
    C. 18.18%.

9. Two components of interest rate risk are:
    A. duration and convexity.
    B. reinvestment risk and price risk.
    C. duration sensitivity and price risk.

10. To immunize a portfolio consisting of a single coupon bond against a future liability, an investor should select a bond that:
    A. has a duration that equals the liability horizon.
    B. has a duration that exceeds the liability horizon.
    C. has a maturity date that extends beyond the liability horizon.

11. An extension of immunization that uses cash matching during the early years of a liability schedule and duration matching in the later years is referred to as:
    A. combination matching.
    B. dual horizon matching.
    C. immunization matching.

12. An investor wishes to immunize a single liability payment that will occur six years from today. Which of the following portfolios *most likely* has the *least* immunization risk?
    A. A 12-year annually compounded coupon bond with duration of six years.
    B. 50% invested in a 2-year zero-coupon bond and 50% invested in a 10-year zero-coupon bond.
    C. 50% investment in a 5-year zero-coupon bond and 50% investment in a 7-year zero-coupon bond.

Use the following information to answer Questions 13 through 17.

An investor has $100 million and would like to institute a contingent immunization strategy over the next six years. Current rates of return for immunization strategies are 10%, but the investor is willing to accept an 8.5% rate of return. His active strategy is to purchase $100 million in 8% coupon, semiannually compounded, 25-year bonds priced to yield 10%.

13.   The cushion spread is *closest* to:
    A. 50 basis points.
    B. 150 basis points.
    C. 200 basis points.

14.   The required terminal value is *closest* to:
    A. $163,146,750.
    B. $164,783,136.
    C. $169,588,143.

15.   The amount of assets necessary to achieve the required terminal value is *closest* to:
    A. $91,757,416.
    B. $92,092,087.
    C. $93,015,784.

16.   The current dollar safety margin is *closest* to:
    A. $5,566,976.
    B. $8,242,584.
    C. $71,389,334.

17.   If interest rates fall to 8% immediately after the purchase of this bond, is immunization necessary?
    A. No, because the dollar safety margin is positive.
    B. No, because the dollar safety margin is negative.
    C. Yes, because the dollar safety margin is negative.

18.   **Explain** how using key rate duration in addition to effective duration is more beneficial to measuring a portfolio's sensitivity to yield curve changes than effective duration alone.

19. Portfolio LTG has a dollar duration of 80,000 and a market value of $3 million. Suppose that one year later the yield curve shifted upward, which consequently decreased the dollar duration to 65,000 and decreased the market value to $2.5 million. Without considering a controlling position, what is the portfolio's rebalancing ratio and total increase in portfolio value required to readjust the portfolio back to its original dollar duration?

	Rebalancing ratio	Dollar adjustment
A.	0.81	$475,000
B.	1.23	$575,000
C.	0.81	$575,000

20. Tim Owens is currently managing his portfolio against a liability structure. However, interest rates have recently declined and some of the bonds in his portfolio have been called. Owens is faced with having to reinvest the principal of those bonds at a lower rate of return. **Identify** the risk(s) that Owens is facing while managing his portfolio.

ANSWERS – CONCEPT CHECKERS

1. **C** Portfolio duration is computed as a weighted average of the individual bond durations.

    duration = $(0.50 \times 2) + (0.40 \times 3) + (0.10 \times 4) = 2.60$

2. **B** Contribution of Bond 2 to the portfolio duration = $0.4 \times 3 = 1.2$.

3. **C** The bond portfolio is potentially exposed to spread risk, default risk, and interest rate risk.

4. **C** The option-adjusted spread (OAS) is determined using a binomial interest-rate tree. The nominal spread is based on the nominal spread between non-Treasury and Treasury securities. The zero-volatility spread uses present value methodology to determine what spread must be added to the Treasury spot rate curve to equate the present value of a bond's cash flows with the market price of the bond plus accrued interest.

5. **C** Tracking error is the standard deviation of alpha, the return to active management. Whenever the manager deviates the composition of the portfolio from that of the index, the portfolio has the potential for generating alpha and, hence, tracking error. However, the non-zero tracking error does not automatically indicate that the manager generated negative alphas over the period. Anytime alpha is not exactly the same for each period, even if it is always positive, it will have a standard deviation.

6. **C** The spread duration for the U.S. Treasuries is zero, and the spread duration of the portfolio is a weighted average of the individual (sector) durations. We can solve for the spread duration (SD) of the corporates as follows:

    $$SD_p = w_C SD_C + w_T SD_T = 5.6$$

    since:

    $$SD_T = 0; \ w_T = \frac{5,000,000}{15,000,000} = 0.333; \ w_C = \frac{10,000,000}{15,000,000} = 0.667$$

    $$0.667(SD_C) + 0.333(0) = 5.6 \Rightarrow SD_C = \frac{5.6}{0.667} = 8.395$$

7. **B** The contribution of a bond or sector to the portfolio duration = $w_i D_i$. In this case, the bond is valued at \$100,000 and the portfolio is valued at \$15 million. The bond's duration is 6, so its contribution to the portfolio duration is $(100,000 / 15,000,000) \times 6 = 0.04$.

    The contribution of a bond or sector to the portfolio dollar duration is the dollar duration of the individual bond or sector. The bond is worth \$100,000 and its duration is 6, so its dollar duration (contribution to the portfolio dollar duration) is $-(6)(100,000)(0.01) = \$6,000$.

    Note: Unless you are asked to specify percentage contributions, the effective duration of the portfolio is irrelevant (i.e., extraneous information).

8. **C** Step 1: Compute the horizon price of the bond using a yield of 9%:

The horizon yield of 9% is determined by adding the credit spread of 100 bps to the treasury yield of 8%. The new credit spread of 100 bps is computed as the difference between the original credit spread of 350 bps and the 250 bps reduction in the spread at the horizon date.

Recognizing that the bond has three years to maturity after one year, the price of this bond when discounted at a flat rate of 9% is:

$N = 6$; $PMT = 5.5$; $I/Y = 4.5$; $FV = 100$; $CPT \rightarrow PV = \$105.16$

Step 2: Calculate the end-of-period value of accumulated coupon income, assuming an annual reinvestment rate of 6% (semiannual rate of 3%):

$N = 2$; $I/Y = 3$; $PMT = 5.5$; $PV = 0$; $CPT \rightarrow FV = \$11.165$

Step 3: Compute the semiannual total return. The end of period value to use in this step is the total value of all cash flows at the end of the investment horizon. This is the sum of the horizon price and the value of the accumulated coupon income that was calculated in Step 1 and Step 2, respectively. This value is: $\$105.16 + \$11.17 = \$116.33$.

$N = 2$; $PV = -98.4321$; $FV = 116.33$; $PMT = 0$; $CPT \rightarrow I/Y = 8.71\%$

Step 4: Compute the effective annual return: rate $= (1.0871)^2 - 1 = 18.18\%$.

Note: The BEY for the investment is $8.71\% \times 2 = 17.42\%$.

9. **B** Interest rate risk is made up of two components: *reinvestment risk* and *price risk*. If interest rates rise, bond prices will fall. At the same time, the amount received from reinvested coupons will rise. The net result is that the two components of interest rate risk move in *opposite* directions.

10. **A** The conditions for immunizing a portfolio against a future liability are (1) the portfolio's duration must equal the duration of the liability and (2) the present value of the assets must equal the present value of the liabilities.

11. **A** Combination matching, also known as horizon matching, involves creating a portfolio that is duration matched with the added constraint that it be cash matched in the early years.

12. **C** The higher the dispersion of cash flows around the horizon date, the greater the reinvestment risk and, hence, the immunization risk. The portfolio in answer choice C contains less dispersion of cash flows than answer choice B. The bond in answer choice A is subject to significant reinvestment risk.

13. **B** The *cushion spread* or *excess achievable return* is the difference between the current immunization rate and minimum acceptable return. In this case, cushion spread = 10% − 8.5% = 1.5% = 150 basis points.

14. **B** The required terminal value $= I(1 + s/2)^{2H}$ (using semiannual compounding), where I = initial portfolio value, s = safety net return, and H = number of years in investment horizon.

In this case, the required terminal value = $100,000,000(1.0425)^{12}$ = \$164,783,136.

Using your financial calculator, PV = \$100,000,000; I/Y = 4.25; PMT = 0; N = 12; CPT → FV = \$164,783,136.

15. **A**   Required assets at any time t = required terminal value / $(1 + i_t)^{2(H-t)}$ (assuming semiannual compounding), where i_t = the immunization rate at time t.

In this case, the required assets = $164,783,136/(1.05)^{12}$ = \$91,757,416.

Using your financial calculator, FV = \$164,783,136; PMT = 0; I/Y = 5; N = 12; CPT → PV = \$91,757,416.

16. **B**   The dollar value of the safety margin at any time t equals the difference between the required assets at time t and the actual value of the assets in the portfolio.

The assets required to meet the minimum required terminal value are $164,783,136/(1.05)^{12}$ = \$91,757,416, and the actual value of the assets in the portfolio is \$100,000,000. Therefore, the dollar safety margin is \$100,000,000 − \$91,757,416 = \$8,242,584.

17. **A**   You initially purchased 122,333 bonds at an individual price of \$817.44 (N = 50; I/Y = 5; PMT = 40; FV = 1,000). At the new immunization rate of 8%, your bonds are priced at par, and your portfolio is worth \$122,333,000.

At 8%, the assets required to meet the required terminal value at 8% are: $164,783,136/(1.04)^{12}$ = \$102,923,061.

Using your financial calculator, FV = \$164,783,136; PMT = 0; I/Y = 4; N = 12; CPT → PV = \$102.92 million.

Since your portfolio is currently worth more than the required assets, the dollar safety margin is positive, and you should not immunize.

18.   The use of effective duration will capture a portfolio's sensitivity to parallel shifts in the yield curve. However, in order to capture twists in the yield curve a portfolio manager should also incorporate key rate durations.

19. **B**   The rebalancing ratio is the old DD / new DD. 80,000 / 65,000 = 1.23. The adjustment to dollar duration is an increase of the new market value of the portfolio times the rebalancing ratio minus 1. 2,500,000 × (1.23 − 1) = \$575,000. Note that in order to incorporate a controlling position we would need to know the market value and dollar duration of each bond in the portfolio. Readjusting the portfolio using a controlling position would most likely require an investment in all bonds that is less than \$575,000.

20.   Since Owens is managing his portfolio against a liability structure he should be concerned about interest rate risk, contingent claim risk (a.k.a. call risk), and cap risk. Note that the risk of having to reinvest the principal of bonds at a lower rate is call risk, but since he is managing a portfolio against a liability structure he should be concerned with all three of the aforementioned risks.

The following is a review of the Management of Passive and Active Fixed-Income Portfolios principles designed to address the learning outcome statements set forth by CFA Institute®. This topic is also covered in:

RELATIVE-VALUE METHODOLOGIES FOR GLOBAL CREDIT BOND PORTFOLIO MANAGEMENT[1]

EXAM FOCUS

This topic review focuses on primary market analysis, liquidity and trading analysis, spread analysis, structural analysis, corporate curve analysis, and credit analysis. Trading rationales and constraints are evaluated, and sector rotation strategies are presented. You should be familiar with the vast terminology that is introduced. This topic review makes use of a considerable amount of applied strategies and trends, which should be studied and understood.

RELATIVE VALUE ANALYSIS

LOS 29.a: Explain classic relative-value analysis, based on top-down and bottom-up approaches to credit bond portfolio management.

In relative value analysis, assets are compared along readily identifiable characteristics and value measures. In comparing firms, for example, we can use measures such as P/E ratios for ranking. With bonds, some of the characteristics used include sector, issue, and structure, which are used to rank the bonds across and within categories by expected performance. You are familiar with two of these methodologies:

1. In the **top-down approach**, the manager uses economy-wide projections to first allocate funds to different countries or currencies. The analyst then determines what industries or sectors are expected to outperform and selects individual securities within those industries.

2. The **bottom-up approach** starts at the "bottom." The analyst selects undervalued issues.

Any bond analysis should focus on total return. The analyst performs a detailed study of how past total returns for markets or individual securities were affected by macroeconomic events, such as interest rate changes and general economic performance. Any trends detected are used to estimate future total returns, based upon predictions for those same macro-trends.

---

1. The terminology presented in this topic review follows industry convention as presented in Reading 29 of the 2011 CFA Level 3 exam curriculum.

Study Session 9
Cross-Reference to CFA Institute Assigned Reading #29 – Relative-Value Methodologies for Global Credit Bond Portfolio Management

Study Session 9

CYCLICAL AND SECULAR CHANGES

LOS 29.b: Discuss the implications of cyclical supply and demand changes in the primary corporate bond market and the impact of secular changes in the market's dominant product structures.

Cyclical changes. Increases in the number of new bond issues are sometimes associated with narrower spreads and relatively strong returns. Even though this seems counter-intuitive, corporate bonds often perform best during periods of heavy supply. A possible explanation is that the valuation of new issues validates the prices of outstanding issues, which relieves pricing uncertainty and reduces all spreads.

Corporate bond returns have even declined, in both relative and absolute terms, when the supply of new issues unexpectedly drops off. An explanation for this occurrence is the loss of the validation provided by the primary markets, which causes uncertainty and accompanying higher spreads.

 Professor's Note: Unlike the fast-moving equity markets, bond markets can be very thinly traded, meaning there isn't an ongoing mechanism for the reassessment of prices. This can make investors uncertain that prices reflect all current information.

Secular changes. In all but the high-yield market, intermediate-term bullets dominate the corporate bond market. Bullet maturities are not callable, putable, or sinkable. Callable issues still dominate the high-yield segment, but this situation is expected to change as credit quality improves with lower interest financing and refinancing.

There are at least three implications associated with these product structures:

1. Securities with embedded options will trade at premium prices due to their scarcity value.

2. Credit managers seeking longer durations will pay a premium price for longer duration securities because of the tendency toward intermediate maturities.

3. Credit-based derivatives will be increasingly used to take advantage of return and/or diversification benefits across sectors, structures, and so forth.

For the Exam: Be sure you know the difference and can discuss cyclical and secular changes.

LIQUIDITY

LOS 29.c: <u>Summarize</u> the influence of investors' short- and long-term liquidity needs on portfolio management decisions.

As you would expect, there is generally a positive relationship between liquidity and bond prices. That is, as liquidity decreases, investors are willing to pay less (increasing yields), and as liquidity increases, investors are willing to pay more (decreasing yields).

The corporate debt market has shown variable liquidity over time, influenced to a great extent by macro shocks (i.e., a variety of economic conditions). And while some investors are willing to give up additional return by investing in issues that possess greater liquidity (e.g., larger-sized issues and government issues), other investors are willing to sacrifice liquidity for issues that offer a greater yield (e.g., smaller-sized issues and private placements). The move in debt markets has been toward increased liquidity (i.e., faster and cheaper trading) mainly due to trading innovations and competition among portfolio managers.

RATIONALES FOR SECONDARY BOND TRADES

LOS 29.d: <u>Discuss</u> common rationales for secondary market trading, including yield-spread pickup trades, credit-upside trades, credit-defense trades, new issue swaps, sector-rotation trades, yield curve-adjustment trades, structure trades, and cash flow reinvestment.

The following are some of the reasons why managers actively trade in the secondary bond markets, rather than simply hold their portfolios. In all cases, the manager must determine whether trading will produce returns greater than the associated costs or not.

Yield/spread pickup trades. The most common rationale for trading is the pickup of additional yield, which is possible within specified duration and credit-quality bounds. For example, suppose that a 10-year, A-rated bond is trading at a spread of 93 basis points, and a 10-year, BBB-rated bond is trading at a spread of 98 basis points. A bond portfolio manager holding the A-rated issue could consider the quality difference virtually meaningless and swap for the BBB issue and pick up a yield of five basis points.

The potential flaw in this rationale is that it does not recognize the limitations of yield measures as an indicator of potential performance (i.e., it is not based within a total return framework). For instance, if the spread on the A bond narrowed during the investment period and the BBB spread remained constant, the A bond would increase in price and outperform the BBB bond on a total return basis.

Credit-upside trades. In credit-upside trades, the bond portfolio manager attempts to identify issues that are upgradeable, before the upgrade is incorporated into their prices. When the upgrade is officially announced, the prices of the affected bonds will increase as their spreads narrow.

Credit upside trades occur most often at the juncture of the highest speculative rating and the lowest investment rating. If the issues that warrant the highest speculative rating (e.g., BB) are considered creditworthy enough to be upgraded to investment grade (e.g., BBB or better), the bonds will benefit from decreased credit spread and increased liquidity.

Credit-defense trades. In credit-defense trades, the opposite of credit-upside trades, managers reduce exposure to (sell) sectors where they expect a credit downgrade.

New issue swaps. Managers often prefer to move into new issues, because new issues, particularly on-the-run Treasuries, are often perceived to have superior liquidity.

 Professor's Note: On-the-run implies the most recent issue of bonds.

Sector-rotation trades. Similar to strategies in the equity market, the idea behind preferred sector trades in the corporate bond market is to shift out of a sector or industry that is expected to underperform and into one that is expected to outperform on a total return basis.

Yield curve-adjustment trades. Yield curve-adjustment trades attempt to align the portfolio's duration with anticipated changes/shifts in the yield curve. That is, if long-term (only) interest rates are expected to fall, the manager may want to shift into longer durations to maximize the positive effect of the change in interest rates.

Structure trades. The rationale behind bond structure trades is to swap into structures that will have strong performance given an expected movement in volatility and yield curve shape. For example, higher volatility tends to result in decreased prices for callable securities because of the increased value to the issuer of the embedded option. Put structures tend to fare better in environments where interest rates are not expected to decrease. Holders of putable bonds sacrifice a small amount of yield for the ability to put the bond to the issuer and seek out higher yielding investments. If interest rates decline, putable bonds tend to underperform nonputable issues as the put feature becomes less valuable.

Cash flow reinvestment trades. The need to reinvest cash flows is a common reason for portfolio managers to trade in the secondary market. This is particularly true when portfolio cash flows do not coincide with new issues in the primary market for corporate bonds.

Based on interest rate expectations, relative-value analysis can be used to identify bonds that will have the greatest price change (and total return) in response to interest rate changes. Duration is a useful tool in the application of relative value analysis, since it is an approximate measure of bond price appreciation or depreciation due to interest rate changes. The following general rules apply:

- If interest rates are expected to rise, buy short-duration bonds and sell long-duration bonds.
- If interest rates are expected to fall, buy long-duration bonds and sell short-duration bonds.

This analysis can also be done on a relative basis in terms of spreads. Assuming the overall level of interest rates remain stable, the following general rules apply:

- If the yield spread for the sector is expected to narrow, choose longer-duration bonds in the sector, as they will gain the most from decreased rates.
- If the yield spread for the sector is expected to widen, choose shorter-duration bonds in the sector.

For the Exam: The material in LOS 29.d may show up in a morning fixed income essay question. A likely form would be statements that you will have to agree or disagree with and provide an explanation if you disagree.

ASSESSING RELATIVE VALUE METHODOLOGIES

LOS 29.e: Discuss and evaluate corporate bond portfolio strategies that are based on relative value, including total return analysis, primary market analysis, liquidity and trading analysis, secondary trading rationales and trading constraints, spread analysis, structure analysis, credit curve analysis, credit analysis, and asset allocation/sector analysis.

For the Exam: There is a plethora of testable material in this LOS, and any of it could show up on the exam as part of an item set or in the morning as part of an essay question. Be sure you understand all the methodologies as you read through them and use Figure 1 as a review tool.

Rationales for Not Trading

There are also circumstances under which managers will not trade or are prohibited from trading:

Trading constraints. Portfolio trading constraints are considered to be a major contributor to inefficiencies in the global corporate bond market. Examples include the following:

- Quality constraints. Some investors, such as state employee pension funds, are limited to investing only in investment grade bonds.
- Restrictions on structures (callables or convertibles not allowed) and foreign bonds.
- High-yield corporate exposure limits for insurance companies.
- Structure and quality restrictions for European investors.
- Floating rate requirements for commercial banks.

Other factors that can contribute to inefficiencies include *story disagreement*, *buy and hold*, and *seasonality*.

Story disagreement refers to the lack of consensus between buy-side and sell-side analysts and strategists, which can lead to conflicting recommendations and uncertainty about optimal trading strategies.

Professor's Note: In some cases "story" disagreement can be similar to anchoring and adjustment, which we discussed in Study Session 3. In this case, the portfolio manager is "anchored" to a long-term forecast and is reluctant to change his forecast and trade on new information because he disagrees with the widely accepted story.

Buy and hold represents an unwillingness to sell and recognize an accounting loss or the desire to keep turnover low. Lack of liquidity has also been cited as a reason for not trading.

Seasonality refers to the slowing of trading at the ends of months, quarters, and calendar years, when portfolio managers are preoccupied with various reports and filings.

YIELD SPREADS

Nominal spread. The nominal spread is simply the yield difference between corporate and government bonds of similar maturity. It is currently the basic unit of both price and relative value analysis for most of the global corporate bond market.

Swap spreads. A swap spread is the spread paid by the fixed-rate payer over the rate on the on-the-run Treasury with the same maturity as the swap. Swap spreads are widely used in Europe as an indication of credit spreads.

Option-adjusted spread. An option-adjusted spread (OAS) is often used when comparing investment-grade corporate securities with mortgage-backed and U.S. Agency issues. It is the effective spread for the class after removing any embedded options. The use of the OAS is declining due to the reduction in corporate structures that contain embedded options.

SPREAD ANALYSIS

Mean-reversion analysis. Probably because of its simplicity, mean-reversion analysis is used extensively for analyzing spreads. The presumption with mean reversion is that spreads between sectors tend to revert toward their historical means.

The procedure is as follows:

- If the current spread is significantly greater than the historic mean, buy the sector or issue. (If yield is high on a relative basis, price is low.)
- If the current spread is significantly less than the historic mean, sell the sector or issue. (If yield is low on a relative basis, price is high.)
- Statistical analysis, using standard deviations and *t*-scores (for determining significance), can be used to determine if the current spread is significantly different from the mean.

Quality-spread analysis. Quality-spread analysis is based on the spread differential between low and high quality credits. Based on this analysis, a manager may buy an issue with a spread wider than that which is justified by its intrinsic quality. However, there is risk that the spread will not narrow or will become even greater.

Study Session 9

Cross-Reference to CFA Institute Assigned Reading #29 – Relative-Value Methodologies for Global Credit Bond Portfolio Management

Percentage yield spread analysis. Percentage yield spread analysis *divides* the yields on corporate bonds by the yields on treasuries with the same duration. If the ratio is higher than justified by the historical ratio, the spread is expected to fall, making corporate bond prices rise. Methodological deficiencies render this form of analysis of little use. For example, the denominator in the ratio (government yields) is just one of many factors that contribute to corporate yields. Supply, demand, profitability, default, liquidity, and other factors can enhance or diminish any insights derived from the ratio of corporate yields to government yields.

BOND STRUCTURES

Structural analysis is the analysis of the performance of structures (e.g., bullet, callable, putable, and sinking fund) on a relative-value basis. This type of analysis is becoming less useful, however, as the U.S. and global corporate bond markets move toward the homogeneous bullet structure of the European corporate bond market. However, it is still a valuable tool that can be used to enhance risk-adjusted returns of corporate portfolios.

Bullet Structures

Short-term bullets have maturities of one to five years and are used on the short end of a barbell strategy. A barbell is a portfolio that contains short- and long-term bonds. As opposed to using short-term Treasuries, corporate securities are used at the front end of the yield curve with long-term Treasuries at the long end of the yield curve.

Medium-term bullets (maturities of five to 12 years) are the most popular sector in the United States and Europe. When the yield curve is positively sloped, 20-year structures are often attractive, because they offer higher yields than 10- or 15-year structures but lower duration than 30-year securities.

Long-term bullets (30-year maturities) are the most commonly used long-term security in the global corporate bond market. They offer managers and investors additional positive convexity at the cost of increased effective duration.

Early Retirement Provisions

Callable bonds. An important consideration in valuing bonds is that the difference between the prices of otherwise identical non-callable and callable bonds is the value of the embedded option. Thus, their price and return differentials are driven by the value of the embedded option.

Due to the *negative convexity* caused by the embedded option, *callable* bonds:

- **Underperform** non-callables when interest rates fall (relative to the coupon rate) due to their negative convexity. They do not realize the gains from a bond market rally (falling rates), because, due to the embedded option, their prices do not rise as much as those of similar non-callables.

- **Outperform** non-callables in bear bond markets with rising rates as the probability of being called falls. (When the current rate is lower than the coupon rate, their negative convexity makes callables respond less to increasing rates.)
- When yields are very high, relative to coupon rates, the callable bond will behave much the same as the non-callable (i.e., the call option has little or no value).

> *Professor's Note: Unless rates are very high (relative to the coupon rate), the embedded option in a callable bond has value. Anytime the option has value, a callable bond will have less interest rate sensitivity than a comparable non-callable.*

Sinking funds. Sinking funds provide for the early retirement of a portion of an issue of bonds. Sinking fund structures priced at a discount to par have historically retained upside price potential during interest rate declines as long as the bonds remain priced at a discount to par (the firm can call the bonds back at par). Furthermore, given that the issuer is usually required to repurchase part of the issue each year, the price of sinking fund structures does not fall as much relative to callable and bullet structures when interest rates rise.

Putable bonds. Due to the relative scarcity of bonds with put options, it is difficult to reach a conclusion regarding their performance and valuation. Thus, managers and investors should only consider putable bonds as an alternative, when there is a strong belief that interest rates will rise (i.e., increases in interest rates increase the value of the embedded put option).

It is worth noting that valuation models for bonds with embedded put options often fail to incorporate the probability that the issuer will be unable to fulfill its obligation to repurchase its bonds. This is particularly relevant to the valuation of putable bonds issued by high-yield issuers. It may be that the creditworthiness of the high-yield issuer is a more relevant indicator of the value of the bond than that calculated using a valuation model.

CREDIT ANALYSIS

Credit analysis involves examining financial statements, bond documents, and trends in credit ratings. It provides an analytic framework in assessing key information in sector selection:

- Capacity to pay is the key factor in corporate credit analysis.
- The quality of the collateral and the servicer are important in the analysis of asset-backed securities.
- The ability to assess and collect taxes is the key consideration for municipal bonds.
- Sovereign credit analysis requires an assessment of the country's ability to pay (economic risk) and willingness to pay (political risk).

The main disadvantage to credit analysis is the need to continually search out and interpret information, which is becoming more arduous with the expansion in the universe of global bonds. In order to be effective, managers must establish and support an effective credit analysis system within their managerial domains to assure that appropriate information is available to make the best possible choices.

Figure 1 is a compilation of the primary relative valuation methodologies along with their descriptions.

Figure 1: Relative Valuation Methodologies

Methodology	Description	Strategy
Total return analysis	Consider coupons (yield) as well as potential price increases or decreases.	Study past bond reactions to macroeconomic changes to project future returns.
Primary market analysis	Supply of and demand for new issues affects returns. Increases (decreases) in new issues tend to decrease (increase) relative yields.	When you expect rates to fall, you expect new issues and refinances to increase.
Liquidity and trading analysis	Liquidity drives bid-ask prices and yields. As liquidity increases, demand increases. As trading increases, prices increase and yields decrease.	Identify issues/sectors that you expect to increase in price from increased liquidity.
Secondary trading rationales	Reasons for trading.	Yield/spread pickup trades. Credit-upside trades. Credit-defense trades. New issue swaps. Sector-rotation trades. Curve-adjustment trades. Structure trades. Cash flow reinvestment.
Secondary trading constraints	Reasons for not trading.	Portfolio constraints. "Story" disagreement. Buy and hold. Seasonality.
Spread analysis	Analyze the various spreads. With increased rate volatility (uncertainty), spreads tend to increase and widen with maturity.	Mean-reversion analysis. Quality-spread analysis. Percentage yield spread analysis.
Structural analysis	Study the structure of bond issues: bullets, callable, sinking funds, put options.	Determine which bond structures will perform best given your macro predictions.
Corporate curve analysis	Study credit and yield curves. With increased rate volatility (uncertainty), spreads tend to increase and widen with maturity.	Corporate spread curves tend to change with the economic cycle (i.e., narrow during upturns and widen during downturns).
Credit analysis	Upgrades cause reduced yields and increased prices. Downgrades cause increased yields and decreased prices.	Identify credit upgrade and downgrade candidates.
Asset allocation/ Sector analysis	Macro allocation is across sectors. Micro allocation is within a sector.	Identify sectors/firms expected to outperform.

KEY CONCEPTS

LOS 29.a

In **relative value analysis**, assets are compared along readily identifiable characteristics and value measures. For example, in comparing firms we can use measures such as P/E ratios for ranking. With bonds, some of the characteristics used include sector, issue, and structure, which are used to rank the bonds across and within categories by expected performance.

- In the **top-down approach**, the manager uses economy-wide projections to first allocate funds to different countries or currencies. Then the analyst determines what industries or sectors are expected to outperform and selects individual securities within those industries.
- The **bottom-up approach** starts at the "bottom." The analyst selects undervalued issues.

LOS 29.b

Cyclical changes relate to the number of new issues. Increases in the number of new bond issues are sometimes associated with narrower spreads and relatively strong returns.

Secular changes relate to the characteristics of bond issues. In all but the high-yield market, intermediate-term bullets dominate the corporate bond market. Bullet maturities are not callable, putable, or sinkable. Callable issues still dominate the high-yield segment, but this situation is expected to change as credit quality improves with lower interest financing and refinancing.

LOS 29.c

Some investors are willing to give up additional return by investing in issues that possess greater liquidity (e.g., larger-sized issues and government issues), other investors are willing to sacrifice liquidity for issues which offer a greater yield (e.g., smaller-sized issues and private placements).

LOS 29.d

Secondary trade rationales include the following:
- Yield/spread pickup trades are the most cited reason for secondary trades.
- Credit-upside trades reflect managers' expectations that an issuer will experience a quality upgrade that is not already reflected in the current spread.
- Credit-defense trades reflect managers' desires to reduce exposure to sectors where a credit downgrade is expected to occur.
- New issue swaps are trades into large, new issues, particularly on-the-run Treasuries that are often perceived to have superior liquidity.
- Sector rotation trades are undertaken to take advantage of sectors that are expected to outperform on a total return basis.
- Yield curve adjustment trades occur because of the desire to alter the duration of a portfolio to be favorably positioned with respect to anticipated yield curve changes.
- Structure trades refers to swaps into structures (callable, bullet, and put) that will have strong performance given an expected movement in volatility and yield curve shape.
- Cash flow reinvestment is a common reason for portfolio managers to trade in the secondary market, particularly when primary issues are scarce.

Study Session 9

Cross-Reference to CFA Institute Assigned Reading #29 – Relative-Value Methodologies for Global Credit Bond Portfolio Management

LOS 29.e

Relative Valuation Methodologies

Methodology	Description	Strategy
Total return analysis	Consider coupons (yield) as well as potential price increases or decreases.	Study past bond reactions to macroeconomic changes to project future returns.
Primary market analysis	Supply of and demand for new issues affects returns. Increases (decreases) in new issues tend to decrease (increase) relative yields.	When you expect rates to fall, you expect new issues and refinances to increase.
Liquidity and trading analysis	Liquidity drives bid-ask prices and yields. As liquidity increases, demand increases. As trading increases, prices increase and yields decrease.	Identify issues/sectors that you expect to increase in price from increased liquidity.
Secondary trading rationales	Reasons for trading.	Yield/spread pickup trades. Credit-upside trades. Credit-defense trades. New issue swaps. Sector-rotation trades. Curve-adjustment trades. Structure trades. Cash flow reinvestment.
Secondary trading constraints	Reasons for not trading.	Portfolio constraints. "Story" disagreement. Buy and hold. Seasonality.
Spread analysis	Analyze the various spreads. With increased rate volatility (uncertainty), spreads tend to increase and widen with maturity.	Mean-reversion analysis. Quality-spread analysis. Percentage yield spread analysis.
Structural analysis	Study the structure of bond issues: bullets, callable, sinking funds, put options.	Determine which bond structures will perform best given your macro predictions.
Corporate curve analysis	Study credit and yield curves. With increased rate volatility (uncertainty), spreads tend to increase and widen with maturity.	Corporate spread curves tend to change with the economic cycle (i.e., narrow during upturns and widen during downturns).
Credit analysis	Upgrades cause reduced yields and increased prices. Downgrades cause increased yields and decreased prices.	Identify credit upgrade and downgrade candidates.
Asset allocation/ Sector analysis	Macro allocation is across sectors. Micro allocation is within a sector.	Identify sectors/firms expected to outperform.

CONCEPT CHECKERS

1. Although all are presented as rationales for secondary trading, which is probably the *most* common rationale?
    A. New issue swaps.
    B. Credit-upside trades.
    C. Yield/spread pickup trades.

2. There is an increase in secondary market trading based on cash flow reinvestment when:
    A. the yield curve is inverted.
    B. the yield curve is relatively flat.
    C. the primary supply is short or the composition of the primary market is not compatible with portfolio objectives.

3. Although the practice is declining, it is common for practitioners to compare the value of mortgage-backed and U.S. Agency securities with investment-grade corporate securities. Which of the following spreads is used for this purpose?
    A. Static spreads.
    B. Nominal spreads.
    C. Option-adjusted spreads.

4. Which of the following is not considered a spread tool widely used in the United States for individually issued corporate bonds?
    A. Swap spread analysis.
    B. Percent yield analysis.
    C. Quality spread analysis.

5. Failure to evaluate future performance on the basis of total return is a common criticism of which of the following rationales for trading?
    A. Credit-defense trades.
    B. Credit-upside trades.
    C. Yield/spread pickup trades.

6. Which of the following is considered the leading contributor to inefficiencies in the global corporate market?
    A. Portfolio constraints.
    B. The reluctance to trade if it will show a loss relative to book value.
    C. The decline in trading activities that occurs during periods when performance reports and government filings are being prepared.

7. Percentage yield analysis examines which of the following values as part of the relative value analytical process? The ratio of:
    A. corporate yields to government yields for securities of similar maturity.
    B. corporate yields to government yields for securities of similar duration.
    C. government yields to corporate yields for securities of similar duration.

ANSWERS – CONCEPT CHECKERS

1. C   It has been estimated that more than half of all secondary trades reflect investor intentions to add additional yield.

2. C   Portfolio managers must search the secondary markets when portfolio cash flows occur during interludes in the primary market or when the composition of the primary market is not compatible with portfolio objectives.

3. C   To compare the volatility of sectors (mortgage-backed securities and U.S. Agencies), practitioners often value investment-grade corporate securities in terms of option-adjusted spreads. The static spread is only used when interest rate volatility is not a concern.

4. A   Mean-reversion analysis, quality spread analysis, and percent yield analysis are commonly used spread tools. A swap spread is a credit spread analysis tool widely used in Europe and Asia for all types of bonds. In the United States, it is used for MBS, CMBS, agency, and ABS.

5. C   Relative yield pickup trades are based on swapping bonds based on YTM and do not include consideration of future price/spread movements.

6. A   Client-imposed portfolio constraints are the biggest contributor to bond market inefficiencies.

7. B   Percentage yield analysis is a popular tool that compares the yields on corporates to the yields on treasuries, keeping duration more or less constant.

The following is a review of the Portfolio Management of Global Bonds and Fixed-Income Derivatives principles designed to address the learning outcome statements set forth by CFA Institute®. This topic is also covered in:

FIXED-INCOME PORTFOLIO MANAGEMENT—PART II

EXAM FOCUS

The significant refinement of the fixed income material along with its persistence at showing up on the exam indicate it is a long-standing favorite of CFA Institute and may show up in free-standing questions, either item set or essay, as well as part of larger portfolio management cases in the morning session of the exam. The country beta material has been in and out of the Level 3 curriculum over the years. Be sure you can discuss its relevance to international bond investments as well as perform the related calculations. Be sure, also, that you can discuss bond risk measures and hedging interest rate risk with futures and that you can perform the calculations to determine the appropriate hedging strategy.

LEVERAGE

LOS 30.a: Evaluate the effect of leverage on portfolio duration and investment returns.

> **For the Exam:** The command word *evaluate* could imply that you will have to calculate the difference in returns and/or durations between an unleveraged and leveraged investment (i.e., determine the effect of leverage).

Leverage refers to the use of borrowed funds to purchase a portion of the securities in a portfolio. Its use affects both the return and duration of the portfolio.

Leverage Effects

If the return earned on the investment is greater than the financing cost of borrowed funds, the return to the investor will be favorably affected. Leverage is beneficial when the strategy earns a return greater than the cost of borrowing.

Although leverage can increase returns, it also has a downside. If the strategy return falls below the cost of borrowing, the loss to investors will be increased. So leverage magnifies both good and bad outcomes.

Additionally, as leverage increases, the dispersion of possible portfolio returns increases. In other words, as more borrowed funds are used, the variability of portfolio returns increases.

Some examples will help illustrate these relationships.

Example: The effect of leverage on return

A portfolio manager has a portfolio worth $100 million, $30 million of which is his own funds and $70 million is borrowed. If the return on the invested funds is 6% and the cost of borrowed funds is 5%, **calculate** the return on the portfolio.

Answer:

The gross profit on the portfolio is: $100 million × 6% = $6 million.

The cost of borrowed funds is: $70 million × 5% = $3.5 million.

The net profit on the portfolio is: $6 million – $3.5 million = $2.5 million.

The return on the equity invested (i.e., the portfolio) is thus:

$$\frac{\$2.5}{\$30} = 8.33\%$$

This calculation can also be approached with the following formula:

$$R_p = R_i + [(B/E) \times (R_i - c)]$$

where:
R_p = return on portfolio
R_i = return on invested assets
B = amount of leverage
E = amount of equity invested
c = cost of borrowed funds

The formula adds the return on the investment (the first component) to the net levered return (the second component in brackets).

Using the example above:

$$R_p = 6\% + [(70/30) \times (6\% - 5\%)] = 8.33\%$$

Practice the use of this formula by checking Figure 1. In the table, we use the same example as above, except that we allow more leverage to be used (than the $70 million above) and allow the return on invested assets to vary (from the 6% above).

Figure 1: Leveraged Returns

Leverage	Return on Invested Assets		
	4%	6%	8%
$70 million	1.67%	8.33%	15.00%
$170 million	−1.67%	11.67%	25.00%
$270 million	−5.00%	15.00%	35.00%

The body of the table shows the leveraged return at combinations of return and leverage. The rows show how leveraged returns increase when asset returns increase. The columns show how leveraged returns either increase or decrease with leverage, depending on whether the return is greater or less than the cost of borrowed funds.

For example, the first row shows the effects of asset returns on leveraged return holding leverage constant at $70 million. Assuming $70 million in leverage, the leveraged return increases from 1.67% to 15% as the return on assets increases from 4% to 8%. Likewise, holding the asset return constant at 4% (which is less than the cost of funds), we see in the first column that the leveraged return decreases from +1.67% to −5% as leverage is increases from $70 million to $270 million.

In summary:

- As leverage increases, the variability of returns increases.
- As the investment return increases, the variability of returns increases.

The Effect of Leverage on Duration

Just as leverage increases the portfolio return variability, it also increases the duration, given that the duration of borrowed funds is typically less than the duration of invested funds.

> **Example: The effect of leverage on duration**
>
> Using the original example above, the manager's portfolio was worth $100 million, $30 million of which was his own funds and $70 million was borrowed. If the duration of the invested funds is 5.0 and the duration of borrowed funds is 1.0, **calculate** the duration on the portfolio.

Answer:

The duration can be calculated with the following formula:

$$D_P = \frac{D_i I - D_B B}{E}$$

where:
D_P = duration of portfolio
D_i = duration of invested assets
D_B = duration of borrowed funds
I = amount of invested funds
B = amount of borrowed funds
E = amount of equity invested

Using the provided information:

$$D_P = \frac{(5.0)100 - (1.0)70}{30} = 14.33$$

Note the use of leverage has resulted in the duration of the portfolio (14.33) being greater than the duration of invested assets (5.0).

Professor's Note: You probably noticed that when we calculate the duration of the levered portfolio, we measure the change in the value of equity rather than the overall portfolio. Until now, we implicitly assumed the portfolio contained no borrowed funds.

REPURCHASE AGREEMENTS

LOS 30.b: Discuss the use of repurchase agreements (repos) to finance bond purchases and the factors that affect the repo rate.

For the Exam: Be sure you fully understand and can discuss the use of repos as well as their characteristics.

To increase the leverage of their portfolios, portfolio managers sometimes borrow funds on a short-term basis using repurchase agreements. In a *repurchase agreement* (or repo), the borrower (seller of the security) agrees to repurchase it from the buyer on an agreed upon date at an agreed upon price (repurchase price).

Although it is legally a sale and subsequent purchase of securities, a repurchase agreement is essentially a collateralized loan, where the difference between the sale and repurchase prices is the interest on the loan. The rate of interest on the repo is referred to as the *repo rate.*

For example, assume a portfolio manager uses a repo to finance a $5 million position. Assuming that the repo term is one day and the repo rate is 4%, the dollar interest can be computed as follows:

$$\text{dollar interest} = \$5 \text{ million} \times 0.04 \times (1 \,/\, 360) = \$555.55$$

This means that the portfolio manager agrees to sell a Treasury security to the lender for $5 million and simultaneously agrees to repurchase the same security the next day for $5,000,555.55. The $555.55 is analogous to the interest on the loan. The portfolio manager gets the use of the $5 million for one day.

The manager ("borrower") obtains funds at a cheap interest rate while the "lender" earns a return greater than the risk-free rate. Although the term of a repo is typically a day or so, they can be rolled over to extend the financing.

The lender in a repurchase agreement is exposed to credit risk, if the collateral remains in the borrower's custody. For instance, the borrower could:

- Sell the collateral.
- Fraudulently use it as collateral for another loan.
- Go bankrupt.

As a result of this risk, repos will be structured with different delivery scenarios:

1. The borrower is required to physically deliver the collateral to the lender. Physical delivery can be costly however.

2. The collateral is deposited in a custodial account at the borrower's clearing bank. This is a cost-effective way to reduce the fees associated with delivery.

3. The transfer of securities is executed electronically through the parties' banks. This is less expensive than physical delivery but does involve fees and transfer charges.

4. Delivery is sometimes not required if the borrower's credit risk is low, if the parties are familiar with one another, or if the transaction is short-term.

The Repo Rate

No single repo rate exists for all repurchase agreements. The particular repo rate depends upon a number of factors.

- The repo rate increases as the **credit risk** of the borrower increases (when delivery is not required).
- As the **quality** of the collateral increases, the repo rate declines.
- As the **term** of the repo increases, the repo rate increases. It is important to note that the repo rate is a function of the repo term, not the maturity of the collateral securities.
- **Delivery**. If collateral is physically delivered, then the repo rate will be lower. If the repo is held by the borrower's bank, the rate will be higher. If no delivery takes place, the rate will be even higher.

- **Collateral.** If the availability of the collateral is limited, the repo rate will be lower. The lender may be willing to accept a lower rate in order to obtain a security they need to make delivery on another agreement.
- The **federal funds rate**, the rate at which banks borrow funds from one another, is a benchmark for repo rates. The higher the federal funds rate, the higher the repo rate.
- As the demand for funds at financial institutions changes due to **seasonal factors**, so will the repo rate.

BOND RISK MEASURES

LOS 30.c: <u>Critique</u> the use of standard deviation, target semivariance, shortfall risk, and value at risk as measures of fixed-income portfolio risk.

Duration is used as a measure of the interest rate risk of a portfolio. The duration for a portfolio is just the weighted average of the duration of its individual bonds. The duration of a portfolio can be adjusted using derivative securities, as we will see later on.

The limitations of duration as a risk measure include the fact that it is not accurate for large yield changes and for bonds with negative convexity. As such, other measures of bond risk should be examined.

Standard Deviation

The standard deviation measures the dispersion of returns around the mean return and is the square root of the variance. Assuming a symmetrical, normal distribution of returns around the mean, 68.3% of the returns will occur within ± one standard deviation of the mean. For example, a normal distribution of investment returns with a mean of 8% and a standard deviation of 4% means that 68.3% of all observed returns lie between 4% and 12% (8 − 4 = 4% and 8 + 4 = 12%).

Drawbacks of Standard Deviation and Variance

The problems with standard deviation and variance are as follows:

- Bond returns are often not normally distributed around the mean. For example, bonds with options will have non-normal return distributions.
- The number of inputs (e.g., variances and covariances) increases significantly with larger portfolios. In fact, if N represents the number of bonds in a portfolio, the number of inputs necessary to estimate the standard deviation of a portfolio is equal to $[N(N + 1)] / 2$.
- Obtaining estimates for each of these inputs is problematic. Historically calculated risk measures may not represent the risk measures that will be observed in the future. Remember from studying duration that bond prices become less sensitive to interest rate changes as the maturity date nears. Therefore, today's volatility will probably not be the same as tomorrow's volatility. Furthermore, a bond's options will change in their influence over time, making the estimation of future portfolio risk even more difficult.

Other measures of risk have been developed to specifically examine downside risk. Downside risk measures focus on the portion of a returns distribution that fall below some targeted return.

Semivariance

As its name implies, semivariance measures the dispersion of returns. Unlike its namesake (variance), semivariance does not measure the total dispersion of all returns above and below the mean. Instead, it measures only the dispersion of returns below a target return, which is the risk that most investors are concerned about.

Drawbacks of Semivariance

Despite its advantage, semivariance is not a commonly used risk measure for the following reasons:

- It is difficult to compute for a large bond portfolio. While computing the portfolio standard deviation is computationally straightforward, there is no easy way of doing so for semivariance.
- If investment returns are symmetric, the semivariance yields the same rankings as the variance and the variance is better understood.
- If investment returns are not symmetric, it can be quite difficult to forecast downside risk and the semivariance may not be a good indicator of future risk.
- Because the semivariance is estimated with only half the distribution, it is estimated with less accuracy.

Shortfall Risk

Whereas the semivariance measures the dispersion of returns below a specified target return, shortfall risk measures the *probability* that the actual return will be less than the target return. For example, the shortfall risk may be specified as: there is a 9.3% chance that returns will be less than the Treasury bill rate this year.

The primary criticism of the shortfall risk measure is:

- Shortfall risk does not consider the impact of outliers so the magnitude (dollar amount) of the shortfall below the target return is ignored. In the example above, we are given no information on how low returns could actually get below the Treasury bill return.

Value at Risk

The value at risk (VAR) provides the probability of a return less than a given amount over a specific time period. For example, VAR could be specified as: "There is a 5% probability that the loss on a bond portfolio will be $242,000 or more over the next month."

The primary criticism of VAR is:

- As in the shortfall risk measure, VAR does not provide the magnitude of losses that exceed that specified by VAR.

Professor's Note: There is an in-depth discussion of three methods of calculating VAR and their respective advantages and disadvantages in Study Session 14.

For the Exam: Be ready to use your knowledge of the risk measure disadvantages in a critique of statements made by analysts or portfolio managers.

FUTURES CONTRACTS

Interest rate futures are a cost-effective means for managing the dollar duration of a bond portfolio. There are interest rate futures contracts on securities of varying maturities, from 30 days to 30 years. The Chicago Board of Trade (CBOT) has a 30-year Treasury futures contract, on which any bond with a maturity or first call of at least 15 years is deliverable. The 30-year contract is very popular, and it is used in most examples and problems.

Just like bond prices, the prices of an interest rate futures contract will change when interest rates change. Also like a bond, the direction of the price change for a long position is opposite to the direction of the change in interest rates. Consequently, futures contracts can be utilized to lengthen or shorten portfolio duration simply by purchasing or shorting the contracts. As you will see, the focus of the next two LOS is dollar duration, which we will discuss shortly.

Cheapest to deliver (CTD) is a very descriptive term for a bond that the counterparty in the short position can deliver to satisfy the obligation of the futures contract. For example, many different bonds can be used to satisfy a CBOT 30-year Treasury bond futures contract. Furthermore, the short position has some choice with respect to the time of delivery. Note that these issues are not addressed in the LOS to follow so this discussion is just to help with your comprehension.

Professor's Note: The option of choosing the bond to deliver on the futures contract is sometimes referred to as the "quality" option or "swap" option. The ability to choose the actual delivery day is referred to as the "timing" option. The "wild card" option is the right to announce, after the exchange has closed, your intent to deliver on the contract.

A **conversion factor** helps determine the price received at delivery by the party with the short position. The quoted price for the CTD is the product of the quoted futures price and the conversion factor. This will be demonstrated in the examples below. Each bond eligible for delivery has a conversion factor provided by the exchange, the computation of which is not important here.

ADVANTAGES OF INTEREST RATE FUTURES

LOS 30.d: <u>Demonstrate</u> the advantages of using futures instead of cash market instruments to alter portfolio risk.

There are three main advantages to using futures over cash market instruments. All three advantages are derived from the fact that there are low transactions costs and a great deal of depth in the futures market.

Compared to cash market instruments, futures:

1. Are more liquid.

2. Are less expensive.

3. Make short positions more readily obtainable, because the contracts can be more easily shorted than an actual bond.

DOLLAR DURATION

> For the Exam: The advantages of using futures over cash instruments are fairly straightforward and, I think, only a secondary consideration here. Your ability to construct a hedge using futures is much more important.

The **dollar duration** is the *dollar* change in the price of a bond, portfolio, or futures contract resulting from a 100 bps change in yield. The relationship between duration and dollar duration is straightforward.

For a given bond with an initial "value":

duration = (%Δvalue) = –(effective duration)(0.01)

Multiplying through by the market value of the bond or portfolio, we get dollar duration, represented by DD:

DD = ($Δvalue) = –(effective duration)(0.01)(value)

The dollar duration of a futures contract is the change in the futures dollar value for a 100 bps interest rate change. The dollar duration of a portfolio can be adjusted by taking a position in futures contracts.

To **increase** dollar duration → **buy** futures contracts.

To **decrease** dollar duration → **sell** futures contracts.

Example: Dollar duration

A manager has a $100 million portfolio with an effective duration of 8. Suppose she is concerned about the possibility that the Fed may increase rates 25 basis points. The manager is interested in limiting her exposure to $1 million. Should the manager hedge, and if so, should she take a long or short position in futures contracts?

Answer:

The change in the value of the portfolio given a 25 basis point increase in rates is:

$$\%\Delta\text{value} = -(8)(0.0025)(\$100,000,000) = -\$2,000,000$$

If her objective is to limit this exposure to $1 million, the manager should short futures contracts. As you will see, determining the actual number of contracts is an important part of this review.

DURATION MANAGEMENT

LOS 30.e: Construct and evaluate an immunization strategy based on interest rate futures.

For this review, controlling interest rate risk means *adding futures positions* (i.e., a derivatives overlay) to an existing portfolio to achieve some *target dollar duration*. Doing this effectively requires accurate measures of the dollar duration of the initial portfolio and the futures contracts.

The problem that you should be ready to solve would provide a current duration and a *target duration* for a portfolio of a given value. The goal is to determine the number of those futures contracts to long/short to achieve the target dollar duration. The logic of the process is seen in the following expression:

$$DD_T = DD_P + DD_{Futures}$$

where:
DD_T = the target dollar duration of the portfolio plus futures
DD_P = the dollar duration of the portfolio before adding futures
$DD_{Futures}$ = the total dollar duration of the added futures contracts

Note that we denote the dollar duration of a single futures contract as DD_f.

The most basic principle of controlling interest rate risk is to take positions in futures contracts that modify DD_P to achieve the specified target dollar duration, denoted DD_T.

For a long futures position, $DD_f > 0$. For a short futures position, $DD_f < 0$.

As an aside, once a given DD_T has been achieved, market conditions will probably change the portfolio's properties, and the manager will usually adjust the futures position to move the dollar duration of the portfolio (which now includes futures) back to DD_T.

It is quite simple to determine the number of contracts needed to achieve a dollar duration if you are given the dollar durations of the current portfolio (usually without futures at the outset), the target portfolio, and one futures contracts.

Example: Achieving the target dollar duration

The manager of a bond portfolio expects an increase in interest rates, so duration should be reduced. The portfolio has a dollar duration of $32,000, and he would like to reduce it to $20,000. The manager chooses a futures contract with a dollar duration of $1,100. How can the manager achieve the target duration?

Answer:

$$\text{number of contracts} = \frac{DD_T - DD_P}{DD_f}$$

$$= \frac{\$20,000 - \$32,000}{\$1,100} = -10.91$$

The manager should short (sell) 11 contracts to reduce the dollar duration.

Dollar Duration of a Futures Contract

Recall that the pricing of a futures contract is based on the cheapest-to-deliver bond. Likewise, the duration of a futures contract will be based on the duration of the cheapest-to-deliver bond.

Given this relationship, the dollar duration for a futures contract can be calculated as:

$$DD_f = \frac{DD_{CTD}}{\text{CTD conversion factor}}$$

In the previous example, you might have been given that the dollar duration of the CTD is $DD_{CTD} = \$1,375$ and the conversion factor is 1.25. In that case, you would have had to compute $DD_f = \$1,375 / 1.25 = \$1,100$.

From what we have so far, we can write:

$$\text{number of contracts} = \frac{DD_T - DD_P}{DD_f}; \text{ then, since } DD_f = \frac{DD_{CTD}}{\text{CTD conversion factor}}$$

$$\text{number of contracts} = \frac{DD_T - DD_P}{DD_{CTD}\Big/\text{conversion factor}}$$

Note: The Level 3 curriculum shows the formula as:

$$\text{number of contracts} = \frac{(D_T - D_P)P_P}{D_{CTD}P_{CTD}}(\text{CTD conversion factor})$$

Remember that dollar duration is calculated as duration multiplied by value (price), so if we multiply the numerator and denominator components together, we have:

$$\text{number of contracts} = \frac{(DD_T - DD_P)}{DD_{CTD}}(\text{CTD conversion factor})$$

Which, when rearranged, is exactly the same as our original equation:

$$\text{number of contracts} = \frac{DD_T - DD_P}{DD_{CTD}\big/\text{conversion factor}}$$

> **For the Exam:** Before entering the exam room, be sure you know and can perform as well as discuss any of the futures hedging calculations.

Hedging Issues

> **For the Exam:** The material on the next several pages is presented as necessary background material. It is not specifically addressed in any LOS.

Although calculating the number of contracts needed to increase or decrease interest rate risk exposure is straight forward, in practice the hedge may not work as planned. The following discusses some of the issues in hedging that may arise in practice.

Basis Risk and Cross Hedging

Price basis refers to the difference between the spot price and the futures price at delivery:

price basis = spot (cash) price – futures delivery price

Basis risk is the variability of the basis. It is an important consideration for hedges that will be lifted in the intermediate term (i.e., before delivery). Basis can change unexpectedly due to difference in the underlying bond and the futures contract.

In a *cross hedge,* the underlying security in the futures contract is not identical to the asset being hedged (e.g., using T-bond futures to hedge corporate bonds). A cross hedge can be either long or short. It must be used if no corresponding futures contract exists for a given position or, if a corresponding contract exists, its liquidity is too low to be effective.

The prices of the bond portfolio and the futures contract will vary over time with changes in interest rates. And since they are not perfectly correlated, they can move closer together or farther apart. In other words, the basis changes over time. If the basis is significantly different than expected at the horizon date for the investment, the hedge could be quite ineffective.

Thus, it is important to note that at the initiation of a hedge, a manager substitutes the uncertainty of the basis for the uncertainty of the price of the hedged security. In other words, the manager may think he has effectively hedged the risk of the bond with a futures contract, when in fact he has not.

When implementing a cross hedge, the manager should evaluate the differences in the relevant risk factor exposures of the bond and the futures contract. If the bond has greater sensitivity to interest rate changes, for example, more of the futures contract will be needed to effectively hedge the bond position.

The desired hedge ratio is given by:

$$\text{hedge ratio} = \frac{\text{exposure of bond to risk factor}}{\text{exposure of futures to risk factor}}$$

For example, if it was determined that 100 futures contracts would be needed to hedge a bond portfolio and the manager subsequently estimates that the hedge ratio is 1.2, the bond portfolio should be hedged with 120 contracts.

Note that the hedge ratio and hence the number of contracts should be estimated for the time at which the hedge is lifted (i.e., the hedge horizon), because this is when the manager wishes to lock in a value. The manager should also have an estimate of the price, because the effect of changes in risk will vary as price and yield vary.

Given that the pricing of the futures contract depends on the cheapest-to-deliver bond, the hedge ratio can also be expressed as:

$$(1) \quad \text{hedge ratio} = \frac{\text{exposure of bond to risk factor}}{\text{exposure of CTD to risk factor}} \times \frac{\text{exposure of CTD to risk factor}}{\text{exposure of futures to risk factor}}$$

In the formula above, the second term on the right-hand side represents the conversion factor for the CTD bond.

If we are examining interest rate risk as the risk factor and we wish to fully hedge the bond, the target dollar duration is zero. Thus we can rewrite the formula for the number of contracts to hedge a bond from the numerical example above as:

$$(2) \quad \text{hedge ratio} = \frac{DD_P}{DD_{CTD}} \times \text{conversion factor for the CTD}$$

Note the similarities between (1) the general expression for hedging risk and (2) the formula specific to hedging interest rate risk.

Yield Beta

Another complication that arises with cross hedges is that the spread in yields between the bond and the futures may not be constant. In the calculations up to now, we have assumed that the yield spread is constant (i.e., the yields change in unison so that the spread remains the same). To adjust for changes in the spread, the **yield beta** is obtained from a regression equation:

$$\Delta \text{yield on bond} = \alpha + \beta(\Delta \text{yield on CTD}) + e$$

The yield beta, β, shows the relationship between changes in the yields on the bond and the CTD. A yield beta of 0.80, for example, would imply that for a yield change of 100 bps on the CTD, the yield on bond changes 80 bps. If the yield spread between the bond being hedged and the CTD issue is assumed to be constant, the yield beta must equal one.

To adjust formula (2) for fully hedging interest rate risk when yield spread is not constant, we must adjust the formula to incorporate the yield beta as follows:

$$\text{hedge ratio} = \frac{DD_P}{DD_{CTD}} \times \text{conversion factor for the CTD} \times \text{yield beta}$$

The formula states that if the yield on the bond is more volatile than that of the CTD (i.e., $\beta > 1$), then more futures contracts will be needed to hedge the bond than would be the case if yield spreads were constant. If the yield on the bond was less volatile, then less contracts would be needed.

 Professor's Note: Whenever you use Treasury futures to hedge a non-Treasury portfolio, you are using a cross hedge. That is, since the two assets are not identical, the basis is subject to change; their yields will not move in tandem.

Evaluating Hedging Effectiveness

The effectiveness of hedging strategies should be evaluated so that future hedging will be more effective. There are three basic sources of hedging error. There can be an error in the:

1. Forecast of the basis at the time the hedge is lifted.

2. Estimated durations.

3. Estimated yield beta.

Estimating the duration of bonds with options can be particularly complicated and should be estimated with care.

 Professor's Note: The material below is covered in more detail in Study Session 15.

LOS 30.f: Explain the use of interest rate swaps and options to alter portfolio cash flows and exposure to interest rate risk.

In an **interest rate swap**, one party typically pays a fixed rate of interest and the other party pays a floating rate. The principal typically acts only as a reference value and is not exchanged. The floating interest rate is based on London Interbank Offered Rate (LIBOR), Treasury bills, or some other benchmark.

Swaps can be used to convert a floating rate loan or bond into a fixed rate, or vice versa. They can also be used to alter the duration of a portfolio. Receiving fixed in a swap increases duration while paying fixed reduces duration. The duration of the floating side is negligible. Swaps are used to hedge interest rate risk because they are lower in cost than futures and other contracts.

Most **interest rate options** are written on interest rate futures contracts, rather than on a debt security. In a call option written on a futures contract, the buyer has the right to buy the futures contract at the strike price. If exercised, the seller would take a short position in the futures contract. In a put option written on a futures contract, the buyer has the right to sell the futures contract at the strike price.

The duration of an option depends on the duration of the underlying contract, the option delta, and the leverage. The option delta measures the change in price of the option relative to the change in the underlying contract. The leverage refers to the price of the underlying contract relative to the price of the option. Out of the money options will be cheaper and hence provide more leverage than in the money options. However, out of the money options will be less sensitive to the underlying contract and hence have a lower delta.

The delta and duration of a call will be positive (it provides the right to go long) and the delta and duration of a put will be negative (it provides the right to go short).

Options can be used to establish a **protective put** or a covered call. In the former, the purchase of a put protects a bond investment from increases in interest rates. If interest rates fall, the bond investment will increase in value and the manager will let the put expire worthless. The cost of the put will, however, reduce the manager's return.

In a **covered call**, the manager believes that the upside on a bond owned is limited and sells a call to earn extra income. If, however, interest rates fall, the call will be exercised against the manager and reduce his return. If interest rates rise, the loss on the bond will be buffered by the income from the sale of the call. However, the call does not provide downside protection as strong as that provided by the protective put.

There are also interest rate **caps** and **floors**. Note that these are written on an interest rate, not on a bond futures contract as in the protective put or a covered call described above. The former is a series of calls that put a cap on the cost of borrowing. The floor provides a minimum return on a held loan. A collar is a combination of a cap and floor, where one is bought and the other sold to finance the purchase of the other.

For example, a bank borrows short-term to lend long-term. To protect against an increase in short-term rates, the bank will buy a cap. If interest rates rise above the strike rate, the cap will provide a payment to the bank that mitigates the increased cost of borrowing. If interest rates fall, the bank will let the cap expire worthless and benefit from the lower rate.

The bank may finance the purchase of the cap by selling a floor. If, however, short-term rates fall below the floor's strike rate, the bank will owe a payment on the floor and the sale of the floor will adversely affect the bank.

On the other hand, an insurance company may have a long-term liability in the form of an annuity contract that calls for fixed payments (i.e., payments at a fixed rate). The proceeds from the sale of the annuity policy might be invested in a floating rate note. The risk of short-term interest rates falling is mitigated by buying a floor. If short-term rates fall below the strike rate, the floor will provide a payment that mitigates the lower return to the insurance company. If short-term rates rise, the insurance company will let the floor expire worthless and benefit from the higher rate.

The insurance company may finance the purchase of the floor by selling a cap. If, however, short-term rates rise above the cap's strike rate, the sale of the cap will reduce the insurance company's profits.

MANAGING DEFAULT RISK, CREDIT SPREAD RISK, AND DOWNGRADE RISK WITH DERIVATIVES

LOS 30.g: Compare and contrast default risk, credit spread risk, and downgrade risk and demonstrate the use of credit derivative instruments to address each risk in the context of a fixed-income portfolio.

Types of Credit Risk

There are three principal credit-related risks that can be addressed with credit derivative instruments:

Default risk is the risk that the issuer will not meet the obligations of the issue (i.e., pay interest and/or principal when due). This risk is unique in the sense that it results from a potential action—failure to pay—of the debt issuer.

Credit spread risk is the risk of an increase in the yield spread on an asset. Yield spread is the asset's yield minus the relevant risk-free benchmark. This risk is a function of potential changes in the market's collective evaluation of credit quality, as reflected by the spread.

Downgrade risk is the possibility that the credit rating of an asset/issuer is downgraded by a major credit-rating organization, such as Moody's. If the credit rating is downgraded, the price of the bond will fall as its yield rises.

Types of Credit Derivative Instruments

Credit derivatives are designed to transfer risk between the buyer and seller of the instrument. They fall into three broad categories: (1) *credit options*, (2) *credit forwards*, and (3) *credit swaps*.

Credit options. Credit options provide protection from adverse price movements related to credit events or changes in the underlying reference asset's spread over a risk-free rate. When the payoff is based on the underlying asset's price, the option is known as a binary credit option. When the payoff is based on the underlying asset's yield spread, the option is known as a credit spread option.

Credit options written on an asset. A binary credit put option will provide protection if a specific **credit event** occurs, and if the value of the underlying asset is less than the option strike price. A credit event is typically a default or an adverse change in credit rating. The option value (OV) or payoff is:

$$OV = max\,[(strike - value),\,0]$$

Example: Using binary credit options to address risk

A portfolio manager holds 1,000 bonds with a face value of $1 million and fears that a credit event may occur. The portfolio manager purchases binary credit puts with a strike price at par. Subsequently a credit downgrade occurs, and the bonds decline in value to $900. What is the option value?

Answer:

$$OV = max\,[(strike - value),\,0] = (1,000 - 900) = \$100$$

If protection were purchased on the entire position, the overall payoff would be $100,000 (= 100 × 1,000), less the cost of purchasing the options. Remember, a positive payoff is contingent upon both a credit event occurring, and the option being in the money. A decline in value alone will not trigger a payoff.

Credit spread options. A credit spread call option will provide protection if the reference asset's spread (at option maturity) over the relevant risk-free benchmark increases beyond the strike spread. The increase in the spread beyond the strike spread (i.e., the option being in the money) constitutes an identifiable credit event, in and of itself. The option value (OV) or payoff is:

$$OV = max\,[(actual\ spread - strike\ spread) \times notional \times risk\ factor,\,0]$$

Example: Using credit spread options to address risk

A portfolio manager holds 1,000 bonds with a face value of $1 million. The current spread over a comparable U.S. Treasury is 200 basis points. The portfolio manager purchases credit spread calls with a strike price of 250 basis points, notional principal of $1 million, and a risk factor of 10. At the option's maturity, the bond price is $900, implying a spread of 350 basis points. What is the option value?

Answer:

$$OV = \max\ [(0.035 - 0.025) \times \$1\ \text{million} \times 10,\ 0] = \$100,000$$

The size of the notional principal and the risk factor are calibrated to the level of protection desired by the portfolio manager. In this case, the level of protection was the same as that derived from the binary credit option.

Credit forwards. Credit spread forwards are forward contracts wherein the payment at settlement is a function of the credit spread over the benchmark at the time the contract matures. The value (FV) or payoff to the buyer of a credit spread forward is:

$$FV = (\text{spread at maturity} - \text{contract spread}) \times \text{notional} \times \text{risk factor}$$

This is a zero sum game in that for one party to gain, the other party to the contract must lose. If the spread at maturity is less than the contract spread, the forward buyer (often the portfolio manager) will have to pay the forward seller.

Example: Using credit spread forwards to address risk

A portfolio manager holds 1,000 bonds with a face value of $1 million. The current spread over a comparable U.S. Treasury is 200 basis points. The portfolio manager purchases a credit spread forward with notional principal of $1 million, a contract spread of 250 basis points, and a risk factor of 10. At the contract's maturity, the bond price is $900, implying a spread of 350 basis points, what is the value of the forward?

Answer:

$$FV = [(0.035 - 0.025) \times \$1\ \text{million} \times 10] = \$100,000$$

Once again, the size of the notional principal and the risk factor are calibrated to the level of protection desired by the portfolio manager. The resulting level of protection was the same as that derived in the previous option examples.

Credit swaps. Credit swaps describe a category of products in the swap family, all of which provide some form of credit risk transfer. Our focus here will be on **credit default swaps** which can be viewed as protection, or insurance, against default on an underlying credit instrument (called the reference asset or reference entity when referring to the issuer).

To obtain the requisite insurance, the protection buyer agrees to pay the protection seller a periodic fee in exchange for a commitment to stand behind an underlying bond or loan should its issuer experience a credit event, such as default. A credit default swap agreement will contain a list of credit events that apply to the agreement.

The terms of a credit swap are custom-designed to meet the needs of the counterparties. They can be cash settled or there can be physical delivery, which generally means the buyer of the swap delivers the reference asset to the counterparty for a cash payment.

Example: Using credit default swaps to address risk

The Rose Foundation enters into a 2-year credit default swap on a notional principal of $10 million of 5-year bonds issued by the Crescent Corporation. The swap specifies an annual premium of 55 basis points and cash settlement. Assume that the Crescent Corporation defaults at the end of the first year, and the bonds are trading at 60 cents to the dollar. **Describe** the cash flows associated with the credit default swap.

Answer:

The Rose Foundation would pay $55,000 (0.0055 × $10 million) at the beginning of the first year to the seller of the credit default swap. If Crescent defaults after one year, the Rose Foundation will receive a payment of $4,000,000 [(1 − 0.6) × $10 million)]. This payment compensates Rose for the decline in value of the bonds.

Note that in all cases, the rules for the calculation of the cash payouts for these credit derivative instruments must be agreed upon when the instrument is created. Of particular importance is the definition of what constitutes a credit event that will trigger payment and the size of the resulting payment. The buyer will only realize adequate protection from a specific type of credit risk if these parameters are correctly specified.

For the Exam: Whenever you see any material on swaps, pay attention. CFA Institute likes swaps, any kind of swaps, and frequently asks questions on them. Be able to offer a suggested swap to achieve the portfolio manager's specified goals.

INTERNATIONAL BOND EXCESS RETURNS

LOS 30.h: Explain the potential sources of excess return for an international bond portfolio.

The phrase *excess return* implies active management. That is, instead of passively overseeing the portfolio, the manager of a bond portfolio actively seeks out sources of additional return beyond that merely compensating for the level of risk. In this LOS, we discuss six of the potential sources of excess return on international bonds: (1) market selection, (2) currency selection, (3) duration management, (4) sector selection, (5) credit analysis, and (6) markets outside the benchmark.

For the Exam: As you read through these sources for excess return, try to imagine their equivalents in equity portfolio management, which will be discussed in Study Session 11. For example, market, sector, and currency selection all have direct counterparts in equity portfolio management. Selecting securities or even markets outside the benchmark can also be compared directly to equity portfolio management. Credit analysis involves selecting bonds whose rating should either improve or fall. This could be compared to selecting equities expected to out- or underperform, based upon the manager's expectations. You might want to refer back to this material as you study the equity portfolio management material.

Market selection involves selecting appropriate national bond markets. The manager must determine which bond markets offer the best overall opportunities for value enhancement.

Currency selection. The manager must determine the amount of active currency management versus the amount of currency hedging he will employ. The manager should remain unhedged or employ hedging strategies to capture value only if she feels confident in her ability to forecast interest rate changes and their resulting impact on exchange rates. Due to the complexities and required expertise, currency management is often treated as a separately-managed function.

Duration management. Once the manager has determined what sectors (i.e., countries) will be held, she must determine the optimal maturities. That is, anticipating shifts or twists, the manager will often utilize segments of the yield curve to add value. Limited maturity offerings in some markets can be overcome by employing fixed-income derivatives.

Sector selection. This is directly analogous to domestic bond portfolio management. Due to increasing ranges of maturities, ratings, and bond types (e.g., corporate, government), the international bond portfolio manager is now able to add value through credit analysis of entire sectors. (Note that sector selection refers to entire sectors, not individual securities.)

Credit analysis refers to recognizing value-added opportunities through credit analysis of individual securities.

Markets outside the benchmark. Large foreign bond indices are usually composed of sovereign (government) issues. With the increasing availability of corporate issues, the manager may try to add value through enhanced indexing by adding corporates to an indexed foreign bond portfolio.

INTERNATIONAL BOND DURATIONS

LOS 30.i: <u>Evaluate</u> 1) the change in value for a foreign bond when domestic interest rates change and 2) the bond's contribution to duration in a domestic portfolio, given the duration of the foreign bond and the country beta.

For the Exam: Evaluating a change in value will probably require supporting calculations.

If interest rates worldwide changed simultaneously by equal amounts (i.e., only parallel shifts in the "global" yield curve), computing and interpreting the duration and duration contribution of each of the bonds in a global bond portfolio would be no different than doing so for a purely domestic portfolio. Unfortunately, we know that interest rate changes are not always the result of parallel shifts and there is no such thing as a "global" yield curve. Interest rates across the globe can change in the same direction by different amounts or even move in opposite directions. They are influenced by local macroeconomic factors and international factors including foreign interest rates.

To assign meaning to the duration measures for foreign bonds, they must be "standardized." In other words, the sensitivity of the bonds to changes in their own (foreign) interest rates has little meaning to the manager trying to measure the sensitivity of his portfolio to changes in the domestic rate, unless the manager knows if and by how much the foreign rate will change if the domestic rate changes. To estimate the sensitivity of the prices of the foreign bonds to changes in the domestic interest rate, the manager must measure the *correlations* between changes in their yields and changes in the domestic interest rate.

 Professor's Note: The word standardized *is used here to indicate that the foreign bond's duration measured against its local interest rate has been adjusted to have the same meaning as the durations of the domestic bonds in the portfolio. In other words, the foreign bond's* standardized *duration measures its sensitivity to domestic rates. This is my term only. You will not find it used in the Level 3 curriculum.*

Assuming there is a relationship (i.e., correlation) between yields on the domestic and foreign bonds, the manager can regress the yield on the foreign bond against the yield on a domestic bond of similar risk and maturity:

$$\Delta yield_{foreign} = \beta(\Delta yield_{domestic}) + e$$

In the regression, β is the *country beta* or *yield beta*, which measures the sensitivity of the yield on the foreign bond to changes in the yield on the domestic bond. Multiplying the country beta times the change in the domestic rate gives the manager the estimated change in the foreign yield. Then, multiplying the change in the foreign yield by the bond's duration gives the estimated change in the foreign bond's price.

Example: Applying the country beta

Suppose the country (yield) beta for Japan is 0.45 and the duration of a Japanese bond is 6.0. **Estimate** the change in the price of the Japanese bond given a 100 bps change in the domestic interest rate.

Answer:

For a 100 bps change in the domestic rate, the Japanese bond's yield will change (0.45)(100 bp) = 45 bps. Multiplying the estimated change in the Japanese rate by the Japanese bond's duration gives the estimated change in the Japanese bond's price.

$$\%\Delta_{price} = duration \times \Delta y \times \beta_{yield}$$

$$\%\Delta_{price} = 6 \times (0.01 \times 0.45) = 0.027 = 2.7\%$$

For the Exam: Remember that the technical definition of modified or effective duration is the percentage change in the price of the bond given a *100 basis point* change in its yield. This means that the duration number can be directly interpreted as the estimated *percentage change* in the bond's price given a change in yield measured in basis points.

Duration Contribution

The duration of a foreign bond must also be adjusted when we calculate its *contribution* to the portfolio duration. Remember that the contribution of a domestic bond to the duration of a purely domestic portfolio is the bond's weight in the portfolio multiplied by its duration. Likewise, the duration contribution for a foreign bond to a portfolio is its *standardized* duration multiplied by its weight in the portfolio.

Example: Duration contribution of a foreign bond

The duration of an Australian bond is 6.0 and the country beta is 1.15. A U.S. portfolio manager has $50,000 in the Australian bond in an otherwise domestic portfolio with a total value of $1,000,000. **Calculate** the Australian bond's duration contribution to the portfolio.

Answer:

First, the bond's *standardized* duration can be estimated as 6 × 1.15 = 6.90. Multiplying the bond's *standardized* duration of 6.90 by its weight in the portfolio (5%) gives the bond's contribution to portfolio duration:

duration contribution = weight × duration
= 0.05 × 6.90 = 0.35

As with a purely domestic portfolio, the duration of a portfolio containing both domestic and foreign bonds can be estimated as the *sum* of the individual bond duration contributions.

Example: Portfolio duration

Assume that you have a portfolio consisting of two bonds. 75% of the portfolio is in a U.S. dollar-denominated bond with a duration of 5.0. 25% of the portfolio is in a foreign bond with a duration of 8.0 and a country beta of 1.2. **Compute** the duration of this portfolio from a U.S. perspective.

Answer:

contribution of domestic bond	= 0.75 × 5	= 3.75
contribution of foreign bond	= 0.25 × 8 × 1.2	= 2.40
portfolio duration	= 3.75 + 2.4	= 6.15

THE HEDGING DECISION

LOS 30.j: <u>Recommend</u> and <u>justify</u> whether to hedge or not hedge currency risk in an international bond investment.

For the Exam: The hedging strategies discussed in this section are all based on interest rate parity (IRP). Before we turn to the hedging strategies, therefore, we review IRP and its implications. The LOS asks you to "recommend and justify whether to hedge or not hedge an international bond investment," and that decision could be made using IRP without even considering the strategies. Had the LOS asked for you to determine the optimal hedging strategy, we could ignore IRP and focus solely on the strategies themselves. The curriculum only vaguely mentions IRP and resulting arbitrage conditions, but I recommend that you know all this material when you enter the test room.

Interest Rate Parity

For any two currencies, there is a unique relationship among the current spot exchange rate, the short-term risk-free rates in the currencies, and the forward exchange rate. This relationship is known as interest rate parity (IRP). The IRP formula summarizes this arbitrage-free relationship:

$$F = S_0 \left(\frac{1 + c_d}{1 + c_f} \right)$$

where:
F = the forward exchange rate (domestic per foreign)
S_0 = the current spot exchange rate (domestic per foreign)
c_d = the domestic short-term rate
c_f = the foreign short-term rate

If we know the current interest rates and the spot exchange rate, we are able to determine what forward exchange rate must prevail in order to prevent arbitrage.

When we compare this forward rate with the spot rate, we can determine the implied currency appreciation or depreciation in percentage terms. Appreciation of the forward foreign currency is called a premium, and depreciation in the forward foreign currency is called a discount.

We can *approximate* the forward premium or discount (i.e., the *currency differential*) as the difference in short-term rates:

$$f_{d,f} = \frac{(F - S_0)}{S_0} \approx c_d - c_f$$

 Professor's Note: $f_{d,f}$ is read as the forward premium or discount (the forward currency differential) of currency f (the foreign currency) relative to currency d (the domestic currency).

We continue the review by calculating a currency differential.

Example: Calculating a forward differential

Suppose that the U.S. dollar is trading at a spot rate of $1.50 per £1.00, and 1-year U.S. dollar Eurocurrency deposits are yielding 6.50%, while 1-year pound sterling Eurocurrency deposits are yielding 5.75%. **Calculate** the equilibrium 1-year forward rate and the pound sterling forward premium or discount.

Answer:

We use IRP to determine the implied forward exchange rate:

$$F = S_0 \left(\frac{1 + c_d}{1 + c_f} \right) = 1.50 \left(\frac{1.065}{1.0575} \right) = 1.51064 \, USD / GBP$$

Once the implied forward exchange rate is calculated, we can calculate the premium or discount using IRP. We can also approximate the premium or discount as the interest rate differential between the two countries.

$$f_{d,f} = \frac{F - S_0}{S_0} = \frac{1.51064 - 1.50}{1.50} = 0.71\%$$

or

$$f_{d,f} \approx c_d - c_f = 6.5 - 5.75 \approx 0.75\% \text{ (approximation)}$$

COVERED INTEREST ARBITRAGE

Covered interest arbitrage forces interest rates toward *parity*, because risk-free rates must be the same across borders when forward exchange rates exist. For example, if the spot and forward rates in the previous example were both \$1.50/£, it would be possible to borrow pounds sterling at 5.75%, convert to dollars, lend in dollars at 6.50%, and fix our repayment in pounds sterling at the forward rate of \$1.50. We would earn potentially infinite profits with no capital at stake! Speculators trying to take advantage of this situation would force rates back into equilibrium. We assume the forward rate would be forced to \$1.51064, at which the arbitrage would not be possible.

Professor's Note: If the nominal domestic interest rate is low relative to the nominal foreign interest rate, the foreign currency must trade at a forward discount (this relationship is forced by arbitrage). Alternatively, if the nominal home interest rate is high relative to the nominal foreign interest rate, the foreign currency must trade at a forward premium.

If a foreign currency is trading at a forward discount, it is expected to depreciate relative to the domestic currency (i.e., the forward rate, specified domestic per foreign, is less than the spot rate). Likewise, if the foreign currency is trading at a forward premium, it is expected to appreciate relative to the domestic currency (i.e., the forward rate, specified domestic per foreign is greater than the spot rate).

We can check for an arbitrage opportunity by using the covered interest differential. The covered interest differential says that the domestic interest rate should be the same as the *hedged* foreign interest rate. More specifically, the difference between the domestic interest rate and the hedged foreign rate should be zero.

The covered interest differential can be viewed by rewriting IRP in the following way:

$$(1 + c_d) = (1 + c_f)\left(\frac{F}{S_0}\right)$$

The left-hand side of the equation is the domestic interest rate, while the right-hand side is the hedged foreign rate (the foreign rate expressed in domestic terms). Arbitrage will prevent this relationship from getting out of balance. To preclude arbitrage, the left-hand side minus the right-hand side should equal zero. Hence, the covered interest differential can be written as:

$$\text{covered interest differential} = (1 + c_d) - (1 + c_f)\left(\frac{F}{S_0}\right)$$

Example: Covered interest differential

You can invest in euros at r = 5.127%, or you can invest in U.S. dollars at r = 5.5%. You live in Germany (which represents the home or domestic country). The current spot rate is 0.96000 €/USD, and the forward rate is 0.95661 €/USD. **Determine** if there are any arbitrage opportunities. Assume you have 1,000 euros.

Answer:

First, insert the numbers and see if the covered interest differential is zero:

$$(1.05127) - (1.055)\left(\frac{0.95661}{0.96000}\right) = 0 \rightarrow \text{no interest arbitrage}$$

This should not be required on the exam, but to test the relationship you could work through the following steps:

Step 1: Convert your 1,000 euros to U.S. dollars at the spot rate:
1,000 / 0.96000 = USD1,041.67

Step 2: Invest your U.S. dollars at 5.5% in the United States. At year-end you will have $1,041.67(1.055) = USD1,098.96.

Step 3: At the same time you invested your U.S. dollars in the United States, you entered into a 1-year forward contract to convert U.S. dollars back to euros at the forward rate of 0.95661 €/USD.

Step 4: When the U.S. dollar investment matures, collect the interest and principal (USD1,098.96) and convert it back to euros:
1,098.96(0.95661) = €1,051.28.

If you had invested the euros directly in Germany, at year end you would have 1,000(1.05127) = €1,051.27. While there is a modest rounding error, there is no arbitrage opportunity here.

Hedging Techniques

There are three primary methods utilized for hedging the currency risk in an international bond investment: (1) the *forward hedge*, (2) the *proxy hedge*, and (3) the *cross hedge*.

The forward hedge. The forward hedge is used to eliminate (most of) the currency risk. Utilizing a forward hedge assumes forward contracts are available and actively traded on the foreign currency in terms of the domestic currency. If so, the manager enters a forward contract to sell the foreign currency at the current forward rate.

The proxy hedge. In a proxy hedge, the manager enters a forward contract between the *domestic currency and a second foreign currency* that is correlated with the first foreign currency (i.e., the currency in which the bond is denominated). Gains or losses on the forward contract are expected to at least partially offset losses or gains in the domestic return on the bond. Proxy hedges are utilized when forward contracts on the first foreign currency are not actively traded or hedging the first foreign currency is relatively expensive.

Notice that in currency hedging, the proxy hedge is what we would usually refer to as a *cross hedge* in other financial transactions. In other words, the manager can't construct a hedge in the long asset, so he hedges using another, correlated asset.

The cross hedge. In a currency cross hedge, the manager enters into a contract to deliver the original foreign currency (i.e., the currency of the bond) for a third currency. Again it is hoped that gains or losses on the forward contract will at least partially offset losses or gains in the domestic return on the bond. In other words, the manager takes steps to eliminate the currency risk of the bond by replacing it with the risk of another currency. The currency cross hedge, therefore, is a means of *changing* the risk exposure rather than eliminating it.

Foreign Bond Returns

The return on an investment in a foreign bond can be broken down into its nominal local return and the currency return implied by the forward currency differential:

$$R_b \approx R_l + R_c$$

where:
R_b = the domestic return on the foreign bond
R_l = the local return on the foreign bond (i.e., in its local currency)
R_c = the expected (by the market) currency return; the forward premium or discount

We can decompose the relationship using IRP, which demonstrates that the forward premium or discount depends upon the interest rate differential:

$$R_b = R_l + R_c \Rightarrow \text{Since } R_c \approx i_d - i_f$$

$$R_b = R_l + R_c \approx R_l + (i_d - i_f) \Rightarrow i_d + (R_l - i_f)$$

So, as shown by decomposing the return, as long as the bonds are similar in maturity and other risk characteristics, choosing between them is determined solely by the bond that offers the greatest excess return denominated in its local currency.

The Hedging Decision

Professor's Note: The ranking of returns on fully hedged international bond investments depends only on the individual bond's risk premiums. That is, when comparing fully hedged strategies, the bond that offers the highest excess return over the risk-free rate in its local currency will provide the highest fully hedged return.

We explore the hedging decision by first determining the optimal bond to purchase and then determining whether to hedge or not.

Example: Selecting the right international bond

Using only the following data on two foreign bonds with the same risk characteristics (e.g., maturity, credit risk), **determine** which bond should be purchased, if the currency risk of either can be fully hedged with a forward contract.

Country	Nominal Return	Risk-Free Rate
i	4.75%	3.25%
j	5.25%	3.80%

Answer:

Since their maturities and other risk characteristics are similar and an investment in either can be hedged using a forward contract, we can determine the better bond to purchase by calculating their excess returns:

Bond i: 4.75% − 3.25% = 1.50%

Bond j: 5.25% − 3.80% = 1.45%

Bond i offers the higher excess return, so given the ability to fully hedge the manager should select Bond i.

Example: To hedge or not to hedge

A U.S. manager is considering a foreign bond. The U.S. risk-free rate (i.e., the domestic rate) is 4% and the risk-free rate in the foreign country (i.e., the local rate) is 4.8%. The manager expects the dollar to appreciate only 0.4% over the expected holding period. Based on this information and assuming the ability to hedge with forward contracts, **determine** whether the manager should hedge the position or leave it unhedged.

Answer:

We start by calculating the forward differential expected by the market:

$$f \approx i_d - i_f = 4.0\% - 4.8\% = -0.8\%$$

The current nominal risk-free interest rates imply a forward differential of −0.8%; the market expects the foreign currency to depreciate 0.8% relative to the dollar. The manager on the other hand expects the dollar to appreciate only 0.4%. If the manager's expectations are correct, the *forward dollar is too expensive*, or alternatively, the forward price of the foreign currency is too cheap. The manager is better off not hedging the currency risk, as the foreign currency will not fall in value as much as predicted by the market.

Example: To hedge or not to hedge (cont.)

Now assume the U.S. risk-free rate is 4% and the risk-free rate in the foreign country is 4.8%, but the manager expects the dollar to appreciate 1.0% over the expected holding period. Based only on this information, **determine** whether the manager should hedge the position or leave it unhedged.

Answer:

Again, start by calculating the forward differential expected by the market:

$$f \approx i_d - i_f = 4.0\% - 4.8\% = -0.8\%$$

In this case, the manager expects the dollar to be *stronger than predicted* by the market. He predicts the dollar to appreciate a full percent against the foreign currency while the market predicts a 0.8% increase. You could also say the *forward dollar is too cheap*, and it will take more of the foreign currency to buy dollars than predicted by the market. In this case the manager is better off hedging.

BREAKEVEN SPREAD ANALYSIS

LOS 30.k: Illustrate how breakeven spread analysis can be used to evaluate the risk in seeking yield advantages across international bond markets.

For the Exam: In this instance, *illustrating* will be hard to do without showing supporting calculations.

Breakeven analysis involves determining the widening in the spread between two bonds that will make their total returns (i.e., coupon plus capital gain or loss) equivalent over a given period. Although it does not address the risk associated with currency movements, breakeven analysis does give the manager an idea of the amount of risk associated with attempting to exploit a yield advantage.

Note that in performing a breakeven analysis, the manager must assume a *set time horizon* and measure the yield change in the bond with the *higher duration*.

Example: Breakeven analysis

A portfolio manager is performing a breakeven analysis to determine the shift in interest rates that would generate a capital loss sufficient to eliminate the yield advantage of the foreign bond. **Determine** the breakeven change in the yield of the foreign bond if the intended holding period is three months.

Bond	Nominal Return	Duration
i (domestic)	4.75%	4.5
j (foreign)	5.25%	6.3

Answer:

The foreign bond is currently at an annual yield advantage of 50 bps, which equates to a quarterly advantage of 12.5 bps. Utilizing the duration of the foreign bond, which is the longer of the two, and the fact that its price will change 6.3 times the percentage change in its yield, we can determine the breakeven yield change:

$$\text{change in price} = -\text{duration} \times \text{breakeven yield change}$$

Solving for Δy:

$$\Delta y = \frac{\text{change in price}}{-\text{duration}}$$

$$\Delta y = \frac{-0.125\%}{-6.3} = 0.0198 = 1.98 \text{ bps}$$

The conclusion is that the yield on the foreign bond would have to increase a little under 2 bps over the holding period for the decrease in its price (i.e., the capital loss) to completely wipe out its yield advantage. The manager can compare this breakeven event against her interest rate expectations and currency expectations to assess whether the yield advantage warrants investment in the foreign bond.

EMERGING MARKET DEBT

LOS 30.l: Discuss the advantages and risks of investing in emerging market debt.

In actively managing a fixed income portfolio, managers often utilize a **core-plus approach**. In a core-plus approach, the manager holds a "core" of investment grade debt and then invests in bonds perceived to add the potential for generating added return. Emerging market debt (EMD) is frequently utilized to add value in a core-plus strategy.

Advantages of investing in EMD include:

- Increased quality in emerging market sovereign bonds. In addition, emerging market governments can implement fiscal and/or monetary policies to offset potentially negative events and they have access to major worldwide lenders (e.g., World Bank, International Monetary Fund).
- Increased resiliency; the ability to recover from value-siphoning events. When EMD markets have been hit by some event, they tend to bounce back offering the potential for high returns.
- Lack of diversification in the major EMD index, the Emerging Markets Bond Index Plus (EMBI+). The index is concentrated in Latin American debt (e.g., Brazil, Mexico). The bond investor can diversify the fixed income portfolio, so an undiversified index offers return-enhancing potential.

Risks associated with EMD include:

- Unlike emerging market governments, emerging market corporations do not have the tools available to help offset negative events.
- EMD returns can be highly volatile with negatively skewed distributions.
- A lack of transparency and regulations gives emerging market sovereign debt higher credit risk than sovereign debt in developed markets.
- Under-developed legal systems that do not protect against actions taken by governments. For example, there is little protection provided (i.e., lack of seniority protection) for prior debt holders when emerging market governments add to their debt.
- A lack of standardized covenants, which forces managers to carefully study each issue.
- Political risk (a.k.a. geopolitical risk).
  - Political instability.
  - Changes in taxation or other regulations.
  - International investors may not be able to convert the local currency to their domestic currency, due to restrictions imposed by emerging market governments.
  - Relaxed regulations on bankruptcy that serve to increase its likelihood.
  - Imposed changes in the exchange rate (e.g., pegging).

SELECTING A FIXED-INCOME MANAGER

LOS 30.m: <u>Discuss</u> the criteria for selecting a fixed-income manager.

The due diligence required to identify managers who can consistently generate superior returns (i.e., positive alpha), entails thoroughly analyzing the managers' organization and personnel as well as trading practices. Since the vast majority of the typical fixed income portfolio is managed actively, the focus should be on active managers. Past performance, however, should not be used as an indicator of future success.

Criteria that should be utilized in determining the *optimal mix* of active managers include *style analysis, selection bets, investment processes,* and *alpha correlations.*

Style analysis. The majority of active returns can be explained by the managers' selected style. The primary concerns associated with researching the managers' styles include not only the styles employed but any additional risk exposures due to style.

Selection bets. Selection bets include credit spread analysis (i.e., which sectors or securities will experience spread changes) and the identification of over- and undervalued securities. By decomposing the manager's excess returns, the sponsor can determine the manager's ability to generate superior returns from selection bets.

Investment processes. This step includes investigating the total investment processes of the managers. What type of research is performed? How is alpha attained? Who makes decisions and how are they made (e.g., committee, individual)? This step typically entails interviewing several members of the organization.

Alpha correlations. Alphas should also be "diversified." That is, if the alphas of the various managers are highly correlated, not only will there be significant volatility in the overall alpha, but the alphas will tend to be all positive or negative at the same time. The sponsor should attempt to find the mix of active managers that optimizes the average alpha with the alpha volatility.

You may have noticed that the process for determining the best mix of fixed income active managers is much the same as that for selecting the best mix of equity portfolio managers. The one consideration that distinguishes the two is the need for a low-fee strategy. That is, fees are an important consideration in selecting any active manager, but the ratio of fees to alpha is usually higher for fixed income managers.

KEY CONCEPTS

LOS 30.a

Leverage is only beneficial when the strategy earns a return greater than the cost of borrowing.

Although leverage can increase returns, it also has a downside. If the strategy return falls below the cost of borrowing, the loss to investors will be increased. So leverage magnifies both good and bad outcomes.

$$\text{leveraged return: } R_p = R_i + [(B/E) \times (R_i - c)]$$

LOS 30.b

To increase the leverage of their portfolios, portfolio managers sometimes borrow funds on a short-term basis using repurchase agreements. In a **repurchase agreement** (or **repo**), the borrower (seller of the security) agrees to repurchase it from the buyer on an agreed upon date at an agreed upon price (repurchase price). Although it is legally a sale and subsequent purchase of securities, a repurchase agreement is essentially a collateralized loan, where the difference between the sale and repurchase prices is the interest on the loan. The rate of interest on the repo is referred to as the *repo rate*.

The lender in a repurchase agreement is exposed to credit risk if the collateral remains in the borrower's custody. For instance, the borrower could sell the collateral, fraudulently use it as collateral for another loan, or go bankrupt.

The repo rate decreases as the credit risk decreases, as the quality of the collateral increases, as the term of the repo decreases, if collateral is physically delivered, if the availability of the collateral is limited, and as the federal funds rate decreases.

LOS 30.c

Standard deviation measures the dispersion of returns around the mean.

Drawbacks of Standard Deviation and Variance
- Bond returns are often not normally distributed around the mean.
- The number of inputs (e.g., variances and covariances) increases significantly with larger portfolios.
- Obtaining estimates for each of these inputs is problematic.

Semivariance measures the dispersion of returns below a target return.

Drawbacks of Semivariance
- It is difficult to compute for a large bond portfolio.
- If investment returns are symmetric, the semivariance yields the same rankings as the variance and the variance is better understood.
- If investment returns are not symmetric, it can be quite difficult to forecast downside risk and the semivariance may not be a good indicator of future risk.
- Because the semivariance is estimated with only half the distribution, it is estimated with less accuracy.

Shortfall risk measures the *probability* that the actual return or value will be less than the target return or value.

Drawback of Shortfall Risk
- Shortfall risk does not consider the impact of outliers so the magnitude (dollar amount) of the shortfall below the target return is ignored.

The value at risk (VAR) provides the probability of a return less than a given amount over a specific time period.

Drawback of VAR
- VAR does not provide the magnitude of losses that exceed that specified by VAR.

LOS 30.d
The main advantages to using futures over cash market instruments are that they are more liquid, less expensive, and make short positions more readily obtainable because the contracts can be more easily shorted.

The general rules for using futures contracts to control interest rate risk are:
- Long futures position → increase in duration.
- Short futures position → decrease in duration.

LOS 30.e
The most basic principle of controlling interest rate risk is to take positions in futures contracts that modify DD_P to achieve the specified target dollar duration, denoted DD_T.

$$DD_T = DD_P + DD_{Futures}$$

where:
DD_T = the target dollar duration of the portfolio plus futures
DD_P = the dollar duration of the portfolio before adding futures
$DD_{Futures}$ = the total dollar duration of the added futures contracts

For a long futures position, $DD_f > 0$. For a short futures position, $DD_f < 0$.

The dollar duration for a futures contract can be calculated as:

$$DD_f = \frac{DD_{CTD}}{CTD \text{ conversion factor}}$$

$$\text{number of contracts} = \frac{DD_T - DD_P}{DD_f}$$

$$\text{and since } DD_f = \frac{DD_{CTD}}{CTD \text{ conversion factor}}$$

$$\text{number of contracts} = \frac{DD_T - DD_P}{DD_{CTD} \big/ \text{conversion factor}}$$

LOS 30.f
In volatile interest rate environments, floating rate assets and liabilities are subject to cash flow risk, and fixed rate assets and liabilities are subject to market value risk. Anticipating rising interest rates the holder of a fixed rate asset might want to swap into a floating rate to increase cash received as well as minimize the decline in market value. The holder of a floating rate liability would want to swap into a fixed rate to minimize the increase in cash paid and to maximize the decline in market value. Interest rate put options are used to protect floating rate assets against falling interest rates. Interest rate calls are used to protect floating rate liabilities against rising interest rates. An option on a swap (i.e., a swaption) provides the holder the option to enter into a swap before, during, or after a change in interest rates.

LOS 30.g
Default risk is the risk that the issuer will not make timely payments of principal and/or interest. This risk can be effectively hedged through the use of credit swaps and credit options.

Credit spread risk is the risk that the market's collective assessment of an issue's credit quality will change, resulting in an increase in the yield spread. This risk can be managed with credit options and credit forwards.

Downgrade risk reflects the possibility that the credit rating of an asset/issuer will be downgraded by a major credit-rating organization. This risk can be managed through the use of credit swaps and credit options.

When the payoff is based on the underlying asset's price, the option is known as a **binary credit option**. When the payoff is based on the underlying asset's yield spread, the option is known as a **credit spread option**.

A **binary credit put option** will provide protection if a specific **credit event** occurs, and if the value of the underlying asset is less than the option strike price. A credit event is typically a default or an adverse change in credit rating. The option value (OV) is:

$$OV = max\ [(strike - value),\ 0]$$

A **credit spread call option** will provide protection if the reference asset's spread over the relevant risk-free benchmark increases beyond the strike spread. The option value (OV) is:

$$OV = max\ [(actual\ spread - strike\ spread) \times notional \times risk\ factor,\ 0]$$

Credit spread forwards are forward contracts wherein the payment at settlement is a function of the credit spread over the benchmark at the time the contract matures. The value (FV) or payoff to the buyer of a credit spread forward is:

$$FV = (spread\ at\ maturity - contract\ spread) \times notional \times risk\ factor$$

This is a zero sum game in that for one party to gain, the other party to the contract must lose. If the spread at maturity is less than the contract spread, the forward buyer (often the portfolio manager) will have to pay the forward seller.

Credit default swaps can be viewed as protection against default on an underlying credit instrument (called the reference asset or reference entity when referring to the issuer).

LOS 30.h

Market selection. The manager must determine which bond markets offer the best overall opportunities for value enhancement.

Currency selection. The manager must determine the amount of active currency management versus the amount of currency hedging he will employ.

Duration management. The manager must determine the optimal maturities. Anticipating shifts or twists, the manager will often utilize segments of the yield curve to add value.

Sector selection. Adding value through credit analysis of entire sectors.

Credit analysis refers to recognizing value-added opportunities through credit analysis of individual securities.

Markets outside the benchmark. The manager may try to add value through enhanced indexing by adding bonds not in the index.

LOS 30.i

The relationship (i.e., correlation) between yields on the domestic and foreign bonds can be determined with:

$$\Delta\text{yield}_{\text{foreign}} = \beta(\Delta\text{yield}_{\text{domestic}}) + e$$

In the regression, β is the *country beta* or *yield beta*, which measures the sensitivity of the yield on the foreign bond to changes in the yield on the domestic bond. Multiplying the country beta times the change in the domestic rate gives the manager the estimated change in the foreign yield. Then, multiplying the change in the foreign yield by the bond's duration gives the estimated change in the foreign bond's price.

The duration contribution for a foreign bond to a portfolio is its duration multiplied by its weight in the portfolio and the country beta.

LOS 30.j

We can *approximate* the forward premium or discount (i.e., the *currency differential*) as the difference in short-term rates:

$$f_{d,f} = \frac{(F - S_0)}{S_0} \approx c_d - c_f$$

The decision of whether or not to hedge a foreign bond is based upon interest rate parity and the manager's expectations for the foreign currency. The difference between the domestic and foreign risk-free interest rates reflects interest rate parity. If the manager expects the foreign currency to appreciate more or depreciate less than interest rate parity implies, the position should not be hedged.

LOS 30.k

Note that in performing a breakeven analysis, the manager must assume a *set time horizon* and measure the yield change in the bond with the *higher duration*.

The breakeven spread tells us by how much the spread between the yields of two bonds will have to widen to offset the advantage of the higher-yielding bond.

$$\text{change in price} = -\text{duration} \times \Delta y$$

Solving for Δy:

$$\Delta y = \frac{\text{change in price}}{-\text{duration}}$$

LOS 30.l

Advantages of investing in emerging market debt (EMD) include:
- Increased quality in emerging market sovereign bonds.
- Increased resiliency; the ability to recover from value-siphoning events.
- Lack of diversification in the major EMD index offers return-enhancing potential.

Risks associated with EMD include:
- Unlike emerging market governments, emerging market corporations do not have the tools available to help offset negative events.
- Highly volatile returns with negatively skewed distributions.
- A lack of transparency and regulations.
- Underdeveloped legal systems that do not protect against actions taken by governments.
- A lack of standardized covenants.
- Political risk.

LOS 30.m

Style analysis. The majority of active returns can be explained by the manager's selected style.

Selection bets. Selection bets include credit spread analysis (i.e., which sectors or securities will experience spread changes) and the identification of over- and undervalued securities.

Investment processes. This step includes investigating the total investment processes of the managers.

Alpha correlations. Alphas should also be diversified. That is, if the alphas of the various managers are highly correlated, not only will there be significant volatility in the overall alpha, but the alphas will tend to be all positive or negative at the same time.

CONCEPT CHECKERS

1. A portfolio manager has a portfolio worth $160 million, $40 million of which is his own funds and $120 million is borrowed. If the return on the invested funds is 7% and the cost of borrowed funds is 4%, the return on the portfolio is *closest* to:
    A. 11.0%.
    B. 12.0%.
    C. 16.0%.

2. A manager's portfolio was worth $160 million, $40 million of which was his own funds and $120 million was borrowed. If the duration of the invested funds is 4.2 and the duration of borrowed funds is 0.8, the duration of the portfolio is *closest* to:
    A. 3.6.
    B. 5.0.
    C. 14.4.

3. Which of the responses *best* describes the relationship between the repo rate and the term of the repo and delivery of the security? Lower repo rates are associated with:

	Term of the repo	Delivery of the security
A.	Intermediate	Held by borrower's bank
B.	Longer	No delivery
C.	Shorter	Physically delivered

4. If the target return for AA Bond Investors, Inc. is 15% and 15 out of 60 return observations fall *below* the target return percentage, then shortfall risk is:
    A. 15%.
    B. 20%.
    C. 25%.

5. Which of the following downside risk measures takes into consideration the effects of outliers below the target return?
    A. Value at risk.
    B. Shortfall risk.
    C. Semivariance.

6. Which of the following is *least likely* to be considered a characteristic of futures, relative to the underlying cash market?
    A. More liquid.
    B. Harder to short.
    C. Less expensive.

7. The effective duration of the futures contract is 3.25. The futures contract has a face value of $100,000 and is currently trading at 102.5. What is the expected change in value for a 75 basis point increase in interest rates?
    A. –$2,437.50.
    B. –$2,498.44.
    C. –$3,250.00.

8. An investor's portfolio has a current dollar duration of £1,555,000. His target is £2,250,000. The dollar duration of the relevant pound sterling futures contract is £3,527.92. To achieve his target duration, he should:
   A. sell 197 contracts.
   B. buy 197 contracts.
   C. buy 435 contracts.

9. With a current dollar duration of $487,500, an investor fears a 25 basis point rise in interest rates and wants to hedge. The dollar duration of the cheapest-to-deliver (CTD) issue is $4,750, and its conversion factor is 0.917. How will she hedge this position?
   A. Sell 94 contracts.
   B. Buy 94 contracts.
   C. Sell 112 contracts.

10. Observing the 6-month futures price, an investor concludes that the CTD Treasury bond has an expected dollar duration of $6,954 six months from today. Using this, he concludes that a corporate bond he holds has an expected dollar duration of $8.559 per $100 six months from today. The value of his holding is $10 million. The conversion factor for the CTD bond is 1.156. If he wants to hedge against a possible rise in rates of 75 basis points, he should:
    A. sell 94 contracts.
    B. buy 94 contracts.
    C. sell 142 contracts.

11. To hedge a bond portfolio against an increase in interest rates, which of the following options positions will be the *best* choice to hedge the downside risk while leaving as much of the upside potential intact?
    A. A collar.
    B. Long puts.
    C. Long calls.

12. There are three principal credit-related risks to which a portfolio manager is exposed and can be addressed with the appropriate derivative securities. For example, a manager owns Bond Q, and is concerned that the firm's management is about to take an action that will affect the value of Bond Q adversely. This describes:
    A. downgrade risk, and this can be most effectively managed with credit spread options or credit forward contracts.
    B. spread risk, and this can be most effectively managed with credit spread options or swaps.
    C. default risk, and this can be most effectively managed with binary credit options or swaps.

13. There are three principal credit-related risks to which a portfolio manager is exposed and can be addressed with the appropriate derivative securities. For example, a manager owns Bond R, and is concerned that market forces may result in a change that will affect the value of Bond R adversely. This describes:
   A. downgrade risk, and this can be most effectively managed with credit binary options or credit forward contracts.
   B. spread risk, and this can be most effectively managed with credit spread options or credit forward contracts.
   C. default risk, and this can be most effectively managed with credit spread options or swaps.

14. There are three principal credit-related risks to which a portfolio manager is exposed and can be addressed with the appropriate derivative securities. For example, a manager owns Bond S, and is concerned that the actions of a third party may result in a change that will affect the value of Bond S adversely. This describes:
   A. downgrade risk, and this can be most effectively managed with binary credit options or swaps.
   B. spread risk, and this can be most effectively managed with credit spread options or swaps.
   C. default risk, and this can be most effectively managed with binary credit options or credit spread options.

15. When considering potential sources of excess return for an international bond portfolio manager, which of the following statements is *most correct*?
   A. Market selection refers to nations in which investments are to occur, currency selection refers to whether or not currency exposures are actively managed or hedged, and sector selection refers to industries, ratings categories, maturity ranges, et cetera.
   B. Sector selection refers to nations in which investments are to occur, currency selection refers to whether or not currency exposures are actively managed or hedged, and market selection refers to industries, ratings categories, maturity ranges, et cetera.
   C. Currency selection refers to nations in which investments are to occur, and sector selection refers to industries, ratings categories, maturity ranges, et cetera.

16. A Canadian bond represents 10% of an international bond portfolio. It has a duration of 7 and a yield beta of 1.2. If domestic interest rates change by 50 basis points, what is the estimated percentage price change for the bond, and what is its duration contribution to the portfolio?

	Price change	Duration contribution
A.	3.5%	0.70
B.	4.2%	0.84
C.	8.4%	0.42

17. An international bond portfolio manager is considering two bonds for investment. The bonds are comparable in terms of risk characteristics, and the following information applies:

Country	Nominal Return	Risk-Free Rate	Exchange Rate #/D
A	9.75%	8.50%	3.00
B	4.75%	3.25%	5.00
Domestic	n/a	5.75	n/a

You expect Currency A to depreciate against the domestic currency by 2.6%, and you expect Currency B to appreciate against the domestic currency by 2.6%. On a fully-hedged basis, which bond should be selected, and, assuming that this bond is selected, should the bond's currency exposure be hedged?
A. Bond A; hedge.
B. Bond A; do not hedge.
C. Bond B; do not hedge.

18. A portfolio manager with investable funds is considering two alternatives:

Bond	Nominal Yield	Duration
Australian Bond	7.65%	6.5
New Zealand Bond	6.85%	5.3

If the target holding period is six months, by how much would either of the yields on these two bonds have to change to offset the current yield advantage of the Australian Bond?
A. Australian increase by 6 bp, New Zealand decrease by 8 bp.
B. Australian decrease by 6 bp, New Zealand increase by 8 bp.
C. Australian increase by 12 bp, New Zealand decrease by 15 bp.

19. From the perspective of an international bond portfolio manager, which of the following is the *least likely* rationale for an allocation to emerging market debt (EMD) securities?
A. EMD credit quality has been improving.
B. Holding EMD issues results in reduced currency risk exposure.
C. EMD issuers are recovering from adverse events more quickly than in the past.

20. With respect to emerging market debt (EMD), one of the main risks to the foreign bondholder is political risk. Which of the following is *least likely* to be a type of political risk?
A. Potential changes in tax and/or regulatory policy.
B. A lack of standardized debt covenants for EMD securities.
C. The possibility that investment capital cannot be repatriated to the investor's home country.

21. Factors that should be evaluated during the due diligence process when selecting a fixed income portfolio manager include:
A. style analysis, selection ability, investment process, and beta correlations.
B. style analysis, selection ability, investment process, and alpha correlations.
C. style analysis, selection ability, risk management process, and alpha correlations.

ANSWERS – CONCEPT CHECKERS

1. **C** The gross profit on the portfolio is: $160 million × 7% = $11.2 million.

   The cost of borrowed funds is: $120 million × 4% = $4.8 million.

   The net profit on the portfolio is: $11.2 million – $4.8 million = $6.4 million.

   The return on the equity invested (i.e., the portfolio) is thus: $6.4 / $40 = 16.0%.

   Alternatively, the problem can be solved as: 7% + [(120 / 40) × (7% – 4%)] = 16.0%.

2. **C** The duration can be calculated with the following formula:

$$D_p = \frac{D_i I - D_B B}{E}$$

   Using the values in the problem:

$$D_p = \frac{(4.2)160 - (0.8)120}{40} = 14.40$$

3. **C** The repo rate decreases: as the credit risk decreases; as the quality of the collateral increases; as the term of the repo decreases; if collateral is physically delivered, if the availability of the collateral is limited: and as the federal funds rate decreases.

4. **C** Shortfall risk is the ratio of number of observations that fall *below* the target return to the total number of observations. Shortfall risk = 15 / 60 = 25%.

5. **C** Like the variance, the semivariance measures the dispersion of returns. Unlike the variance, semivariance does not measure the total dispersion of all returns above and below the mean. Instead it only measures the dispersion of returns below a target return.

   Of the responses, only the semivariance takes into consideration the effects of outliers below the target return. By measuring all returns in the left hand side of the distribution, outliers are considered by the semivariance. None of the other methods evaluate outliers.

6. **B** The advantages to using futures over cash market instruments are that they are more liquid, less expensive, and make short positions more readily obtainable because the contracts can be more easily shorted. There is a great deal of depth in the futures market which explains their liquidity and low cost.

7. **B** −3.25 × 0.0075 × $102,500 = −$2,498.44

8. **B** $\text{number of contracts} = \dfrac{DD_T - DD_P}{DD_f} = \dfrac{2,250,000 - 1,555,000}{3,527.92} = \dfrac{695,000}{3,527.92} \cong +197$;

   buy 197 contracts.

9. **A** $\text{number of contracts} = \dfrac{-487,500}{\dfrac{\$4,750}{0.917}} \cong -94$; sell 94 contracts.

10. **C**   number of contracts $= \dfrac{-\left(\dfrac{8.559}{100}\right) \times \$10 \text{ million}}{\dfrac{\$6,954}{1.156}} \cong -142$; sell 142 contracts.

11. **B**   Using a long put with the bond portfolio (a protective put) will provide downside protection below the option strike price but will leave most of the upside potential intact.

12. **C**   Although there are obviously many actions that a firm's management could take to the detriment of the bondholders, of the three principal credit-related risks, this most accurately describes default risk. In this event, the firm's management fails to pay principal or interest when due, causing the issue to default. Default risk can be best managed with binary credit put options or credit default swaps.

13. **B**   Market forces come to bear on bonds via required yields. The credit-related risk most closely associated with market forces is credit spread risk, which is the difference between the yield on the reference asset (Bond R in this case), and the appropriate risk-free benchmark. If the spread increases, reflecting a deterioration in the market's assessment of the creditworthiness of the issue or issuer, the value of Bond R will be adversely affected. Credit spread risk can be best managed with credit spread options or credit spread forward contracts.

14. **A**   The type of credit-related risk most closely associated with the actions of a third party is downgrade risk. In this case, a major rating agency reduces its assessment of the issue/issuer's credit quality, and the value of the bond is adversely affected. This type of credit risk can be best managed with binary credit options or swaps. In the case of both instruments, the specified credit event is a downgrade below some level.

15. **A**   There are at least six potential sources of excess return. Market selection concerns determining which national bond markets may afford the best opportunities. Currency selection concerns currency exposure management: should we hedge our exposures or should we actively manage our exposures? Duration management refers to managing interest rate risk and exposure so as to take advantage of any anticipated changes in rates. Sector selection involves seeking out the best performing industries, ratings categories, maturity ranges and other sector classifications. Credit analysis concerns the evaluation of credit qualities in an attempt to identify securities that may experience positive credit quality changes. The degree to which we are willing to deviate from our benchmark, which is often referred to as enhanced indexing.

16. **B**   The estimated price change is:

$\%\Delta_{price} = \text{duration} \times \Delta y \times \beta = 7 \times 0.005 \times 1.2 = 4.2\%$

The duration contribution is:

$DC = \text{weighting} \times \text{duration} \times \beta = 0.10 \times 7 \times 1.2 = 0.84$

17. **C**   Assuming a comparable level of risk and a fully hedged position, the bond selection is based upon the bond's excess return:

Bond A excess return = 9.75 – 8.50 = 1.25%

Bond B excess return = 4.75 – 3.25 = 1.50%

Bond B should be selected under the assumption that the position will be fully-hedged.

Once Bond B has been selected, if the hedging decision is revisited, the decision will depend upon the change in currency values implied by the differential in the risk-free rates, relative to the portfolio manager's expectations.

Change in Currency B implied by the interest rate differential = 5.75 – 3.25 = +2.50%. Since you expect Currency B to appreciate by 2.60%, you should not hedge.

18. **A**   The current yield advantage to the Australian Bond is 7.65 – 6.85 = 0.8% or 80 bp. Since the target holding period is six months, this represents 40 bp over the investment horizon. Next, we calculate the required change for each bond:

$$\Delta y_{AU} = \frac{-0.40\%}{-6.5} = 0.06\% \rightarrow \text{The yield would need to increase by 6 bp.}$$

$$\Delta y_{NZ} = \frac{0.40\%}{-5.3} = -0.08\% \rightarrow \text{The yield would need to decrease by 8 bp.}$$

In either case, the yield advantage is offset by the spread widening.

19. **B**   Emerging market currencies can be extremely volatile, especially during negative market events. Thus, even if the choice is between a bond in a developed country/currency and an EMD issue, the currency risk is most likely to be greater for the EMD issue. The other points are valid rationales for an allocation to EMD.

20. **B**   A lack of standardized debt covenants is certainly an issue, and creates risks for the EMD holder. If the covenants were changed arbitrarily, that could constitute political risk. However, the lack of standardization itself is not political risk. The other points are all forms of political risk.

21. **B**   Four principal factors that should be evaluated during the due diligence process surrounding the selection of a fixed income portfolio manager are (1) style analysis (which includes portfolio management policy), (2) security selection ability, (3) investment process (which includes how research is conducted and decisions are made), and (4) the correlation of the manager's alpha with other current and prospective managers.

The following is a review of the Portfolio Management of Global Bonds and Fixed-Income Derivatives principles designed to address the learning outcome statements set forth by CFA Institute®. This topic is also covered in:

HEDGING MORTGAGE SECURITIES TO CAPTURE RELATIVE VALUE

EXAM FOCUS

Hedging mortgage securities requires special considerations, such as dealing with negative convexity, which means the increase in value from a given yield decrease is less than the decrease in value from an equal yield increase. Twists of the yield curve become more important for mortgage securities, because they do not have a large bullet payment at maturity. For the exam, therefore, focus on the concept of negative convexity and its implications when hedging with an instrument that has positive convexity. I would say that understanding and being able to discuss the underlying concepts for LOS 31.b and LOS 31.d are critical for the exam.

NEGATIVE CONVEXITY AND MORTGAGE SECURITIES

This material focuses on the behavior and hedging of securities whose payoffs are determined by an underlying pool of mortgages. Since the focus is on the mechanics, we use the term *mortgage securities* in a general sense to apply to securities that pay interest and/or principal as an annuity over the life of the security and have a prepayment option embedded in them. When interest rates decline, people tend to refinance at the new, lower rate and prepay the old, higher-rate mortgage. The embedded option increases in value when interest rates decrease, resulting in a lower value for the mortgage security compared to similar, non-callable, fixed-income instruments. A key point is that duration is difficult to assess because of the inherent prepayment risk. To form an effective hedge on a mortgage security, a cash flow projection must model prepayment patterns.

We should also recall that a mortgage security is designed to be an annuity, which it is, if no prepayments are made. This makes it different from the standard bond, which has a large cash flow at maturity when the principal is returned to the investor. Hedging an annuity requires more attention to twists of the yield curve.

Despite their complexities, mortgage securities can offer an attractive spread over Treasury bonds (T-bonds). In analyzing the spread, analysts find it beneficial to adjust it for the embedded options to get an option-adjusted spread (OAS), which is a concept from Level 2.

 Professor's Note: If you would like to review the basics of mortgage-backed securities, check out the free Schweser Level 3 online library volume entitled Mortgage-Backed Securities.

Convexity refers to the nonlinear relationship between the value of a fixed income instrument and its yield. For a given interest rate increase, the capital loss effect is smaller than the capital gain effect that occurs with an equal interest rate decrease. For **negative convexity** this relationship reverses (i.e., a given decrease in the market interest rate produces a smaller capital gain than the absolute value of the capital loss produced by an equal increase in the market rate).

Figure 1 shows the familiar price-yield curve of a non-callable bond (i.e., bullet).

Figure 1: Positive Convexity in Bond Prices (Bullets)

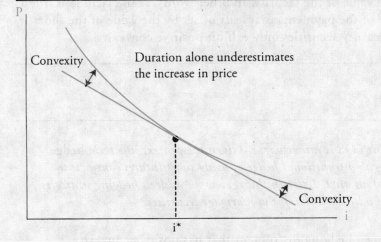

The (positive) convexity in the relationship is indicated by the distance between the price curve and a straight line tangent to the curve, in this case at i^*, which demonstrates the price change predicted using duration alone. Positive convexity means the price of the bond increases at an increasing rate as the interest rate falls below the coupon rate. Positive convexity also means the price of the bond falls at a decreasing rate as the interest rate rises above the coupon rate. Note that the straight line represents the change in price predicted by the bond's duration, when its yield changes from i^*. This demonstrates how duration alone will underestimate the increase in price with falling rates and overestimate the decrease in price with rising rates.

Figure 2 shows the price-yield relationship for the same bond, assuming it is now callable.

Figure 2: Price-Yield Function of a Callable Bond

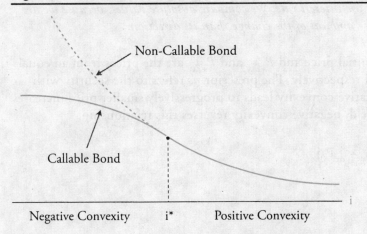

As indicated, when the yield on the bond is below its coupon rate, i^*, the bond exhibits negative convexity; that is, the price of the bond increases at a decreasing rate. Above i^*, the call option on the bond is out-of-the-money, so the bond behaves as if it were non-callable.

From the perspective of the investor, a mortgage security essentially has an embedded short call option because the mortgage payers have a **prepayment option**. When this option is out-of-the-money, the mortgage security will exhibit (positive) convexity. When the option is in-the-money, the mortgage security will tend to exhibit negative convexity, because the price will be compressed from the prepayment option going into the money and reducing the value of the security. In other words, as the yield falls, the increase in the present value of the payments is at least offset by the value of the short call position, In contrast, Treasury securities only exhibit positive convexity.

LOS 31.a: <u>Demonstrate</u> how a mortgage security's negative convexity will affect the performance of a hedge.

Professor's Note: This LOS is rather vague. Given the context, the term hedge seems to be referring to a traditional hedge of using short futures contracts to preserve the value of an asset. Later in this review we address hedging strategies that can better deal with the behavior of mortgage securities.

There is a problem with using a hedging instrument that has positive convexity (indicated below by the prescript pc) to hedge an asset with negative convexity. If the downside risk from a yield increase is hedged exactly, then the portfolio will likely lose value when interest rates decrease. To demonstrate this, we recall that for a security exhibiting *positive convexity*, we can write:

$$\left|\, _{pc}P_{-\Delta y} - \, _{pc}P_0 \,\right| > \left|\, _{pc}P_{+\Delta y} - \, _{pc}P_0 \,\right|$$

Professor's Note: The two sides of the above equation represent the increase in price from a decrease in interest rates (i.e., the left side of the equation) and the decrease in price from an increase in rates (i.e., the right side of the equation). The equation states that the absolute value of the increase in price from a decrease in the interest rate is greater than the absolute value of the decrease in price from an equal increase in the interest rate. We compare absolute values, because we are interested more in the amount of the change than its direction.

In this expression, P_0 is the initial price and $P_{-\Delta y}$ and $P_{+\Delta y}$ are the prices from an equal decrease and increase in yield respectively. The prescript nc refers to the security with negative convexity. Since negative convexity leads to progressively smaller price increases from each unit decrease in yield, negative convexity reverses this relationship:

$$\left|\, _{nc}P_{-\Delta y} - \, _{nc}P_0 \,\right| < \left|\, _{nc}P_{+\Delta y} - \, _{nc}P_0 \,\right|$$

Let us look at the use of a short position of an instrument with positive convexity, such as a Treasury futures contract, to hedge an instrument with negative convexity such as a mortgage security.

If the hedge has been set up to preserve value in the face of a given *increase* in yield, then:

$$(N)\big|_{pc}P_{+\Delta y} - {}_{pc}P_0\big| = \big|{}_{nc}P_{+\Delta y} - {}_{nc}P_0\big|$$

where:
pc = a futures contract with positive convexity
N = the number of futures contracts used in the hedge

Since the *pc* position is short and the *nc* position is long, the net effect from $+\Delta y$ would be a zero change in the value of the portfolio from the *increase* in yield (above the coupon rate on the MBS):

$$(N)({}_{pc}P_{+\Delta y} - {}_{pc}P_0) + ({}_{nc}P_{+\Delta y} - {}_{nc}P_0) = 0$$

However, if a positive change in yield produces that result, then the following would result from negative change in yield, $-\Delta y$ (below the coupon rate on the MBS):

$$(N)({}_{pc}P_{-\Delta y} - {}_{pc}P_0) + ({}_{nc}P_{-\Delta y} - {}_{nc}P_0) < 0$$

This means that for a decline in yield, the increase in value of the hedged position, which has negative convexity, will be less than the associated increase in value of the short position in the hedging instrument. The combined position will lose value from a decrease in yield.

MORTGAGE SECURITY RISKS

LOS 31.b: Explain the risks associated with investing in mortgage securities and discuss whether these risks can be effectively hedged.

For the Exam: You should be able to discuss the following five risks and their identifying features.

1. **Spread risk** is the risk of the mortgage security's yield spread over the corresponding T-bond widening, and thus lowering the value of mortgage security relative to the T-bond. Usually the manager focuses on the option-adjusted spread (OAS).

2. **Interest rate risk** is the price fluctuation caused by the volatility of the yield on Treasuries with which the yields on mortgage securities are highly correlated. (It is considered distinct from spread risk, because the interest rate can change without the spread changing.)

3. **Prepayment risk** is the cause of the negative convexity, which means the mortgage security loses more from a given increase in yield than it gains from a corresponding decrease in yield. This is why an unhedged mortgage security is called a *market directional* investment.

4. **Volatility risk** is associated with the embedded prepayment option. As we know from option pricing theory, an increase in volatility increases the value of an option. Since the mortgage security is short the option:

   > increased yield volatility → increased value of option → decreased value of mortgage security

5. **Model risk** can be from naively projecting past patterns of interest rates into the future. Another source is not recognizing the effects of technological and institutional innovations, which make prepayment more convenient to the borrower, thus increasing the risk from that source.

Although spread risk is part of the overall yield or interest rate on the mortgage security, a manager should consider spread risk separately from interest rate risk. One strategy would be to hedge away the risk caused by movements in T-bond yields (i.e., the interest rate risk). This leaves the manager with a risk-free rate of return plus the spread. The manager who does not hedge spread risk can take advantage of the price changes that result. An increase (decrease) in the spread makes the mortgage securities cheaper (more valuable) relative to Treasuries. The strategy would be:

- If the spread increases, increase the exposure to mortgage securities.
- If the spread decreases, decrease the exposure to mortgage securities.

Hedging spread risk would eliminate the possibility of profiting from these movements.

YIELD CURVE RISK

LOS 31.c: <u>Contrast</u> an individual mortgage security to a Treasury security with respect to the importance of yield-curve risk.

Unless explicitly stated otherwise, most discussions of interest rate risk usually only pertain to parallel shifts in the yield curve. Duration is often adequate in such cases. Very undesirable results can come from nonparallel shifts or *twists*, however, and that is *yield curve risk*. The usual approach to handling yield curve risk for a portfolio is to focus on a few particular **key rate durations**.

For a single noncallable bond issue, a manager may generally focus on only one rate, because of the comparatively large bullet in the form of the bond's principal. Even when the yield curve twists, changes in the yield corresponding to the maturity of the bond will explain most of the changes in the price of the bond. In summary, for a single noncallable bond, yield curve risk is not as important because of the comparatively large cash flow at maturity.

Yield curve risk is much more important for mortgage securities because there is no bullet payment at the end [i.e., rather than interest-only payments (coupons) with the principal paid at the end, mortgage security payments can contain interest, principal, or both]. A manager has to consider hedging against changes in more than a single key rate. Additional complication is added with principal and interest strips. Principal-only (PO) strips have negative key rate durations in the short and intermediate rates, which turn positive for longer (e.g., 10-year) rates. Interest-only (IO) strips start out with positive key rate durations, which turn negative.

> *Professor's Note: Key rate duration refers to the change in the value of the asset given a change in key interest rates (e.g., individual maturities, such as the 5-year rate). A negative key rate duration implies that values move in the same direction as the change in the key interest rate. For the exam you probably won't have to explain why IOs and POs have some negative key rate durations.*

HEDGING MORTGAGE SECURITIES

LOS 31.d: <u>Compare</u> and <u>contrast</u> duration-based approaches with interest rate sensitivity approaches to hedging mortgage securities.

Given the complications mentioned to this point (i.e., call risk, the need for more key rates and negative convexities), using only a duration-based framework will generally not be adequate for hedging mortgage securities. First, as demonstrated earlier for a security with negative convexity, a duration-based hedge that removes the risk associated with an increase in rates can produce a net loss on the hedged position when rates decrease. Second, a duration-based framework does not effectively deal with two crucial points: (1) observed patterns of yield curve changes over time and (2) the effect yield curve changes have on the propensity for the prepayment by homeowners.

Research has shown that more than 95% of changes in interest rates can be explained by yield curve shifts and twists. Addressing the possibility of *twists* requires more assumptions in forming the hedge. Under a given set of assumptions, managers can form a hedge by using two hedging instruments from two maturity sectors of the yield curve (e.g., a 2-year and a 10-year). Those assumptions are that the manager:

- Incorporates reasonable possible yield curve shifts.
- Uses an adequate model for predicting prepayments given certain changes in yield.
- Includes reliable assumptions in the Monte Carlo simulations of interest rates.
- Knows the security's price change given a small change in yield.
- Knows that the average price change method (a demonstration follows) yields good approximations.

> *Professor's Note: In hedging a long position in an asset like a mortgage security, a two-bond hedge strategy can refer to selling short two bonds of different maturities or taking a short position in futures on the bonds. The LOS does not make a distinction, and the procedure is basically the same.*

If the previous assumptions are valid, the manager can use a *two-bond hedge* to hedge the risk associated with both a parallel shift and a twist in the yield curve. The following steps summarize how to hedge a mortgage security, denoted MS, using two hedging instruments, denoted H1 and H2, with different maturities. The prices are P_{MS}, P_{H1}, and P_{H2}, respectively.

Step 1: Determine the **average absolute price change** per \$100 of the mortgage security and each of the hedging instruments resulting from equal positive and negative **shifts** in the yield curve ($\pm\Delta y$). Label these $\Delta P_{MS\Delta y}$, $\Delta P_{H1\Delta y}$, and $\Delta P_{H2\Delta y}$.

Step 2: Determine the **average absolute price change** per \$100 of the mortgage security and each of the hedging instruments resulting from a given **twist** in the yield curve. Label these $\Delta P_{MStwist}$, $\Delta P_{H1twist}$, and $\Delta P_{H2twist}$.

Step 3: Using the changes in the values of the three instruments, solve a system of two simultaneous equations for the required amounts of H1 and H2 needed to exactly offset the change in the value of MS:

Shift: $(H1)(\Delta P_{H1\Delta y}) + (H2)(\Delta P_{H2\Delta y}) = -\Delta P_{MS\Delta y}$

Twist: $(H1)(\Delta P_{H1twist}) + (H2)(\Delta P_{H2twist}) = -\Delta P_{MStwist}$

 Professor's Note: In both equations we set the sum of the changes in the values of the hedging instruments equal to but opposite the change in the value of the mortgage security, such that the net change in the portfolio of three securities is zero.

The following example uses numbers that reflect positive convexity in the hedging instruments, H1 and H2, and negative convexity in the mortgage security, MS. The manager assumes a value for the parallel shifts in the yield curve, $\pm\Delta y$, based on an historical average yield change and computes the average price changes for the three instruments. The manager then defines a likely yield curve twist and computes the resulting average price changes for MS, H1, and H2.

Example: 2-bond hedge of MS

A manager has used historical data and Monte Carlo simulation to determine how \$100 of a mortgage security will change in value from (1) a given parallel shift in the yield curve, Δy, and (2) for a forecasted twist in the yield curve. The manager uses the forecasts of Δy and the twist to compute the changes in prices of two hedging instruments and the mortgage security. Results are shown in the following figures.

Price Changes from Parallel Shifts in the Yield Curve

Instrument	Initial Price	Price After $+\Delta y$	Price After $-\Delta y$	Average Absolute Change in Value
MS	100.00	99.00	100.50	0.75
H1	99.40	99.20	99.68	0.24
H2	102.00	100.40	104.00	1.80

Price Changes from a Twist in the Yield Curve

Instrument	Initial Price	Price After Positive Twist	Price After Negative Twist	Average Absolute Change in Value
MS	100.00	99.70	100.34	0.32
H1	99.40	99.24	99.54	0.15
H2	102.00	101.40	102.60	0.60

Professor's Note: Looking at the first figure we see that when its yield is increased by Δy, MS falls \$1.00 in value, but when its yield is decreased by Δy, it increases only 50 cents in value. For equal positive and negative changes in its yield, then, the increase in the price of MS is less than the decrease in price. This is an important indicator of negative convexity. In comparison, note that the increases for H1 and H2 are greater than the decreases, indicative of instruments with positive convexity.

Using the average absolute value changes in the last columns, we solve for H1 and H2, the required amounts of the hedging instruments.

Remember, the general form of each equation is:

(value change in H1 + value change in H2) = – (value change in MS)

For a parallel shift: $(H1)(\Delta P_{H1\Delta y}) + (H2)(\Delta P_{H2\Delta y}) = -\Delta P_{MS\Delta y}$

$$(H1)(0.24) + (H2)(1.8) = -0.75$$

For a twist: $(H1)(\Delta P_{H1twist}) + (H2)(\Delta P_{H2twist}) = -\Delta P_{MStwist}$

$$(H1)(0.15) + (H2)(0.6) = -0.32$$

Remember that we place a negative sign on the right-hand side of the equations (i.e., –0.75, –0.32), because we want the movements in H1 and H2 to *offset* the movements in MS. That is, we want the sum of the value changes in the three instruments to be zero.

Solve the simultaneous equations by first multiplying the second equation by (–3):[1]

Multiply the second equation by (–3):

$$-(3) \times [(H1)(0.15) + (H2)(0.6) = -0.32] = -(3)(H1)(0.15) - (3)(H2)(0.6) =$$
$$-(3)(-0.32) = -0.45H1 - 1.8H2 = 0.96$$

Now add the equations one and two:

$$0.24H1 + 1.8H2 \quad = -0.75$$
$$\underline{-0.45H1 - 1.8H2 = \quad 0.96}$$
$$-0.21H1 + 0 \qquad = \quad 0.21 \rightarrow H1 = -1.0$$

By substituting –1.0 for the value of H1 into one of the equations, we can solve for H2:

$$(H1)(0.24) + (H2)(1.8) = -0.75$$

$$(-1)(0.24) + (H2)(1.8) = -0.75$$

$$1.8H2 = -0.51 \rightarrow H2 = -0.2833$$

Therefore, for every $1 of MS, the manager should take a short position of $1 of H1 and a short position of $0.2833 of H2.

---

1. No doubt there are numerous ways of solving this set of equations. Multiplying the second equation by –3 and adding the equations is only one of eliminating one of the unknowns.

KEY CONCEPTS

LOS 31.a

Negative convexity means the security loses more from a given increase in yield than it gains from a corresponding decrease in yield. In mortgage securities it is caused by the prepayment option. Mortgage securities can exhibit positive convexity, however, if the prepayment option is out of the money (i.e., interest rates are higher than mortgage rates).

Due to negative convexity, a standard hedge against an increase in interest rates will likely result in a loss if rates decrease.

LOS 31.b

Spread risk is the risk of the mortgage security's yield spread over the corresponding T-bond widening, and thus lowering the value of mortgage security.

Interest rate risk is the price fluctuation caused by the volatility of the yield on Treasuries with which the yields on mortgage securities are highly correlated.

Prepayment risk is the cause of the negative convexity, which means the mortgage security loses more from a given increase in yield than it gains from a corresponding decrease in yield.

Volatility risk is associated with the embedded prepayment option. An increase in volatility increases the value of an option. Since the mortgage security is short the option:

increased yield volatility → increased value of option → decreased value of mortgage security

Model risk can be from naively projecting past patterns of interest rates into the future. Another source is not recognizing the effects of technological and institutional innovations, which make prepayment more convenient to the borrower, thus increasing the risk from that source.

One strategy would be to hedge interest rate risk and not hedge spread risk. The strategy would be:
- If the spread increases, increase the exposure to mortgage securities.
- If the spread decreases, decrease the exposure to mortgage securities.

LOS 31.c

Unless explicitly stated otherwise, most discussions of interest rate risk usually pertain only to parallel shifts in the yield curve. Duration is often adequate in such cases. However, very undesirable results can come from nonparallel shifts or "twists," called **yield curve risk**. The usual approach to handling yield curve risk for a portfolio is to focus on a few particular key rate durations.

For a single noncallable Treasury bond issue, a manager may generally focus on only one rate because of the comparatively large bullet in the form of the bond's principal. Even when the yield curve twists, changes in the yield corresponding to the maturity of the bond will explain most of the changes in the price of the bond. In summary, *for a single noncallable Treasury bond, yield curve risk is not as important because of the comparatively large cash flow at maturity.*

Yield curve risk is much more important for mortgage securities because there is no bullet payment at the end.

LOS 31.d

A duration-based hedge that removes the risk associated with an increase in rates can produce a net loss on the hedged position when rates decrease. Second, a duration-based framework does not effectively deal with observed patterns of yield curve changes over time and the effect that yield curve changes have on the propensity for the prepayment by homeowners.

A two-bond hedge can, given certain assumptions, hedge against both a change in interest rates and a twist in the yield curve. This is done by forecasting a given rate and curve twist and the associated average price change for the mortgage security and the two bonds being used to hedge. This gives a two-equation and two-unknown system to determine the positions needed for the two-bond hedge.

CONCEPT CHECKERS

1. Just after the issue of a mortgage security, interest rates increase. This makes the mortgage security *more likely* to exhibit:
    A. negative convexity.
    B. zero convexity.
    C. positive convexity.

2. A manager composes an effective hedge against the fall in the value of a mortgage security by taking a short position in a T-bond futures contract. The hedged position will *likely* decline in value if interest rates:
    A. decrease.
    B. stay the same.
    C. increase.

3. The volatility risk of a mortgage security refers to the:
    A. negative relationship between yield volatility and the security's price.
    B. positive relationship between yield volatility and the security's price.
    C. volatility of the yield caused by the volatility of Treasury securities.

4. To focus on capturing profits from changes in the spread, a manager of mortgage security investments should hedge which of the following?
    A. The option-adjusted spread (OAS).
    B. The entire spread, which includes both the OAS and credit spread.
    C. Interest rate risk.

5. Yield curve risk refers to price changes from all of the following except:
    A. a flattening of the yield curve.
    B. a steepening of the yield curve.
    C. a parallel shift of the yield curve.

6. In hedging mortgage securities, a duration-based framework will be inadequate because the mortgage securities:
    A. have a high correlation with Treasury bonds and exhibit negative convexity.
    B. have a high correlation with Treasury bonds and have a high probability of default.
    C. exhibit negative convexity and have yield curve risk.

7. In contrast to a 1-bond hedge, a 2-bond hedge requires:
    A. some but fewer assumptions.
    B. the same amount of assumptions.
    C. more assumptions.

ANSWERS – CONCEPT CHECKERS

1. **C** Although we usually think of mortgage securities as having negative convexity, they will exhibit positive convexity as interest rates increase. When the embedded call is essentially out of the money, the price/yield relationship of a mortgage security resembles that of a noncallable fixed income instrument.

2. **A** If the hedge is designed to protect the mortgage security against a fall in value, which would be from an interest rate increase, then a loss is likely to result from a decrease in interest rates. This is because when rates decline, the loss in the value of the hedging instrument (e.g., a short futures contract) is likely to be larger than the gain in the mortgage security itself.

3. **A** An increase in volatility will increase the value of the call (a.k.a. the prepayment option) and lower the value of the mortgage security.

4. **C** Managers may choose not to hedge spread risk. To capture profits from changes in the spread, a manager should hedge the interest rate risk and then purchase mortgage securities when the spread widens and the price falls relative to Treasury securities. When the spread narrows, the manager should sell.

5. **C** Yield curve risk is caused by the probability of any nonparallel shift of the yield curve.

6. **C** This is true because a duration-based framework assumes a parallel shift of the yield curve. The correlation with the Treasury securities is true, but it is not a valid answer to the question. Default risk is not an issue that is necessarily associated with mortgage securities. Also, many mortgage securities are issued by government-sponsored agencies and thus have a low probability of default.

7. **C** A two-bond hedge requires assumptions such as a particular change in interest rates and twist of the yield curve. If the assumptions are not valid, the hedge may not work.

Use the following information for Questions 1 through 6.

John Wortek and Jack Benson are advisors with Pheifer Advisors, located in New York. Pheifer provides investment advice to wealthy investors and institutional investors and has been doing so for over ten years. Pheifer has a full staff of analysts, traders, portfolio managers, and economists.

The chief economist is Paul Worthington. Based on the Federal Reserve's latest Federal Open Market Committee meeting minutes and a decrease in purchases of U.S. bonds by Chinese investors, Worthington is forecasting an increase in U.S. interest rates. At the same time, Worthington is also forecasting a slowdown in the economy, because he believes that the Federal Reserve has been too aggressive in fighting inflation through increases in interest rates.

Wortek and Benson are in discussions with the Jane Sumner, the portfolio manager of the defined benefit pension plan for Alpha Seed. Alpha is a firm that specializes in the production of bio-engineered seed for farmers so that they can increase crop yield without using as many costly insecticides. Alpha has been a publicly traded firm for just three years. Wortek has calculated the duration of Alpha's liabilities to be approximately 12 years. Currently Alpha's portfolio consists of large cap U.S. stocks, bonds, and adjustable-rate mortgage-backed securities.

Sumner is considering the addition of three bonds to Alpha Seed's pension plan. The bond prices and their corresponding effective durations are as follows:

Bond	Price	Duration
A	95	4.5
B	90	6.0
C	85	7.8

Sumner would also like to keep the fixed income portfolio structured so that it is dedicated to the firm's obligations and is immunized against interest rate risk. Benson states that a barbell strategy exploits a flattening of the yield curve but can immunize a portfolio against interest rate risk in a manner similar to a bullet bond portfolio. Discussing mortgages, Wortek states that the effective duration will drop precipitously when interest rates fall and that the convexity properties are different from a traditional fixed income instrument.

Wortek and Benson also recommend more active strategies for their less risk-averse customers who do not need to immunize against a liability. One strategy Wortek has had particular success with is quality-spread analysis. Wortek describes quality spread analysis as the purchase of bonds with a yield that is higher than that justified by its credit risk. The appropriate yield spread is determined by examining the yields on high-quality and low-quality bonds. Benson suggests that a superior trading strategy would be to use percentage yield spread analysis.

1.   Suppose Worthington's forecast of interest rates and the economy is correct; which of the following strategies would be *most* applicable?
     A. Total return analysis.
     B. Wortek's strategy that is based on quality-spread analysis.
     C. Benson's strategy that is based on percentage yield spread analysis.

2.   The adjustable rate MBS in Alpha's pension plan are subject, at least to some degree, to which of the following risks?
     A. Cap risk, call risk, and interest rate risk.
     B. Call risk and interest rate risk only.
     C. Cap risk and call risk only.

3.   Given that the Fed raises interest rates by 100 basis points and the information on the bonds Sumner is considering for addition to the plan, **calculate** the dollar duration of Bond A and **determine** what Sumner should do if she wishes to increase the dollar duration of this bond.

Bond A	Increasing DD
A. $4.50	Sell futures contracts
B. $4.28	Buy futures contracts
C. $4.50	Buy futures contracts

4.   Sumner uses shortfall risk to measure the risk of the bonds in Alpha's pension plan. What is the primary drawback that Sumner should be aware of when using this measure? Shortfall risk:
     A. does not consider the magnitude of losses.
     B. is difficult to compute for a large bond portfolio.
     C. may not represent the risk measures that will be observed in the future.

5.   Regarding Wortek's and Benson's statements concerning mortgages and portfolio immunization:
     A. one is correct.
     B. both are incorrect.
     C. both are correct.

6.   Regarding Wortek's and Benson's statements concerning active strategies for bonds:
     A. one is correct.
     B. both are incorrect.
     C. both are correct.

SELF-TEST ANSWERS: FIXED INCOME PORTFOLIO MANAGEMENT

1. **A**   If Worthington is correct, there will be an increase in interest rates and a slowdown in the economy. In this case, short duration bonds should be purchased and long duration bonds should be sold. Furthermore, if the economy slows, the spreads on credit risky bonds should increase. Bond trading based only on yields, such as Wortek's and Benson's strategies, will ignore the potential price decrease from an increase in credit spreads. Total return analysis examines both the yield and the potential price change and is most appropriate in this situation where spreads are projected to increase.

2. **A**   Even though the MBS are adjustable-rate, they are still subject to some degree of call risk, because borrowers may prepay their mortgages for reasons other than a change in the level of interest rates. The degree is obviously less than that for fixed-rate MBS. Once again, even though the MBS are adjustable-rate, they are still, to a small degree, subject to interest rate risk between reset periods. Finally, floating rate assets, such as MBS backed by adjustable-rate mortgages, are subject to cap risk if the underlying mortgage rates adjust upward to the point that they reach the cap.

3. **B**   Bond A's dollar duration for a 100 basis point move in rates is: $(4.5)(0.01)(\$95) = \$4.28$. To increase the dollar duration, Sumner should buy futures contracts.

4. **A**   Shortfall risk does not consider the impact of outliers so the magnitude (dollar amount) of the shortfall below the target return is ignored. *Semivariance* is difficult to compute for a large bond portfolio and since it is estimated with only half the distribution, it is estimated with less accuracy. *Standard deviation* is a historically calculated risk measure that may not represent the risk that will be observed in the future.

5. **C**   Wortek is correct. The effective duration of a mortgage will drop precipitously when interest rates drop because the effective maturity of the bond decreases sharply as the bond is more likely to be called. Benson is also correct. A barbell strategy exploits a flattening of the yield curve but can immunize the duration of a portfolio just as a bullet bond portfolio could. The barbell invests in both a short-term and a long-term bond. When the yield curve flattens, the decrease in the long-term yield results in a stronger price increase than the decrease in the short-term bond's price because the long-term bond has a longer duration.

6. **A**   Wortek is correct. Quality spread analysis uses the spread on high-quality and low-quality bonds to identify the bonds that have a yield higher than that justified by its credit risk. Benson is incorrect. Percentage yield spread analysis, which divides a bond's yield by a government bond's yield so that mispriced bonds may be identified, is of little use because there are many additional factors that affect a bond's yield.

EQUITY PORTFOLIO MANAGEMENT

EXAM FOCUS

This topic review is very comprehensive, as it seems to cover almost everything related to managing an equity portfolio. Many individual topics (e.g., tracking risk) are discussed in greater detail in other topic reviews, but in general, this entire topic review is likely to show up somewhere on the exam. I have noted what I consider to be some of the more important areas, but do not neglect any part of this review.

EQUITIES IN A PORTFOLIO

LOS 32.a: <u>Discuss</u> the role of equities in the overall portfolio.

Equities are a substantial portion of the investment universe, and U.S. equity typically constitutes about half of the world's equity. The amount of equity in an investor's portfolio varies by locale. In the United States, institutional investors hold about 60% of their portfolio in equities. In Europe, the percentage is closer to 20%. Investing internationally provides diversification as well as the opportunity to invest in companies not available in the investor's home market.

An inflation hedge is an asset whose nominal returns are positively correlated with inflation. Bonds have been a poor inflation hedge because their future cash flows are fixed, which makes their value decrease with increased inflation. This drop in price reduces or eliminates returns for current bondholders. The historical evidence in the United States and in other countries indicates that **equities** have been a good inflation hedge. There are some important qualifiers, however. First, because corporate income and capital gains tax rates are not indexed to inflation, inflation can reduce the stock investor's return, unless this effect was priced into the stock when the investor bought it. Second, the ability of an individual stock to hedge inflation will depend on its industry and competitive position. The greater the competition, the less likely the firm will be able to pass inflation on to its consumers, and its stock will be a less effective hedge.

Examining the historical record in 17 countries from 1900–2005, equities have had consistently positive real returns. Equities have also had higher real returns than bonds in all 17 countries.[1]

---

1. Elory Dimson, Paul Marsh, and Mike Staunton, "The Worldwide Equity Premium: A Smaller Puzzle," *EFA 2006 Zurich Meetings Paper* (April 7, 2006), http://papers.ssrn.com/sol3/papers.cfm?abstract_id=891620. Accessed August 2010.

ACTIVE, PASSIVE, AND SEMIACTIVE STRATEGIES

LOS 32.b: <u>Discuss</u> the rationales for passive, active, and semiactive (enhanced index) equity investment approaches and <u>distinguish</u> among those approaches with respect to expected active return and tracking risk.

Passive equity managers do not use forecasts to influence their investment strategies. The most common implementation of passive management is indexing, where the manager invests so as to mimic the performance of a security index. Though indexing is passive in the sense that the manager does not try to outperform the index, the execution of indexing requires that the manager buy securities when the security's weight increases in the index (e.g., the security is added to the index or the firm sells new stock) or sell stock when the security's weight decreases in the index (e.g., the security is dropped from the index or the firm repurchases stock). Indexing has grown in popularity since the 1970s and often constitutes an investor's core holding.

Active equity management is the other extreme of portfolio management. Active managers buy, sell, and hold securities in an attempt to outperform their benchmark. Even with the growth of indexing, active management still constitutes the vast majority of assets under management.

The middle road between the two previous approaches is **semiactive** equity management (a.k.a. enhanced indexing or risk-controlled active management). A semiactive manager attempts to earn a higher return than the benchmark while minimizing the risk of deviating from the benchmark.

To differentiate the three approaches, their investment characteristics are summarized in Figure 1. *Active return* is the excess return of a manager relative to the benchmark. *Tracking risk* is the standard deviation of active return and is a measurement of active risk (i.e., volatility relative to the benchmark).

Figure 1: Active Return and Tracking Risk for Equity Investment Approaches

Passive Management	Semiactive Management	Active Management
Low	Expected Active Return	*High*
Low	Tracking Risk	*High*

The **information ratio** combines expected active return and tracking risk into one risk-adjusted return measure. It is the expected active return divided by the tracking risk, so it shows the manager's active return per unit of tracking risk (a.k.a. tracking error). Historically, it has been highest for semiactive management and lowest for passive management with active management falling in the middle.

Example: Computing and interpreting information ratios

Suppose there are two managers, Cirrus Managers and Cumulus Managers. **Calculate** the information ratios and comment on their relative performance.

	Cirrus Managers	Cumulus Managers
Active return	0.40%	0.62%
Tracking risk	5.60%	9.20%

Answer:

The information ratio for Cirrus Managers is 0.40%/5.60% = 0.071.

The information ratio for Cumulus Managers is 0.62%/9.20% = 0.067.

Even though Cumulus has the higher active return, on a risk-adjusted basis it slightly underperforms Cirrus as its information ratio is lower. For every 1% in tracking risk, Cirrus Managers delivered 0.071% in active return whereas Cumulus delivered 0.067%.

THE IPS, MARKET EFFICIENCY, AND EQUITY STRATEGIES

LOS 32.c: Recommend an equity investment approach when given an investor's investment policy statement and beliefs concerning market efficiency.

For the Exam: You should notice how well this material fits with constructing a portfolio for an individual investor as presented in Study Session 4. You are likely to see questions related to recommending the appropriate investment approach in a morning case for either a wealthy individual investor or an institutional investor or even in a stand-alone essay question or item set on equity portfolio management.

If an investor's **investment policy statement** (IPS) states that the investor is taxable, the asset allocation is more likely to favor passive management. This is because active management requires higher portfolio turnover such that capital gains and their associated taxes are realized more frequently. Additionally, each particular investor will have required liquidity, time horizon, and/or ethical investing concerns that will provide direction on which investment strategy to follow.

If an investor believes that markets are **efficient**, he is likely to choose a passive strategy because he does not believe the returns of active management will justify the costs of research and trading. Historical data suggests that such investors would be justified in their thinking because active management, on average, does not outperform passive management after consideration of expenses. The level of active manager underperformance is about the same as their average expenses, which suggests that active manager performance before expenses is about the same level as passive management.

Passive strategies are appropriate in a wide variety of markets. When investing in large-cap stocks, indexing is suitable because these markets are usually informationally efficient. In small-cap markets, there may be more mispriced stocks, but the high turnover associated with active strategies increases transaction costs. In international equity markets, the foreign investor may lack information that local investors have. In this case, active investing would be futile and the manager would be wise to follow a passive strategy.

EQUITY INDEX WEIGHTING SCHEMES

LOS 32.d: <u>Distinguish</u> among the predominant weighting schemes used in the construction of major equity share indices and <u>evaluate</u> the biases of each.

Stock indices are used to benchmark manager performance, provide a representative market return, create an index fund, execute technical analysis, and measure a stock's beta. The weighting schemes for stock indices are price-weighted, value-weighted, float-weighted, and equally weighted.

A *price-weighted index* is simply an arithmetic average of the prices of the securities included in the index. Computationally, a price-weighted index adds together the market price of each stock in the index and then divides this total by the number of stocks in the index. The divisor of a price-weighted index is adjusted for stock splits and changes in the composition of the index (i.e., when stocks are added or deleted), so the total value of the index is unaffected by the change. A price-weighted index implicitly assumes the investor holds one share of each stock in the index.

The primary advantage of a price-weighted index is that it is computationally simple. There is also a longer history of data for price-weighted indices, so they can provide a long record of performance.

A *market capitalization-weighted index* (or just "value-weighted") is calculated by summing the total market value (current stock price times the number of shares outstanding) of all the stocks in the index. The value-weighted index assumes the investor holds each company in the index according to its relative weight in the index. This index better represents changes in aggregate investor wealth than the price-weighted index.

Unlike the price-weighted index where a stock's representation is determined by its price, the representation of a stock in the value-weighted index is determined by the stock's total market value. This method thus automatically adjusts for stock splits of individual firms so that high priced firms are not overrepresented in the index.

A subtype of a value-weighted index is the *free float-adjusted market capitalization index*. The portion of a firm's outstanding shares that are actually available for purchase is known as the *free float*. A problem with some equity benchmarks is that market capitalization weighting can overstate the free float. For example, a large fraction of a firm's shares may be closely held by a small number of investors. This means that not all of the firm's shares are truly investable from the viewpoint of outside investors. A free float-adjusted market capitalization index is adjusted for the amount of stock that is actually available to the public.

For the Exam: Free float is also discussed in LOS 34.a of Topic Review 34.

A free float-adjusted market cap-weighted (e.g., value-weighted) index assumes the investor has bought all the *publicly available* shares of each company in the index. The major value-weighted indices in the world have been adjusted for free-float. The float-adjusted index is considered the best index type by many investors because it is more representative and can be followed with minimal tracking risk.

In an *equal-weighted index*, all stock returns are given the same weight (i.e., the index is computed as if an investor maintains an equal dollar investment in each stock in the index). These indices must be periodically rebalanced to maintain equal representation of the component stocks.

Biases in the Weighting Schemes

The price-weighted index has several biases. First, higher priced stocks will have a greater impact on the index's value than lower priced stocks. Second, the price of a stock is somewhat arbitrary and changes through time as a firm splits its stock, repurchases stock, or issues stock dividends. As a stock's price changes through time, so does its representation in the index. Third, the price-weighted index assumes the investor purchases one share (or the same number of shares) of each stock represented in the index, which is rarely followed by any investor in practice.

The primary bias in a value-weighted index and the free float-adjusted market capitalization index is that firms with greater market capitalization have a greater impact on the index than firms with lower market capitalization. This feature means that these indices are biased toward large firms that may be mature and/or overvalued. Another bias is that these indices may be less diversified if they are overrepresented by large-cap firms. Lastly, some institutional investors may not be able to mimic a value-weighted index if they are subject to maximum holdings and the index holds concentrated positions.

The equal-weighted index is biased toward small-cap companies because they will have the same weight as large-cap firms even though they have less liquidity. Many equal-weighted indices also contain more small firms than large firms, creating a further bias toward small companies. Secondly, the required rebalancing of this index creates higher transactions costs for index investors. Lastly, the emphasis on small-cap stocks means that index investors may not be able to find liquidity in many of the index issues.

The Composition of Global Equity Indices

The best-known price-weighted index in the United States is the Dow Jones Industrial Average. It was created in 1896 and has undergone many changes in composition through time. The Nikkei Stock Average is also a price-weighted index, and it contains 225 stocks listed on the Tokyo Stock Exchange.

There are many examples of value-weighted indices, and most of them are float-adjusted. They include the Standard & Poor's 500 Index Composite and the Russell Indices. International indices that are value-weighted include the Morgan Stanley Capital

International Indices. Non-U.S. indices include the Financial Times Actuaries Share Indices, which represents stocks on the London Stock Exchange, and the Tokyo Stock Exchange Price Index (TOPIX). European examples include the CAC 40 in France and the DAX 30 in Germany.

An example of an equal-weighted index is the Value Line Composite Average, which is an equally weighted average of approximately 1700 U.S. stock returns.

Regardless of the weighting scheme, the investor should be aware of differences in methodologies across indices. Index reconstitution refers to the process of adding and deleting securities from an index. Indices that are reconstituted by a committee will have lower turnover, and hence, lower transactions costs and taxes for the index investor. These indices may drift from their intended purpose, though, if they are reconstituted too infrequently. In contrast, an index regularly reconstituted by a mechanical rule will have more turnover and less drifting. Another difference in index methodologies concerns minimum liquidity requirements. The presence of small-cap stocks may create liquidity problems but also offers the index investor a potential liquidity risk premium.

METHODS OF PASSIVE INVESTING

LOS 32.e: <u>Compare</u> and <u>contrast</u> alternative methods for establishing passive exposure to an equity market, including indexed separate or pooled accounts, index mutual funds, exchange-traded funds, equity index futures, and equity total return swaps.

Index Mutual Funds and Exchange-Traded Funds

There are five main differences between **index mutual funds** and **exchange-traded funds** (ETFs). First, index mutual funds are less frequently traded. In the United States, a mutual fund's value (as calculated using the net asset value) is typically only provided once a day at the end of the day when trades are executed. In contrast, an ETF trades throughout the day.

> *Professor's Note: Exchange-traded funds (ETF) are similar to mutual funds; shares of stock are held by a trustee and shares representing ownership in the fund, not the underlying shares, are sold to investors. Shares in the first ETF, Standard and Poor's Depository Receipts (SPDRs), were first sold in January of 1993. These SPDRs contain every stock in the S&P 500 in its appropriate weight, so the S&P 500 SPDR is effectively an index fund. Each S&P 500 SPDR share contains a claim on one-tenth of the S&P index and trades at roughly one-tenth of its dollar-value. Owing to the success of the original S&P SPDRs, other SPDRs have been created including energy, technology, industrial, utility, consumer staples, and health care.*

> *To create ETF shares, authorized participants (typically market makers/ specialists) first purchase shares of the underlying stocks in large quantities. For example, in 2007 one creation unit for S&P 500 SPDRs called for the creation of 50,000 ETF shares and cost approximately $64 million. The authorized participant then deposits the shares with the fund trustee and sells and redeems ETF shares using this account.*

Second, ETFs do not have to maintain recordkeeping for shareholders, whereas mutual funds do. These expenses can be significant, especially if the fund has many small shareholders. As a consequence, some mutual funds charge expenses to shareholders based on the amount they have invested. Note, however, that there are trading expenses associated with ETFs because they trade through brokers like ordinary shares.

Third, index mutual funds usually pay lower license fees to Standard & Poor's and other index providers than ETFs do.

Fourth, ETFs are generally more tax efficient than index mutual funds. Typically, when an investor wants to liquidate their ETF shares, they sell to another investor, which is not a taxable event for the ETF, or when an ETF redeems a large number of ETF shares for an institutional investor, the ETF may exchange the shares for the actual basket of stocks underlying the ETF. This also is not a taxable event for the ETF. In an index mutual fund, redemptions by shareholders might require the sale of securities for cash, which could be a taxable event for the mutual fund that is passed on to shareholders. The bottom line is that an ETF structure is more tax efficient for the investor than a mutual fund structure.

Fifth, although ETFs carry brokerage commissions, the costs of holding an ETF long-term is typically lower than that for an index mutual fund. Due to the differences in redemption described previously, the management fees arising from taxes and the sale of securities in an ETF are usually much lower than that for a mutual fund. Thus, an ETF investor does not pay the cost of providing liquidity to other shareholders the way a mutual fund investor does.

Separate or Pooled Accounts

Indexed institutional portfolios may be managed as **separate** or **pooled accounts**. Pooling is advantageous to smaller funds, which cannot afford a dedicated manager. The drawback for these smaller funds is it is difficult to differentiate the performances of the separate, pooled funds and the manager may have to hold excess cash to provide liquidity for all the pooled funds. The firm managing these accounts may also be responsible for the management of ETFs and index mutual funds. Comparing indexed institutional portfolios against both index mutual funds and ETFs, the former have lower management costs. The expenses could be just a few basis points, and sometimes securities are lent out to other investors, which may offset or exceed expenses. The lending of securities to offset expenses can also be utilized by index mutual funds, which partially accounts for performance differences of as much as 2% amongst index mutual funds.

Professor's Note: As the names suggest, the difference between separate and pooled accounts is the way they are managed. In a pooled account the indexed portfolio is combined (pooled) with others under one manager rather than each portfolio being managed by a separate manager.

Equity Futures

The most popular **equity index future** in the United States is the contract based on the S&P 500. There are also futures contracts on a variety of global indices. The growth of equity futures contracts has been driven partly by the availability of *portfolio trades* (a.k.a. basket or program trades), where a basket of stocks is traded all at the same time.

Compared to ETFs, equity futures have two disadvantages. First, the futures contracts have a finite life and must be periodically rolled over into a new contract, at potentially less attractive terms. Second, using basket trades and futures contracts in combination for risk management may be problematic because a basket may not be shorted if one of the components violates the *uptick rule*. The uptick rule states that a security may not be shorted if the last price movement was a decline. ETFs are not usually subject to the uptick rule.

 Professor's Note: Although mentioned in the curriculum, the uptick rule was eliminated as of July 6, 2007. The SEC is currently considering reinstatement of the rule with modifications.

Equity Total Return Swap

In an **equity total return swap**, an investor typically exchanges the return on an equity security or an interest rate for the return on an equity index. By doing so, the investor can synthetically diversify a portfolio in one transaction. This portfolio rebalancing can often be performed more cheaply than trading in the underlying stocks. Their lower costs makes equity swaps ideal for tactical asset allocation.

There are also tax advantages to equity swaps. Suppose a U.S. investor wanted to buy European stocks but did not want to be responsible for the withholding taxes on them. The investor would exchange the return on a security for the return on the foreign portfolio. The swap dealer would be responsible for the tax payments and may be tax-advantaged relative to the investor.

For the Exam: In Topic Review 33, equity swaps are discussed as part of a potential moral hazard problem with upper management. They are discussed in more depth in Topic Review 43.

INDEXING A PORTFOLIO

LOS 32.f: <u>Compare</u> and <u>contrast</u> full replication, stratified sampling, and optimization as approaches to constructing an indexed portfolio and <u>recommend</u> an approach when given a description of the investment vehicle and the index to be tracked.

Full Replication

To create an indexed portfolio using **full replication**, all the stocks in the index are purchased according to the weighting scheme used in the index. Full replication is more likely to be used when the number of stocks in the index is less than 1,000 and when the stocks in the index are liquid. A prime example of an index that can be replicated is the S&P 500. Replication is also more likely when the manager has more funds to invest.

The *advantage* of replication is that there is low tracking risk and the portfolio only needs to be rebalanced when the index stocks change or pay dividends. The return on a replicated fund should be the index returns minus the administrative fees, cash drag, and transactions costs of tracking the index. Cash drag results because a fund must set aside cash for shareholder redemptions. Transactions costs arise due to reinvesting dividends and changes in index composition. Note that a replicated fund will underperform the index to a greater extent when the underlying stocks are illiquid and, thus, have higher trading costs. The index does not bear the trading costs that the replicating fund does.

Stratified Sampling

As the number of stocks in the index increases and as the stocks decrease in liquidity, stratified sampling or optimization become more likely. In **stratified sampling** (a.k.a. representative sampling), the portfolio manager separates the stocks in an index using a structure of two or more dimensions. For example, the dimensions might be industry, size, and price-earnings ratio. The market caps for each cell in a matrix are calculated given the total market cap of all the stocks in that cell. Within each cell, the manager picks a few representative stocks and makes an investment in them equaling the total market cap for that cell.

The *advantage* of stratified sampling is that the manager does not have to purchase all the stocks in an index. This is particularly useful when the number of stocks in an index is large and/or when the stocks are illiquid. The tracking risk from stratified sampling decreases as the number of cells increases in the structure (i.e., the cells are differentiated into finer divisions). Note that some government regulations restrict funds from investing too much in any one security. A stratified sampling process can be used to mimic the performance of concentrated positions within an index without taking the actual concentrated positions.

> **For the Exam:** Stratified sampling is also discussed as an enhanced indexing strategy for bond portfolio managers in Topic Review 28.

Optimization

An **optimization** approach uses a factor model to match the factor exposures of the fund to those of the index. It can also incorporate an objective function where tracking risk is minimized subject to certain constraints. The advantage of an optimization is that the factor model accounts for the covariances between risk factors. In a stratified sampling procedure, it is implicitly assumed that the factors (e.g., industry, size, price-earnings ratios) are uncorrelated.

There are three main *disadvantages* of the optimization approach. First, the risk sensitivities measured in the factor model are based on historical data and may change once the model is implemented. Second, optimization may provide a misleading model if the sample of data is skewed by a particular security or time period of data. Third, the optimization must be updated to reflect changes in risk sensitivities, and this leads to frequent rebalancing.

Regardless of its limitations, an optimization approach leads to lower tracking risk than a stratified sampling approach. This is particularly true when optimization is combined with replication. In this case, a few of the largest securities are purchased and the rest of the securities in the index are mimicked using an optimization approach.

EQUITY STYLE

LOS 32.g: Explain and justify the use of equity investment-style classifications and discuss the difficulties in applying style definitions consistently.

LOS 32.h: Explain the rationales and primary concerns of value investors and growth investors and discuss the key risks of each investment style.

For the Exam: Equity style and equity style benchmarks are important topics for the Level 3 exam. You will see style mentioned in several sections of the study notes, especially Study Session 17, Topic Reviews 46 and 47, Book 5.

There are three main categories of investment style: value, growth, and market-oriented. A value investor focuses on stocks with low price multiples [e.g., low price-earnings (P/E) ratio or low price-to-book value of assets (P/B) ratio]. A growth investor favors stocks with high past and future earnings growth. Market-oriented investors cannot be easily classified as value or growth. Equity investment styles can also be defined using market cap.

It is important to define a manager's style so that performance measurement is conducted fairly. The differentiation between a value and a growth manager is often not clear, however, especially when a manager's portfolio is characterized based on its expected future performance. For example, a stock may have respectable earnings growth that is expected to increase in the future. The current P/E ratio may be low because the market hasn't yet recognized the stock's potential. Based on the P/E ratio, it appears to be a value stock, but based on expectations, it appears to be a growth stock.

Value Investing

Value investors focus on the numerator in the P/E or P/B ratio, desiring a low stock price relative to earnings or book value of assets. The two main justifications for a value strategy are: (1) although a firm's earnings are depressed now, the earnings will rise in the future as they revert to the mean; and (2) value investors argue that growth investors expose themselves to the risk that earnings and price multiples will contract for high-priced growth stocks.

The philosophy of value investing is consistent with behavioral finance, where investors overreact to the value stock's low earnings and price them too cheaply. Market efficiency proponents argue, however, that the low price of value stocks reflects their risk. Still others argue that value stocks are illiquid and that the excess return earned by value investors is actually a liquidity risk premium. Regardless of the explanation, a value investor must realize that there may be a good reason why the stock is priced so cheaply.

The value investor should consider what is needed for the stock to increase in price and how long this will take.

There are three main *substyles* of value investing: high dividend yield, low price multiple, and contrarian. Value investors favoring high dividend yield stocks expect that their stocks will maintain their dividend yield in the future. The dividend yield has constituted a major part of equity return through time. Low price multiple investors believe that once the economy, industry, or firm improves, their stocks will increase in value. Contrarian investors look for stocks that they believe are temporarily depressed. They frequently invest in firms selling at less than book value.

Growth Investing

Growth investors focus on the denominator in the P/E ratio, searching for firms and industries where high expected earnings growth will drive the stock price up even higher. The risk for growth investors is that the earnings growth does not occur, the price-multiple falls, and stock prices plunge. Growth investors may do better during an economic contraction than during an expansion. In a contraction, there are few firms with growth prospects, so the growth stocks may see their valuations increase. In an expansion, many firms are doing well, so the valuation premiums for growth stocks decline.

There are two main *substyles* of growth investing: consistent earnings growth and momentum. A consistent earnings growth firm has a historical record of growth that is expected to continue into the future. Momentum stocks have had a record of high past earnings and/or stock price growth, but their record is likely less sustainable than that of the consistent earnings growth firms. The manager holds the stock as long as the momentum (i.e., trend) continues, and then sells the stock when the momentum breaks.

Market-Oriented Investing

The term market-oriented investing is used to describe investing that is neither value nor growth. It is sometimes referred to as blend or core investing. Market-oriented investors have portfolios that resemble a broad market average over time. They may sometimes focus on stock prices and other times focus on earnings. The risk for a market-oriented manager is that she must outperform a broad market index or investors will turn to lower cost indexing strategies.

The *substyles* of market-oriented investing are market-oriented with a value tilt, market-oriented with a growth tilt, growth at a reasonable price (GARP), and style rotation. Value and growth tilting is not full-blown value or growth, and these investors hold diversified portfolios. GARP investors search for stocks with good growth prospects that sell at moderate valuations. Style rotators adopt the style that they think will be popular in the near future.

Market Capitalization-Based Investing

Besides the three previous characterizations of investment style, investors can also be classified by the market cap of their stocks. *Small-cap* investors believe smaller firms are more likely to be underpriced than well-covered, larger cap stocks. They may also believe that small-cap stocks are likely to have higher growth in the future and/or that higher returns are more likely when an investor is starting from a smaller stock price base. *Micro-cap* investors focus on the smallest of the small-cap stocks.

Mid-cap investors believe that stocks of this size may have less coverage than large-cap stocks but are less risky than small-cap stocks. *Large-cap* investors believe that they can add value using their analysis of these less risky companies. Investors in the different capitalization categories can be further classified as value, growth, or market-oriented.

STYLE IDENTIFICATION

LOS 32.i: <u>Compare</u> and <u>contrast</u> techniques for identifying investment styles and <u>characterize</u> the style of an investor when given a description of the investor's security selection method, details on the investor's security holdings, or the results of a returns-based style analysis.

One method of determining a portfolio manager's style is to ask the manager to explain their security selection methods. For example, if the manager focuses on stocks with minimal analyst coverage that are underpriced relative to their earnings, we would characterize the manager as a *small-cap value manager*.

However, managers do not always invest as stated. For this reason, we may want to examine a manager's portfolio returns or holdings to determine style. There are two main methods of more accurately identifying an investor's style. Style can be identified using either returns-based style analysis or through an examination of an investor's holdings. These methods can be used for performance evaluation or to predict a manager's future performance.

> **For the Exam:** I strongly recommend that you are able to discuss returns-based style analysis as well as interpret the regression output to characterize a manager's style or to compare managers.

Returns-Based Style Analysis

In **returns-based style analysis**, the returns on a manager's fund are regressed against the returns for various security indices (e.g., large-cap value stocks, small-cap value stocks). The regression coefficients, which represent the portfolio's exposure to an asset class, are constrained to be nonnegative and to sum to one.

To demonstrate the use of returns-based style analysis, we regress the returns on a manager's portfolio against the returns on four indices: a small-cap growth index; a large-cap growth index; a large-cap value index; and a small-cap value index. As with any regression, the coefficients on the independent variables indicate the change in the dependent variable (in this case the return on the portfolio) given changes in the returns on the independent variables (in this case the returns on the four indices).

Assume an analyst has run the following regression:

$$R_p = b_0 + b_1 SCG + b_2 LCG + b_3 SCV + b_4 LCV + e$$

where:
R_p = returns on our manager's portfolio
SCG = returns on a small-cap growth index
LCG = returns on a large-cap growth index
SCV = returns on a small-cap value index
LCV = returns on a large-cap value index

output: $b_1 = 0$; $b_2 = 0$; $b_3 = 0.15$; $b_4 = 0.85$
      (SCG) (LCG) (SCV)   (LCV)

From the values of the regression coefficients, we would conclude that the manager's portfolio has no exposure to growth stocks ($b_1 = 0$ and $b_2 = 0$). The manager is primarily a large-cap value manager ($b_4 = 0.85$) with an exposure to small-cap value stocks ($b_3 = 0.15$). We would construct a custom benchmark for this manager consisting of 85% large-cap value stocks (i.e., a large-cap value index) and 15% small-cap value stocks (i.e., a small-cap value index).

The security indices used in the regression should be mutually exclusive of one another, be exhaustive in the sense that all the manager's exposures are represented, and represent distinct, uncorrelated sources of risk. If the indices don't have these characteristics, then the results of the returns-based style analysis can be misleading. In the previous example, if we had omitted the small-cap indices and just used the large-cap value and growth indices, then the regression might force the coefficient on the large value index to equal one. Using this misspecified regression, we could have mistakenly concluded that the investor had no exposure to small-cap stocks, when in fact he did.

Suppose that instead of four indices in the regression, we just used two broad indices: large-cap stocks and small-cap stocks. In this case, the regression would show some exposure to both indices, but there would be no indication as to whether the manager was a value manager or a growth manager. In that case, the indices (i.e., independent variables) are not well specified and the regression will not provide much useful information.

From the regression, we are also provided with the coefficient of determination (R^2). This provides the amount of the investor's return explained by the regression's style indices. It measures the *style fit*. One minus this amount indicates the amount unexplained by style and due to the manager's security selection. For example, suppose the style fit from the regression is 79%. This would mean that 21% of the investor's returns were unexplained by the regression and would be attributable to the manager's security selection (i.e., the manager made active bets away from the securities in the style indices). The error term in the regression, which is the difference between the portfolio return and the returns on the style indices, is referred to as the manager's *selection return*.

 Professor's Note: Selection return is the excess or surplus return earned by selecting superior investments (e.g., undervalued or over-valued securities) and trading accordingly.

One of the benefits of returns-based style analysis is that it helps determine if the manager's reported style and actual style are the same. For a mutual fund, the investment objective of the manager is contained in the fund's prospectus, and in some cases the investment objective can be determined by the fund's name. However, not all aggressive growth funds invest in the same asset categories or even in the same proportions. Returns-based style analysis helps to determine the reality—not what the manager says, but what she does.

Figure 2 shows the returns-based style analysis of two hypothetical funds, ABC and PDQ, which claim to be large-cap growth funds. The first column shows the indices (benchmarks) against which the portfolio returns were regressed. The second and third columns show the weights each manager has in each category. These are the coefficients from the regression analysis.

Figure 2: Returns-Based Style Analysis of ABC and PDQ Funds

Style Category	ABC Fund Weight %	PDQ Fund Weight %
Large-cap growth	52.0	86.0
Large-cap value	23.0	9.0
Mid-cap growth	11.0	1.5
Mid-cap value	5.0	0.0
Small-cap growth	1.9	1.7
Small-cap value	0.0	0.0
T-bond (1–10 yr.)	0.0	0.0
T-bond (10+ yr.)	0.0	0.0
Corporate bond	1.1	1.3
T-bills	6.0	0.5
Foreign equity	0.0	0.0
Total	100.0	100.0

The results show that although ABC has exposure to large-cap growth, it also has substantial exposure to large-cap value and mid-cap stocks. PDQ's main exposure is to large-cap growth (86%) and some exposure to large-cap value (9%).

Both ABC and PDQ funds claim to be large-cap growth funds. However, ABC fund has substantial exposure to large-cap value and mid-cap stocks. PDQ fund, on the other hand, had style exposure more consistent with its investment objective.

Multi-Period Returns-Based Style Analysis

A single regression in a returns-based style analysis provides the average fund exposures during the time period under analysis. A series of regressions can be used to check the style consistency of a manager. That is, does the manager pursue the same style consistently over time?

Consider a hypothetical fund—Spark Growth and Income Fund. There are five years of monthly data from January 2006 to December 2010 (i.e., T = 60 monthly data points).

We use 36 months in each regression analysis and form 25 overlapping samples of 36 months each:

- The first sample starts at t = 1 (January 2006) and ends at t = 36 (December 2008).
- The second sample starts at t = 2 (February 2006) and ends at t = 37 (January 2009) and so forth.
- The last sample starts at t = 25 (January 2008) and ends at t = 60 (December 2010).

For each of the data samples, we run the returns-based style analysis regression and compute the weights (exposures) of each of the style asset categories. Thus, there are 25 regressions in total. Results for the first and the last samples are shown in Figure 3. Figure 4 shows the plot of all the changes in exposure over the five years, using the results of the 25 regressions.

Figure 3: 5-Year Rolling 36-Month Returns-Based Style Analysis

Style Category	Sample 1 (t = 1 to 36) Weight %	Sample 25 (t = 25 to 60) Weight %
Large-cap growth	12	8
Large-cap value	62	49
Mid-cap value	20	37
Cash	6	6
Total	100	100

Figure 4: Style Consistency of Spark Growth and Income Fund

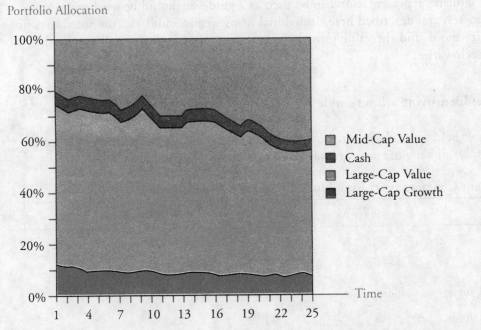

The heights (thickness) of the colored bands indicate that the fund's exposures have changed over time. The exposures to large-cap growth and large-cap value have declined, while the exposure to mid-cap value increased, and the exposure to cash stayed the same. This type of analysis helps to check the manager's style consistency over time. If the manager was hired to focus on large-cap investments, the investor should be concerned about the manager's increasing focus on mid-cap stocks.

Holdings-Based Style Analysis

A second method of verifying a portfolio manager's style is to evaluate the characteristics of the securities in the manager's portfolio. This method is referred to as holdings-based style analysis or composition-based style analysis. The manager would characterize securities based on the following attributes:

Value or growth: Does the manager invest in low P/E, low P/B, and high dividend yield stocks? If so, the manager would be characterized as a value manager. A manager with high P/E, high P/B, and low dividend yield stocks would be characterized as a growth manager. A manager with average ratios would be characterized as market-oriented.

Expected earnings per share growth rate: Does the manager have a heavy concentration in firms with high expected earnings growth? If so, the manager would be characterized as a growth manager.

Earnings volatility: Does the manager hold firms with high earnings volatility? If so the manager would be characterized as a value manager because value managers are willing to take positions in cyclical firms.

Industry representation: Value managers tend to have greater representation in the utility and financial industries because these industries typically have higher dividend yields and lower valuations. Growth managers tend to have higher weights in the technology and health care industries because these industries often have higher growth. Although industry representation can be used as a guide, it should be used with the other characteristics described here. Individual firms within industries do not always fit the industry mold, and the value/growth classification of an industry will vary as the business cycle varies.

Example: Identifying a fund's style

In the table below, the characteristics of a mutual fund and a broad market index are provided. Using only the data provided, **identify** the style of the fund.

Investment Characteristics for a Mutual Fund and Broad Market

	Mutual Fund	*Broad Market*
P/E ratio	18.47	22.33
P/B ratio	2.27	4.09
Dividend yield	2.2%	1.7%
EPS growth for 1 year	11.9%	22.7%
EPS growth for 5 years	6.0%	11.0%
Median market cap ($ billion)	$8.5	$47.9
Industry Weight		
Basic industries	13%	12%
Business services	7%	5%
Consumer goods	5%	8%
Consumer services	9%	8%
Energy	3%	10%
Financials	37%	21%
Information technology	7%	17%
Health	2%	13%
Media	2%	3%
Utilities	15%	3%
Total	100%	100%

Answer:

The manager appears to be a *value manager* because the P/E and P/B ratio are below that of the broad market, and we would expect the portfolios of value managers to have higher dividend yields than that of the broad market. The manager is also invested in stocks with lower EPS growth and overweighted in financials and utilities, which is also characteristic of a value style. The manager is underweighted in technology and health care stocks, which are favored by growth managers. Additionally, we would conclude that the manager has a small-cap focus, because the median market cap is much lower than that of the broad market.

Returns-based style analysis is compared to holdings-based style analysis in Figure 5. Note that both methods can be performed on the same portfolio. By doing so, the analyst can gain further insight into the portfolio manager's processes and holdings. For example, whereas returns-based analysis is useful for easily characterizing an entire portfolio, it will not detect changes in style (i.e., style drift) as quickly as holdings-based analysis. The reason is that the regression in returns-based analysis typically uses monthly returns over the past several years. Thus, a portion of the analysis is based on data that may no longer reflect the manager's emphasis. In contrast, holdings-based style analysis uses the portfolio's current contents to characterize the portfolio and provides a more up-to-date picture of the portfolio's contents.

Figure 5: Advantages/Disadvantages of Returns-Based Analysis and Holdings-Based Style Analysis

Advantages of Returns-Based Analysis	*Advantages of Holdings-Based Analysis*
Characterizes an entire portfolio	Characterizes each security
Enables comparisons of entire portfolios	Enables comparisons of securities
Summarizes the result of the investment process	Can detect style drift more quickly than returns-based analysis
Methodology backed by theory	
Low information requirements	
Different models usually result in the same conclusions	
Low cost and can be executed rapidly	

Disadvantages of Returns-Based Analysis	*Disadvantages of Holdings-Based Analysis*
May be inaccurate due to style drift	Is not consistent with the method used by many managers to select securities
Misspecified indices can lead to misleading conclusions	Requires subjective judgment to classify securities
	Requires more data than returns-based analysis

For the Exam: Be able to identify a manager's style when given portfolio weights or the output from a returns-based style analysis and be able to contrast the two methods of style analysis as well as discuss their advantages and disadvantages.

EQUITY STYLE INDICES

LOS 32.j: <u>Compare</u> and <u>contrast</u> the methodologies used to construct equity style indices.

There are several providers of style indices, each of whom competes to earn the business and licensing fees of ETFs and others who would like to create a financial product based on their index. Some providers differentiate their style using just a few variables whereas others use several. Style may be differentiated using price multiples, earnings growth rates, dividends, and other variables. Most indices use holdings-based style analysis to characterize securities.

There are three different methods used to assign a security to either a value or growth index. In the first method the stock is assigned to value or growth. In the second method, the stock can be assigned to value, growth, or to a third neutral category. In the third method, a stock can be split between categories. For example, if its predominant characteristics are value but there are also some features of the stock that suggest growth, the stock may be classified as 70% value and 30% growth. In the first two methods, style is perceived as a category, whereas in the third method style is perceived as a quantity.

Viewing style as a category means that there will be no *overlap* when a style index is constructed (i.e., an individual security will be assigned to only one style). Viewing style as a quantity means that there will be overlap. Some of a stock's market cap may be assigned to value and another part could be assigned to growth. This occurs when a stock is not clearly value or growth.

Examples of style indices with style overlap are the Russell value and growth indices, where the growth ranking is determined by the price/book ratio as well as by a long-term growth estimate. There is no neutral category, just value or growth. Some stocks are split between the growth and value indices, with, for example, 20% of the stock's market capitalization in the Russell Growth and 80% in the Russell Value Index. The FTSE and S&P/Citigroup Style Index series also have overlap.

Most indices are constructed with no overlap. For example, the Dow Jones Wilshire, Morningstar, Morgan Stanley Capital International (MSCI), and S&P/Citigroup Pure Style Index series have no overlap. Additionally most indices have just two categories, value and growth (i.e., there is no neutral style index). The justification for just two categories is that many investment managers have a clear value or growth directive they must follow.[2]

---

2. For more information on these indices, see www.djindexes.com, www.ftse.com/Indices/, http://indexes.morningstar.com, www.mscibarra.com, www.russell.com, and www.spglobal.com.

Another distinguishing characteristic among index methodologies is the presence of **buffering**. When an index has buffering rules, a stock is not immediately moved to a different style category when its style characteristics have changed slightly. The presence of buffering means that there will be less turnover in the style indices and, hence, lower transactions costs from rebalancing for managers tracking the index.

THE EQUITY STYLE BOX AND STYLE DRIFT

LOS 32.k: Interpret the results of an equity style box analysis and discuss the consequences of style drift.

Another method of characterizing a portfolio's style is to use a **style box**. This method is used by Morningstar to characterize mutual funds and stocks. In this approach, a matrix is formed with value/growth characteristics across the top and market cap along the side. Morningstar uses holdings-based style analysis to classify securities.

In Figure 6, we have provided the Morningstar style box for a hypothetical small-cap value fund. The numbers in each cell represent the percent of the fund's market cap in each category (total of the cells = 100%). Note that most of the fund's component stocks are classified as small-cap value, although other categories are represented as well.

Figure 6: Morningstar Style Box for a Hypothetical Small-Cap Value Fund

	Value	Core	Growth
Large-cap	2%	1%	0%
Mid-cap	17%	12%	1%
Small-cap	60%	5%	2%

Categorizing portfolios by size is fairly standard in that market cap is the usual metric for evaluating size. However, different providers use different categorizations of value and growth attributes. For this reason, the categorization of portfolios can differ a great deal depending on the provider. Usually price-multiples are used to define value stocks, whereas earnings or sales growth rates are used to define growth stocks.

Style drift is when a portfolio manager strays from his original, stated style objective. There are two reasons why this can be problematic for an investor. First, the investor will not receive the desired style exposure. This is a concern because value and growth stocks will perform quite differently over time and over the course of business cycles. Second, if a manager starts drifting from the intended style, she may be moving into an area outside her expertise.

As mentioned previously, returns-based style analysis and holdings-based style analysis can both be used to evaluate style drift, with holdings-based style analysis considered to be the more effective of the two methods. To determine whether a manager has drifted using holdings-based style analysis, we would evaluate the same factors mentioned earlier (i.e., the portfolio's value or growth characteristic, expected earnings growth, earnings volatility, and industry representation).

SOCIALLY RESPONSIBLE INVESTING

LOS 32.l: Explain the use of stock screens based on socially responsible investing criteria and discuss their potential effect on a portfolio's style characteristics.

Socially responsible investing (SRI), also known as ethical investing, is the use of ethical, social, or religious concerns to screen investment decisions. The screens can be negative, where the investor refuses to invest in a company they believe is unethical; or positive, where the investor seeks out firms with ethical practices. An example of a negative screen is an investor who avoids tobacco and alcohol stocks. An example of a positive screen would be when the investor seeks firms with good labor and environmental practices. Most SRI portfolios utilize negative screens, some use both negative and positive screens, and even less use only positive screens. An increasing number of portfolio managers have clients with SRI concerns.

For the Exam: Look for socially responsible investing in developing the IPS for an individual or institutional investor.

A SRI screen may have an effect on a portfolio's style. For example, some screens exclude basic industries and energy companies, which typically are value stocks. SRI portfolios thus tend to be tilted toward growth stocks. SRI screens have also been found to have a bias toward small-cap stocks. There are two main benefits to monitoring the potential style bias resulting from SRI screens. First, the portfolio manager can take steps to minimize the bias, if it is inconsistent with the investor's risk and return objectives. Second, with knowledge of the portfolio's style bias, the manager can determine the appropriate benchmark for the SRI portfolio. Returns-based style analysis can detect the presence of style bias and monitor the success of its remedy.

LONG-SHORT AND LONG-ONLY INVESTMENT STRATEGIES

LOS 32.m: Compare and contrast long-short versus long-only investment strategies, including their risks and potential alphas, and explain why greater pricing inefficiency may exist on the short side of the market.

Long-only strategies focus on using fundamental analysis to find undervalued stocks. In contrast, **long-short** strategies focus on exploiting the constraints many investors face. Specifically, many investors such as institutions are unable to take short positions, which may lead to overvalued stocks.

Whereas long-only strategies can only buy undervalued stocks and avoid overvalued stocks, long-short strategies can both buy undervalued stocks and short overvalued stocks. In essence, the long-short strategy can earn **two alphas**, one on long positions and one on short sales. A long-only strategy can only earn the long alpha through security selection (the excess return relative to its benchmark).

Another way of viewing the advantage of long-short strategies is to consider an investor who is attempting to outperform a market index. If he would like to express a negative view of an index security in a long-only strategy, he is limited to avoiding the stock. For example, if a stock's market cap constitutes 4% of an index, the minimum possible underweighting is 4%, created by not holding the stock. Here the *active weight* is −4%. If the investor wanted an active weight of 6%, on the other hand, the investor would overweight the stock, and it would constitute 10% of the market cap in the investor's portfolio. Thus, the distribution of potential active weights in a long-only portfolio is asymmetric (i.e., underweighting is limited to the security's weight in the portfolio, whereas overweighting is unlimited).

In contrast, a long-short investor can create a symmetric distribution of active weights, provided there is sufficient information regarding the stock's under or overvaluation. The long-short investor can create as short a position as desired (i.e., he is not limited to just avoiding the stock).

In regard to *risk*, a long-only investor is potentially exposed to both systematic and unsystematic risk. In contrast, the long-short investor can eliminate expected systematic risk by using a pair trade (also known as pairs arbitrage) in a *market neutral strategy*. In a pair trade, the investor buys one stock and shorts another in the same industry, thus eliminating exposure to marketwide risk. Systematic risk can be added, if desired, through the use of equity futures or ETFs, which is discussed in the next LOS. The investor, however, still has company specific risk, and if the short position rises in value while the long falls, the results could be disastrous for the long-short investor.

The potential returns and risks of a long-short trade are also magnified by leverage (borrowed funds). Many long-short investors, for example hedge funds, will use leverage of two to three times their capital in a long-short trade. Leverage increases the likelihood that an investor will have to unwind her position early in order to satisfy a margin call.

> **For the Exam:** Hedge fund managers often employ market neutral strategies to enable them to capitalize on their abilities to identify over- and under-priced securities. See Topic Review 36, Book 4.

Pricing Inefficiencies on the Short Side

There are **four reasons for pricing inefficiencies** on the short side of equity trades:

1. There are barriers to short sales that do not exist for long trades. Because of these barriers, some investors do not pursue short strategies. One barrier is that to short a stock, the short seller must find someone who will lend the shares. When the lender requests the shares to be returned, the short seller may have to buy the shares in the open market at an adverse price.

2. Firm management is more likely to promote their firm's stock through accounting manipulations and other means than they are to disparage it. Thus, stock is more likely to be overvalued than undervalued.

3. Analysts on the sell-side are more likely to issue buy recommendations than sell recommendations. The reason is that there is a larger pool of potential buyers of a stock than sellers. The latter is limited to those investors who already own the stock or short sellers. Additionally, analysts will anger large stockholders if they issue a sell recommendation.

4. Sell-side analysts face pressure from firm management against issuing sell recommendations because managers often have stock holdings and options in their firm and may threaten analysts with a cutoff of communications and lawsuits, if the analysts issue sell recommendations. The analyst's firm may also be shut out from investment banking and other corporate finance business if the analyst issues a sell recommendation. Note that such corporate actions are inconsistent with the Best Practice Guidelines Governing Analyst/Corporate Issue Relations supported by the CFA Centre for Financial Market Integrity and the National Investor Relations Institute.[3] Additionally, CFA members, candidates, and charterholders are bound to independence and objectivity by Standard I(B) of the Code of Ethics and Standards of Professional Conduct.

EQUITIZING A LONG-SHORT PORTFOLIO

LOS 32.n: Explain how a market-neutral portfolio can be "equitized" to gain equity market exposure and compare and contrast equitized market-neutral portfolios with short-extension portfolios.

Recall that a long-short strategy in the same industry has no systematic risk. An investor may, however, wish to add systematic risk to the market neutral strategy to earn a higher return. This can be established by taking a **long position in an equity futures** contract with a notional principal equal to the cash from the short sales. The investor's total profit is then the net profit or loss from the long and short position, the profit or loss from the futures contract, and interest earned on the cash from the short sale. To calculate a return, we would divide this amount by the equity the investor has put up for the transaction.

Professor's Note: Two things. First, the proceeds from the short sale are usually deposited with the broker and placed in Treasuries. Interest on the Treasuries that is not paid to the lender of the shares as a fee is passed onto the short seller. The portion received by the short seller is referred to as the "short rebate." Next, pairs trading is a relative value strategy. That is, the manager purchases undervalued shares and shorts overvalued shares with approximately the same market sensitivity (i.e., equal betas). The manager's primary goal is profiting from security selection. If the manager feels the overall market will gain or lose ground, he can buy or sell equity futures, respectively. Thus, pair trades and trading equity futures represent two separate strategies.

A market neutral strategy can also be *equitized using ETFs*. ETFs may be more cost effective and convenient than futures contracts. ETFs do not expire like futures contracts,

---

3. See www.niri.org for more details on the guidelines. Accessed August 2010.

so they don't have to be rolled over. They also have low expenses and are usually available for shorting, if the investor wants to de-equitize after having added them.

Because a long-short, market neutral strategy has no systematic risk, its benchmark should be the risk-free rate (i.e., the return on T-bills). If the strategy is equitized, the benchmark is the index underlying the futures contract or the ETF. Note that a market neutral strategy need not always be equitized. The strategy can be exposed to the risk of other asset classes (e.g., fixed income) using the derivative contracts for other assets.

Short Extension Strategies

 Professor's Note: Market neutral strategies are often employed by hedge fund managers and other arbitrageurs. As such, the market generally considers market neutral strategies to be alternative investments.

Short extension strategies are seen by the market as extensions to long-only investing. In a short extension strategy, the manager shorts an amount of securities equal to a set percentage of his long portfolio and then purchases an equal amount of securities. For example, in a 120/20 short extension strategy (120/20 and 130/30 are the most common), the manager shorts an amount of securities equal to 20% of the market value of the long portfolio and then purchases an equal amount of stocks. Notice that the net position remains 100% (100% – 20% + 20%).

The difference between this short extension strategy and two separate strategies, one 100% long and the other 20/20 market neutral, is the nature of the securities. If the strategy is managed like two separate portfolios, the securities are totally unrelated; the stocks in the long portfolio are different from the long-short portfolio. A short extension strategy, on the other hand, is effectively a single portfolio. The shorted securities can come from the long portfolio, and purchases can be totally new or increased active weights in current securities.

Short extension strategies provide benefits not available to the long-only manager. First, in a market neutral strategy, the manager ends up with zero market exposure and can only add such an exposure with futures, swaps, et cetera. In a short extension strategy, the manager could start out with a beta of 1.0, short a percentage of stocks (above we assumed 20%), go long that same percentage in other stocks, and end up with the same or a different net portfolio beta. The short extension strategy needs no other position to gain exposure to market factors.

 Professor's Note: The net portfolio beta is calculated as the total weight of long positions times their average beta minus the total weight of short positions times their average beta.

Next, the short extension strategy provides the potential to out-perform a long-only strategy by enabling the manager to capitalize to a limited extent on short selling. Remember that in a long-only strategy, the manager can only demonstrate distaste for a benchmark stock by not holding it. The manager's negative active position in the stock is limited by its weight in the index. In a short extension strategy the manager can short the over-priced stock and increase the positive active weight on an under-priced stock.

Professor's Note: An active weight is the difference between the stock's weight in the actively managed portfolio and its weight in the benchmark. If an over-priced stock has a weight of 4% in an index, for example, the only way the long-only manager can capitalize on the mispricing is to not hold the stock. That is, the manager's maximum active weight is –4%. With the ability to short the stock, the manager can push the stock's active weight well beyond –4%.

A drawback to short extension strategies is that they earn their market returns and alphas from the same set of investments. Remember that in a market neutral strategy, the manager earns alpha on the long-short portfolio and then adds the market return with derivatives. In the short extension strategy, the manager earns the market related return on the portfolio while generating alpha through security selection (long and short) in the same portfolio.

SELLING DISCIPLINES

LOS 32.o: <u>Compare</u> and <u>contrast</u> the sell disciplines of active investors.

An investor may need to sell holdings to rebalance the portfolio, to alter the asset allocation for liquidity, or to update the portfolio's security selection. The use of various strategies can help the investor decide when to sell.

Substitution is replacing an existing security with another with brighter prospects. Considering the transactions costs and tax consequences of the sale of the existing security and the purchase of the new security, this approach is referred to as an *opportunity cost sell discipline*. After careful research, a manager may also conclude that a firm's business will worsen in the future. This is referred to as a *deteriorating fundamentals sell discipline*.

Other, more technical, selling disciplines are based on rules. For example, in a *valuation-level sell discipline*, a value investor may sell a stock if its P/E or P/B ratio rises to the ratio's historical mean. In a *down-from-cost sell discipline*, the manager may sell a stock if its price declines more than say 20% from the purchase price. In an *up-from-cost sell discipline*, the manager may sell a stock once it has increased, for example, either a percentage or a dollar amount from the purchase price. In a *target price sell discipline*, the manager determines the stock's fundamental value at the time of purchase and later sells the stock when it reaches this level.

These selling disciplines are not mutually exclusive within an investor's portfolio, as different stocks may call for different disciplines. Also, the consequences of sell disciplines should be appraised on an after-tax basis according to the investors' tax status.

The frequency of buying and selling in a portfolio is driven by the manager's style. Value investors are typically long-term investors, who buy undervalued stocks and hold them until they appreciate. Annual turnover for value managers varies from 20% to 80%. Growth managers base their decisions on earnings growth and are less patient. They often sell after the next quarterly, semiannual, or annual earnings statement comes out (the frequency of the statements depends on the country of the firm's incorporation). Thus, it is not unusual to see annual turnover of 60% to several hundred percent for these investors.

ENHANCED INDEXING

LOS 32.p: Contrast derivatives-based versus stock-based enhanced indexing strategies and justify enhanced indexing on the basis of risk control and the information ratio.

> **For the Exam:** Enhanced indexing applied to bond portfolio management is discussed in Topic Review 28, Book 3. In general the concept of enhanced indexing is important to the Level 3 curriculum.

As discussed previously, semiactive or enhanced indexing strategies attempt to earn an active return (a return greater than a benchmark) while minimizing deviations in performance from the benchmark (tracking risk or active risk). Enhanced indexing strategies are expected to result in higher information ratios (active return divided by tracking risk) than passive or active strategies.

Stock-Based and Derivatives-Based Enhanced Indexing Strategies

An enhanced indexing strategy can be executed using either actual stocks or derivative contracts such as equity futures. Using a **stock-based enhanced indexing strategy**, the manager underweights or overweights index stocks based on beliefs about the stocks' prospects. Risk is controlled by monitoring factor risk and industry exposures. The portfolio resembles the index, except where the manager has a specific belief about the value of an index security.

To understand a stock-based enhanced indexing strategy, it may help to compare it to full-blown active management. If the manager does not have an opinion about an index stock in full-blown active management, she doesn't hold the stock. If the manager does not have an opinion about an index stock in a stock-based enhanced indexing strategy, she holds the stock at the same level as the benchmark.

In a **derivatives-based enhanced indexing strategy**, the manager obtains an equity exposure through derivatives. A common method of doing so is to *equitize cash*. Here the manager holds a cash position and a long position in an equity futures contract. The manager can then attempt to generate an excess return by altering the duration of the cash position. If the yield curve is upward sloping, the manager invests longer-term, if she thinks the higher yield is worth it. If, on the other hand, the yield curve is flat, the manager invests in short-duration, fixed income securities because there would be no reward for investing on the long end.

> **For the Exam:** Using equity futures contracts to "equitize" a position in cash is discussed in Topic Review 41, Book 5.

There are two *limitations* to enhanced indexing in general. First, successful managers will be copied and their alpha will disappear, unless they change their strategy through time. Second, models obtained from historical data may not be applicable to the future, if the economy changes.

The Fundamental Law of Active Management

The **fundamental law of active management** states that an investor's information ratio (IR) is a function of his depth of knowledge about individual securities (the information coefficient—IC) and the number of investment decisions (the investor's breadth—IB).[4]

More formally:

$$IR \approx IC\sqrt{IB}$$

where:
IR = information ratio
IC = information coefficient
IB = investor breadth

For the Exam: The LOS asks you to justify enhanced indexing on the basis of the information ratio, so you may need to use this calculation on the exam. In any case, be sure you are familiar with the concepts and the components of the equation. You will know which information ratio is referenced by the data provided.

The IC is measured by comparing the investor's forecasts against actual outcomes. The closer they are, the higher the correlation between them, and the greater the IC. More skillful managers will have a higher IC.

Note that investor breadth measures the number of *independent* decisions an investor makes, which does not necessarily increase with the number of securities followed. For example, if an investor buys ten energy stocks because she thinks the sector will do well, the IB equals one, not ten.

The narrower an investor's breadth, the greater her knowledge of each security must be to produce the same information ratio. Unfortunately it is difficult for most investors to realize a high IC. A stock-based enhanced indexing strategy can produce higher information ratios because the investor can systematically apply her knowledge to a large number of securities, each of which would have different attributes requiring independent decisions.

---

4. Richard C. Grinold and Ronald N. Kahn. *Active Portfolio Management*. (McGraw Hill, 1995).

©2010 Kaplan, Inc.

Example: Using the fundamental law of active management

Manager X follows the stocks in a broad market index and has made independent forecasts for 400 of them. Her IC is 0.05.

Manager Y has made independent forecasts for 150 stocks. His IC is 0.07.

Which manager has the best performance as measured by the information ratio?

Answer:

The information ratio for each manager can be approximated as:

$$IR_X = 0.05\sqrt{400} = 1.00$$
$$IR_Y = 0.07\sqrt{150} = 0.86$$

Although manager X's depth of knowledge is not as great, she has better performance because she has a greater breadth of decisions. Performance here is measured by the information ratio, so Manager X earns more excess return per unit of active risk.

Note that a derivatives-based enhanced indexing strategy will have less breadth than a stock-based enhanced indexing strategy because the investor uses a derivatives contract to gain exposure to equity *and* earns an excess return using the duration strategy described earlier. Due to its lower breadth, it will require a higher information coefficient to earn as high an information ratio as a stock-based strategy.

ALLOCATING TO MANAGERS

LOS 32.q: <u>Discuss</u> and <u>justify</u>, in a risk-return framework, the optimal portfolio allocations to a group of investment managers.

Given funds to invest, an investor has a series of decisions to make. The investor must first decide which asset classes to allocate the funds to and in what weights. At this level, the focus is on maximizing expected return for a given level of risk.

Once an equity allocation is made, the investor needs to focus on choosing passive or active equity management. Passive equity management has zero active return and zero active risk. Think of passive equity management as the *baseline*. As one moves from passive management to enhanced indexing to active management, the expected active return and active risk increase.

So just as in asset allocation, the investor must choose the tradeoff between risk and return. However, once the investor has made a decision to invest in equity, the tradeoff focuses on **active risk** and **active return**.

The gist of the steps to follow is that the investor must decide how much active risk he is willing to accept and what the best combination of equity managers is to achieve that active risk while maximizing active return.

In the first step in deciding how much equity to allocate to a group of equity managers, the investor will want to maximize the utility of his active return. The utility function for active return is similar to the utility function for expected return. The utility of the active return increases as active return increases, as active risk decreases, and as the investor's risk aversion to active risk decreases.

Next, given his utility function, the investor needs to investigate the performance characteristics of available equity managers. An efficient frontier analysis is useful here, except instead of using expected return and risk, this efficient frontier plots expected active return and active risk using combinations of available equity managers.

Investors are usually more risk averse when facing active risk than they are when dealing with total risk for the following three reasons. First, if an investor were willing to accept zero active return, it would be easy enough to just index. However, to believe that a positive active return is possible, the investor must think that an active manager can deliver an active return, and the investor must believe they can pick that active manager. Second, an investor who must answer to a superior (e.g., a pension plan) for their equity managers' performance will be judged relative to a passive benchmark. It is difficult to produce a positive alpha, and investors are reluctant to take risk positions away from the index. Third, if an investor wants higher active return positions, they must be willing to invest more in the highest active return manager. This results in less diversification across managers. Most institutional investors have an active risk target in the range of 1.5% to 2.5%.[5]

In the following LOS, we present an example of an investor using a group of equity managers to target a specified target active risk level. It is assumed that the correlations between the equity managers' active returns are zero. This is not an unreasonable assumption, if the managers are following different styles.

CORE-SATELLITE AND COMPLETENESS FUND APPROACHES

LOS 32.r: <u>Explain</u> the core-satellite approach to portfolio construction and <u>discuss</u> the advantages and disadvantages of adding a completeness fund to control overall risk exposures.

In a **core-satellite approach** to managing active equity managers, the investor has a core holding of a passive index and/or an enhanced index that is complemented by a satellite of active manager holdings. The idea behind a core-satellite approach is that active risk is mitigated by the core, while active return is added by the satellites. The core is benchmarked to the asset class benchmark, whereas the satellites are benchmarked to a more specific benchmark.

A core-satellite approach can be executed using an informal approach or using a more formal approach as described in LOS 32.q. As part of the latter process, a manager targets an active risk and return and then uses optimization to find the best mix of equity managers to deliver that performance. In the following example, the manager has

---

5.   Barton Waring, Duane Whitney, John Pirone, and Charles Castille. "Optimizing manager structure and budgeting manager risk." *Journal of Portfolio Management*. Vol. 26, Iss. 3; p. 90. (New York, Spring 2000).

a 50% core in the passive index and the enhanced indexed portfolio, with satellites of 25%, 15%, and 10% in the active managers.

Example: Applying the core-satellite approach

The investor has an active risk target of no more than 1.75% and a target information ratio of at least 0.9. The investor can choose from passive management, enhanced indexing, or three active managers (X, Y, and Z) in the figure below. Given the targeted active risk, the investor makes the allocations to maximize return. Note that, by definition, the active return and risk to passive indexing is 0%. Assume that the correlations between the equity managers' active returns are zero.

Active Return, Active Risk, and Allocations to Equity Managers

	Expected Active Return	Expected Active Risk	Allocations
Passive index	0.00%	0.00%	10%
Enhanced indexing	1.40%	2.20%	40%
Active Manager X	1.70%	2.80%	25%
Active Manager Y	3.00%	5.10%	15%
Active Manager Z	3.70%	7.00%	10%

Calculate the investor's active return given the above allocations. **Determine** if the investor has met the targeted active risk and information ratio.

Answer:

To calculate the investor's active return given the equity manager allocations listed in the figure above, we would calculate a weighted average return using the following formula. Note that it is similar to the formula for portfolio expected return except now we use active return instead of total return.

$$\text{expected active portfolio return} = \sum_{i=1}^{n} w_{a,i}(\hat{R}_{a,i})$$

where:
$w_{a,i}$ = weight invested with ith manager
$\hat{R}_{a,i}$ = expected active return of ith manager

Using the active returns and allocations in the figure above, we calculate an expected active portfolio return of 1.81%:

expected active portfolio return =
$(0.10 \times 0\%) + (0.40 \times 1.4\%) + (0.25 \times 1.7\%) + (0.15 \times 3.0\%) + (0.10 \times 3.7\%) = 1.81\%$

To calculate the portfolio active risk, we assume that the correlations between the equity managers' active returns are zero. Assuming zero correlation, the formula for portfolio active risk is:

$$\text{portfolio active risk} = \sqrt{\sum_{i=1}^{n} w_{a,i}^2 \sigma_{a,i}^2}$$

Using the active risks and allocations, we calculate the portfolio active risk:

portfolio active risk

$$= \sqrt{(0.10)^2(0)^2 + (0.40)^2(0.022)^2 + (0.25)^2(0.028)^2 + (0.15)^2(0.051)^2 + (0.10)^2(0.07)^2}$$
$$= \sqrt{0.000234} = 0.0153 = 1.53\%$$

The investor's information ratio is 1.81% / 1.53% = 1.18. The investor has satisfied the active risk target of no greater than 1.75% and the information ratio of at least 0.9.

The Completeness Fund Approach

In contrast to the formalized process followed for the core-satellite approach, many managers use a less exact approach. Given that the resulting portfolio will still be benchmarked against a broad market index, the manager's portfolio will have a number of industry or other biases relative to the benchmark. This is particularly true when examining the portfolios of bottom-up managers, where industry exposures are not given a priority in stock selection.

To minimize the differences in risk exposures between the portfolio and the benchmark, the investor can use a **completeness fund**. The completeness fund is combined with the active portfolio, so that the combined portfolios have a risk exposure similar to the benchmark. The advantage of the completeness fund approach is that the active return from the managers can be maintained while active risk is minimized. The completeness fund must be rebalanced regularly as the active manager's exposures change. The fund can be managed passively or semiactively.

The disadvantage of a completeness fund is that it may result in a reduction of active returns arising from misfit risk. (As described in the next LOS, misfit risk results from differences between the manager's normal portfolio and the broader asset class benchmark.)

COMPONENTS OF TOTAL ACTIVE RETURN

LOS 32.s: <u>Distinguish</u> among the components of total active return ("true" active return and "misfit" active return) and their associated risk measures and <u>explain</u> their relevance for evaluating a portfolio of managers.

Recall that a manager's *normal portfolio* reflects the securities she normally chooses from for her portfolio. It is an appropriate benchmark for the manager, because it reflects the manager's style.

In contrast, an investor who hires a manager may use a broad-based benchmark for the manager's asset class that does not reflect the manager's style. This portfolio would be referred to as the **investor's benchmark**.

Using these two benchmarks, we can then decompose the manager's total active return into two parts, the true active return and the misfit active return, as follows:

true active return = manager's total return – manager's normal portfolio return

misfit active return = manager's normal portfolio return – investor's benchmark return

The **true active return** is "true" in the sense that it measures what the manager earned relative to the correct benchmark. The **misfit active return** is "misfit" in the sense that it measures that part of the manager's return from using a benchmark that is not suited to the manager's style.

Using these components of return, we can decompose the manager's total active risk into the true risk and misfit risk. The total active risk is the volatility of the manager's portfolio relative to the investor's benchmark.

$$\text{total active risk} = \sqrt{(\text{true active risk})^2 + (\text{misfit active risk})^2}$$

Using the true active return and true active risk, we can define an information ratio that better represents the manager's skills:

$$\text{true information ratio} = \frac{\text{true active return}}{\text{true active risk}}$$

There are two uses of the decomposition of the manager's performance into true and misfit components. The first use is to more accurately evaluate the manager's performance using the manager's true return as in the following example.

Example: Decomposing performance into true and misfit components

Bob Davis is a small-cap growth manager who invests in U.S. equities. He was hired by a pension fund that benchmarks him against a broad U.S. market index. Using the information in the figure below, **calculate** the manager's information ratio that most accurately reflects his abilities.

Decomposing Active Risk and Return

Manager return	18.0%
Broad market return	15.0%
Normal portfolio return	20.0%
Total active risk	5.0%
Misfit active risk	3.5%

Answer:

Comparing the manager's return to the broad market, the manager appears to have generated an excess return of 3% (18% – 15%). That is an inappropriate benchmark. If one uses the normal portfolio as the benchmark, the manager has actually underperformed the appropriate benchmark by 2% (18% – 20%). The true and active returns are measured as follows:

$$\text{true active return} = 18\% - 20\% = -2\%$$
$$\text{misfit active return} = 20\% - 15\% = 5\%$$

The true active risk is backed out of the total and misfit risk:

$$\text{total active risk} = \sqrt{(\text{true active risk})^2 + (\text{misfit active risk})^2}$$

$$5\% = \sqrt{(\text{true active risk})^2 + (3.5\%)^2}$$

$$(5\%)^2 = (\text{true active risk})^2 + (3.5\%)^2$$

$$(5\%)^2 - (3.5\%)^2 = (\text{true active risk})^2$$

$$\sqrt{(5\%)^2 - (3.5\%)^2} = \text{true active risk}$$

$$\text{true active risk} = 3.57\%$$

The true information ratio demonstrates underperformance as it is negative, resulting from the negative true active return:

$$\text{true information ratio} = \frac{-2\%}{3.57\%} = -0.56$$

The decomposition of the total active performance into true and misfit components is also useful for optimization. The objective is to maximize the total active return for a given level of total active risk while allowing for an optimal amount of misfit risk. Note that misfit risk is not optimized at zero because a manager may be able to generate a level of true active return for some level of misfit risk. In other words, if you let the manager concentrate in the style he is familiar with, the manager is more likely to generate an excess return relative to his normal portfolio.

ALPHA AND BETA SEPARATION

LOS 32.t: <u>Explain</u> alpha and beta separation as an approach to active management and <u>demonstrate</u> the use of portable alpha.

In an **alpha and beta separation approach**, the investor gains a systematic risk exposure (beta) through a low-cost index fund or ETF, while adding an alpha through a long-short strategy. This strategy may be particularly suitable for markets that are highly efficient and difficult to generate an alpha from.

For example, the investor may pick up a beta exposure in an S&P 500 index fund. The stock prices in this large-cap index are highly efficient with respect to information, and it would be difficult to generate an alpha with this index. The investor could pick up alpha by hiring a manager who specializes in long-short strategies in less efficient small-cap markets. If the manager decides to take a different index exposure, she could keep the small-cap alpha and pick up the beta exposure in some index (e.g., a MSCI World Index ETF). This strategy is referred to as a portable alpha strategy.

An advantage of this approach is that the investor can gain access to equity styles and asset classes outside of a systematic risk class. The investor can also better understand and manage the risks in an alpha and beta separation approach because they are more clearly defined. In contrast, in a long-only strategy, the risks are not as clearly delineated. Lastly, by partitioning the alpha and beta, the investor has a better idea of the costs of investing. A passive beta exposure is typically cheaper than an active alpha exposure.

A limitation of the alpha and beta separation approach is that it may be difficult or costly to implement short positions in markets such as emerging markets or small-cap markets. Secondly, some long-short strategies are not truly market neutral and may have a degree of systematic risk. Lastly, long-short investing may be off-limits to some investors. These investors, however, could create an alpha and beta separation approach exposure using equity futures. For example, suppose the investor wants a beta from large-cap U.S. stocks and an alpha from European equities. The investor can take a long position in the S&P 500 index futures contract and invest with a European equity manager to generate the alpha. To become market neutral in the European equity market, the investor would then short a futures contract based on European equities.

SELECTING EQUITY MANAGERS

LOS 32.u: <u>Review</u> the process of identifying, selecting, and contracting with equity managers, including the development of a universe of suitable candidates based on both qualitative and quantitative factors, the composition of equity manager questionnaires, and the analysis of fee structures.

The process of selecting investment managers is particularly important for institutions and high net worth individuals. The process may be performed in-house or by outside consultants. Consultants research performance records and interview investment managers to determine which managers are worthy of consideration. Qualitative considerations are the strength of the firm's investment approach and research as well as the manager's personnel. Quantitative considerations include the manager's fees, performance, and style. The manager should also have consistency between stated and actual investment approaches.

Past Performance

Past performance is often no guarantee of future performance. In fact, a contrarian strategy often works as well with managers as it does with stocks. Although consistency in superior performance is rare, managers with poor historical performance are unlikely to be hired. That is, without some evidence that a manager can generate an alpha, the investor will passively index. Additionally, a manager who achieves superior performance with a consistent staff and investment philosophy is more likely to be hired.

Manager Questionnaires

In the hiring process, a manager questionnaire is used to screen potential managers. If the manager's responses to the questionnaire are promising, the questionnaire will be followed by personal interviews with the manager.

There are five sections of the questionnaire. The first section regards the manager's staff and organizational structure. Investing is a labor-intensive process, and having the right people and compensation structure in place is key to a manager's potential success. This part of the questionnaire also covers topics such as the vision of the firm, the qualifications and experience of the staff, and how long the staff has worked as a team.

The second section of the questionnaire concerns investment philosophy and procedures. This section provides details on the firm's investment philosophy, how it intends to capture alpha, how research is conducted, how risk is managed and monitored, the firm's stock selection techniques, and how portfolios are composed.

The third section focuses on resources and how research is conducted and used. Other details provided here include portfolio turnover and how quantitative models are utilized.

The fourth section concerns performance: the manager's benchmark, the expected alpha, the sources of risk, and portfolio holdings.

The fifth section provides details on the fee schedule, which are discussed in the next section.

For the Exam: Don't worry about which part of the questionnaire contains what. Just be familiar with the information provided by the questionnaire.

Fee Schedules

Fees can be charged on an *ad valorem* basis or based on performance. (Ad valorem is Latin for "according to the value.") Ad valorem fees are also referred to as asset under management fees (AUM) and are charged based on the asset value managed and may be on a sliding schedule (e.g., 0.50% for the first $10 million managed and 0.40% for asset amounts over $10 million).

A *performance-based fee* is often charged as a base fee plus some percentage of the alpha. For example, the fee may be 0.40% of all assets managed plus 10% of any profit above the benchmark. The performance-based fee may also include *fee caps* and *high water marks*. A fee cap specifies a maximum performance fee. The intent is to prevent managers from undertaking too much risk to earn higher fees. A high water mark condition requires the manager to compensate for past underperformance before receiving a performance-based fee. For example, the manager might have underperformed the benchmark in the previous year (i.e., generated a negative alpha). This year the manager must beat the benchmark, not just improve the value of the fund over last year. Note that the manager would still receive the base fee in both years under most contracts.

For the Exam: High water marks are also discussed as part of hedge fund performance evaluation in Topic Review 36, LOS 36.q, Book 4.

The *advantage* of ad valorem fees is that they are straightforward and known in advance. This is useful when the investor is budgeting investment fees. Their *disadvantage* is that they do not align the interests of managers and investors the way performance-based fees do.

Performance-based fees have two *disadvantages*. First, performance-based fees are more complicated and require detailed specifications. Second, they also increase the volatility of the manager's compensation, which may create problems for a manager attempting to retain staff and provide consistent performance. This is particularly true in years when the manager has underperformed its competitors.

The advantage of performance-based fees is that they align the interests of the manager and the investor, especially if they are *symmetric* (i.e., contain penalties for poor performance and rewards for good performance). This should motivate the manager to work harder on the investor's behalf.

STRUCTURING EQUITY RESEARCH

LOS 32.v: <u>Contrast</u> the top-down and bottom-up approaches to equity research.

Some investors begin their investment process by examining an economy to determine its future state. If, for example, the investor determines the economy is going to expand, cyclical stocks would be favored. Next, specific firms within cyclical industries are examined for attractiveness. This approach is known as a **top-down approach** because the investor starts at the economy level and works her way down. Using a global perspective, the investor would also look at global economic factors and the projections for currencies.

In a **bottom-up approach**, the investor starts at the individual stock level. Stocks are chosen on the basis of their individual characteristics and valuation. For this type of investor, macroeconomic and industry conditions are not as important.

Some investors use a combination of the two approaches. For example, the investor forecasting an economic expansion may select cyclical stocks based on their valuations.

Another way to differentiate investment approaches is by whether the research is conducted by sell-side or buy-side analysts. A *buy-side* analyst composes a portfolio for an investment management firm. The analyst in this case usually must present recommendations to and get approval from a committee. Buy-side research is not usually available to those outside the firm because this is how the firm hopes to establish their competitive advantage.

In contrast, *sell-side* analysts often work for an investment bank that uses the research to promote stocks the bank is selling. Sell-side research is also conducted by independent firms available for hire by investment managers. Thus, sell-side research is available to those outside the firm. It is the research that the public is most familiar with, as sell-side analysts often appear in the financial news or on investment television shows. This research is often organized by industry or sector and provides a buy, sell, or hold recommendation. Formal sector and industry classifications are provided by governmental organizations and private firms such as MSCI.

KEY CONCEPTS

LOS 32.a

Equities are a good inflation hedge, especially when firms can pass inflation on to the consumer. Equities have had consistently positive real returns and higher real returns than bonds in 17 countries over 106 years.

LOS 32.b

Passive managers do not use forecasts to influence their investment strategies. The most common implementation of passive management is indexing, where the manager invests so as to mimic the performance of a security index.

Active managers buy, sell, and hold securities in an attempt to outperform their benchmark. Even with the growth of indexing, active management still constitutes the vast majority of assets under management.

Semiactive (enhanced indexing) managers attempt to earn a higher return than the benchmark while minimizing the risk of deviating from the benchmark.

Active return is the excess return of a manager relative to the benchmark. *Tracking risk* is the standard deviation of active return and is a measurement of active risk. Passive managers have the lowest active return and tracking risk whereas active managers have the highest, with semiactive managers between the two.

LOS 32.c

Passive strategies may be preferable when the investor is taxable, has an informational disadvantage in global markets, is investing in informationally efficient large-cap markets, or wants to avoid the high transactions costs in small-cap markets. The evidence is that the returns to active management do not justify their higher costs.

LOS 32.d

A price-weighted index is an arithmetic average of the prices of the securities included in the index. Computationally, a price-weighted index adds together the market price of each stock in the index and then divides this total by the number of stocks in the index. The divisor of a price-weighted index is adjusted for stock splits and changes in the composition of the index, so that the total value of the index is unaffected by the change. A price weighted index assumes the investor holds one share of each stock in the index. A bias of the price-weighted index is that higher priced stocks are overrepresented in the index.

A value-weighted index is calculated by summing the total market cap of all the stocks in the index. A free float-adjusted market capitalization index is adjusted for the amount of stock that is actually available to the public, and it is considered the best index type because it is the most representative of what an investor could achieve. The primary bias of these indices is that large-cap, possibly mature and/or overvalued firms are overrepresented in the index. These indices can also be less diversified and contain stocks in proportions that are unavailable to investors subject to maximum holdings restrictions.

In an equal-weighted index, all stock returns are given the same weight. Its bias is that it favors small-cap companies. Tracking this index also requires costly periodic rebalancing and exposure to illiquid stocks.

LOS 32.e

In the United States, a mutual fund's value (as calculated using the net asset value) is typically only provided once a day, at the end of the day, when trades are executed. In contrast, an ETF trades throughout the day. ETFs do not have to maintain recordkeeping for shareholders, whereas mutual funds do. These expenses can be significant, especially if the fund has many small shareholders. Index mutual funds usually pay lower license fees than ETFs pay to Standard & Poor's and other index providers.

ETFs are generally more tax efficient than index mutual funds. Typically, when an investor wants to liquidate their ETF shares, they sell to another investor, which is not a taxable event for the ETF. In an index mutual fund, redemptions typically involve a sale of the underlying securities for cash, which is a taxable event that is passed on to shareholders.

The costs of holding an ETF long-term are typically lower than that for an index mutual fund. The management fees and taxes from the sale of securities in an ETF are usually much lower than that for a mutual fund. Indexed institutional portfolios may be managed as separate or pooled accounts. In a pooled account the indexed portfolio is combined (pooled) with others under one manager rather than each portfolio being managed by a separate manager. Comparing indexed institutional portfolios against both index mutual funds and ETFs, the former have lower management costs.

The most popular equity index future in the United States is the contract based on the Standard & Poor's 500. There are also futures contracts on a variety of global indices.

Compared to ETFs, equity futures have two disadvantages. First, futures contracts have a finite life and must be periodically rolled over into a new contract. Second, using basket trades and futures contracts in combination for risk management can be problematic because a basket may not be shorted if one of the components violates the uptick rule.

In an equity total return swap, an investor typically exchanges the return on an equity security or an interest rate for the return on an equity index. Portfolio rebalancing using swaps can often be performed more cheaply than trading in the underlying stocks. There may also be tax advantages to equity swaps, if the swap dealer is responsible for the tax payments and is in a more favorable tax position.

LOS 32.f

Full replication, where all the stocks in an index are purchased, is more appropriate for smaller indices when the index stocks are liquid and when the manager has more funds to invest. The advantage of replication is that there is low tracking risk and the portfolio only needs to be rebalanced when the index stocks change or pay dividends.

In stratified sampling, the manager chooses stocks to match the index using two or more dimensions. Stratified sampling is more appropriate when the number of stocks in the index is large and/or the stocks are illiquid.

Optimization uses a factor model to match the factor exposures of the index. It accounts for the covariances between the risk factors, but the risk sensitivities may change through time. It may also provide misleading results and lead to frequent rebalancing. An optimization approach, however, leads to lower tracking risk than stratified sampling.

LOS 32.g

There are three main categories of investment style: value, growth, and market-oriented.

- A value investor focuses on stocks with low price multiples (e.g., P/E ratio, P/B ratio).
- A growth investor favors stocks with high past and future earnings growth.
- Market-oriented investors cannot be easily classified as value or growth.

The differentiation between a value and a growth manager is often not clear. The current P/E ratio can be low because the market hasn't yet recognized the stock's potential. Based on the P/E ratio, it appears to be a value stock, but based on expectations, it appears to be a growth stock.

LOS 32.h

Value investors focus on the numerator in the P/E or P/B ratio, desiring a low stock price relative to earnings or book value of assets. A value investor must realize that there can be a good reason why the stock is priced so cheaply.

Growth investors focus on the denominator in the P/E ratio, searching for firms and industries where high expected earnings growth will drive the stock price up even higher. The risk for growth investors is that the earnings growth does not occur, the price-multiple falls, and stock prices plunge.

The term market-oriented investing is used to describe investing that is neither value nor growth. It is sometimes referred to as blend or core investing. The risk for a market-oriented manager is that she must outperform a broad market index or investors will turn to lower cost indexing strategies.

Investors can also be classified by the market cap of their stocks. Small-cap investors believe smaller firms are more likely to be underpriced than well-covered, larger cap stocks. They might also believe that small-cap stocks are likely to have higher growth in the future. Mid-cap investors believe that stocks of this size may have less coverage than large-cap stocks but are less risky than small-cap stocks. Large-cap investors believe that they can add value using their analysis of these less risky companies.

LOS 32.i

Style can be identified using either returns-based style analysis or through examination of an investor's holding using a holdings-based style analysis. In returns-based style analysis, the returns on a manager's fund are regressed against the returns for various security indices (e.g., large-cap value stocks, small-cap value stocks). The regression coefficients, which represent the portfolio's exposures to the asset classes, are constrained to be nonnegative and to sum to one. The security indices used in the regression should be mutually exclusive, be exhaustive in the sense that all the manager's exposures are represented, and represent distinct, uncorrelated sources of risk.

From the regression, we are also provided with the coefficient of determination (R^2), which provides the amount of the investor's return explained by the regression's style indices. It measures the style fit. One minus this amount indicates the amount unexplained by style and due to the manager's security selection.

Holdings-based style analysis evaluates portfolio characteristics using the following attributes: value or growth, expected earnings growth, earnings volatility, and industry representation. Returns-based style analysis has the advantage of being a low cost, quick, and consistent method of characterizing an entire portfolio. Its disadvantages are that it may lead to misleading results if misspecified, and it may detect style changes slowly. Holdings-based style analysis has the advantage that it can characterize individual securities and will detect style changes more quickly than returns-based analysis. Its disadvantage is that it subjectively classifies securities, requires more data, and is not consistent with how most managers invest.

LOS 32.j

There are three different methods used to assign a security to either a value or growth index. In the first method the stock is assigned to value or growth. In the second method, the stock can be assigned to value, growth, or to a third neutral category. In the third method, a stock can be split between categories.

Viewing style as a category means that there will be no overlap when a style index is constructed (i.e., an individual security will be assigned to only one style). Viewing style as a quantity means that there will be overlap.

Most indices are constructed with no overlap. Additionally most indices have just two categories: value and growth (i.e., no neutral category). Another distinguishing characteristic among index methodologies is the presence of buffering. When an index has buffering rules, a stock is not immediately moved to a different style category when its style characteristics have changed slightly.

LOS 32.k

A **style box** is a method of characterizing a portfolio's style. Morningstar uses holdings-based style analysis to classify securities. The Morningstar style box for a hypothetical small-cap value fund is shown below. The numbers in each cell represent the percent of the fund's market cap in each category (total of the cells = 100%).

	Value	Core	Growth
Large-cap	2%	1%	0%
Mid-cap	17%	12%	1%
Small-cap	60%	5%	2%

Style drift is when a portfolio manager strays from his original stated style objective. There are two reasons why this can be problematic for an investor. First, the investor will not receive the desired style exposure. This is a concern because value and growth stocks will perform quite differently over time and over the course of business cycles. Second, if a manager starts drifting from the intended style, they may be moving into an area outside their expertise.

LOS 32.l

Socially responsible investing (SRI), also known as ethical investing, is the use of ethical, social, or religious concerns to screen investment decisions. The screens can be negative, where the investor refuses to invest in a company they believe is unethical; or positive, where the investor seeks out firms with ethical practices.

An SRI screen may have an effect on a portfolio's style. For example, some screens exclude basic industries and energy companies, which typically are value stocks. SRI portfolios thus tend to be tilted toward growth stocks. SRI screens have also been found to have a bias toward small-cap stocks.

LOS 32.m

Long-only strategies focus on using fundamental analysis to find undervalued stocks. In contrast, long-short strategies focus on exploiting the constraints many investors face. Specifically, many investors are unable to take short positions, which may lead to overvalued stocks.

Whereas long-only strategies can only buy undervalued stocks and avoid overvalued stocks, long-short strategies can both buy undervalued stocks and short overvalued stocks. In essence, the long-short strategy can earn two alphas, one on long positions and one on short sales. A long-only strategy can only earn the long alpha through security selection (the excess return relative to its benchmark).

A long-only investor is potentially exposed to both systematic and unsystematic risk. In contrast, the long-short investor can eliminate expected systematic risk by using a pair trade (also known as pairs arbitrage) in a market neutral strategy. In a pair trade, the investor buys one stock and shorts another in the same industry, thus eliminating exposure to market-wide risk.

The reasons for pricing inefficiencies on the short side of equity trades include impediments to short sales, management is more likely to promote the firm's stock, analysts are more likely to issue buy recommendations than sell recommendations, and the pressure analysts face from management against issuing sell recommendations.

LOS 32.n

A long-short strategy in the same industry has no systematic risk. An investor may, however, wish to add systematic risk to the market neutral strategy to earn a higher return. This can be established by taking a long position in equity futures.

A market neutral strategy can also be equitized using ETFs. ETFs may be more cost effective and convenient than futures contracts. ETFs do not expire like futures contracts, so they don't have to be rolled over. They also have low expenses and are usually available for shorting.

In a short extension strategy, the manager shorts an amount of securities equal to a set percentage of his long portfolio and then purchases an equal amount of securities. For example, in a 120/20 short extension strategy, the manager shorts an amount of securities equal to 20% of the market value of the long portfolio and then purchases an equal amount of stocks.

In a market neutral strategy, the manager ends up with zero market exposure and can only add such an exposure with futures, swaps, etc. In a short extension strategy, the manager shorts a percentage of stocks, goes long that same percentage in other stocks, and needs no other position to gain exposure to market factors.

LOS 32.o

Substitution is replacing an existing security with another that has brighter prospects. Considering the transactions costs and tax consequences of the sale of the existing security and the purchase of the new security, this approach is referred to as an **opportunity cost sell discipline**. After careful research, a manager may also conclude that a firm's business will worsen in the future. This is referred to as a **deteriorating fundamentals sell discipline**.

Other more technical selling disciplines are based on rules. For example, in a **valuation-level sell discipline**, a value investor may sell a stock if its P/E or P/B ratio rises to the ratio's historical mean. In a **down-from-cost sell discipline**, the manager may sell a stock if its price declines more than say 20% from the purchase price. In an **up-from-cost sell discipline**, the manager may sell a stock once it has increased, for example, either a percentage or a dollar amount from the purchase price. In a **target price sell discipline**, the manager determines the stock's fundamental value at the time of purchase and later sells the stock when it reaches this level.

LOS 32.p

In a stock-based enhanced indexing strategy, the manager uses analysis to underweight or overweight index stocks and controls risk by monitoring factor risk and industry exposures. In a derivatives-based enhanced indexing strategy, the manager may take a long position in an equity futures contract and earn an excess return by altering the duration of the cash position.

The limitations to enhanced indexing are that successful managers' alpha will be competed away, and models obtained from historical data may not be applicable to the future.

The fundamental law of active management states that an investor's information ratio is a function of their depth of knowledge and the number of independent investment decisions. More formally: $IR \approx IC\sqrt{IB}$. Enhanced indexed strategies can produce higher information ratios because the investor can apply his knowledge to a large number of securities.

LOS 32.q

The equity investment decision focuses on the trade-off between active risk and active return. Investors are usually more risk averse when facing active risk than they are when facing total risk.

The investor must decide how much active risk they are willing to accept and what the best combination of equity managers is to achieve that active risk while maximizing active return.

In the first step in deciding how much equity to allocate to a group of equity managers, the investor will want to maximize the utility of their active return. The utility function for active return is similar to the utility function for expected return. The utility of the active return increases as active return increases, as active risk decreases, and as the investor's risk aversion to active risk decreases. Next, given their utility function, the investor needs to investigate the performance characteristics of available equity managers. An efficient frontier analysis is useful here, except instead of using expected return and risk, this efficient frontier plots expected active return and active risk using combinations of available equity managers.

LOS 32.r

In a **core-satellite approach** to managing active equity managers, the investor has a core holding of a passive index and/or an enhanced index that is complemented by a satellite of active manager holdings. The idea behind a core-satellite approach is that active risk is mitigated by the core, while active return is added by the satellites. The core is benchmarked to the asset class benchmark, whereas the satellites are benchmarked to a more specific benchmark.

To minimize the differences in risk exposures between the portfolio and the benchmark, the investor can use a **completeness fund**. The completeness fund complements the active portfolio so that the combined portfolios have a risk exposure similar to the benchmark. The advantage of the completeness fund approach is that the active return from the managers can be maintained while active risk is minimized. The completeness fund must be rebalanced regularly as the active manager's exposures change. The fund can be managed passively or semiactively.

The disadvantage of a completeness fund is that it may result in a reduction of active returns arising from misfit risk (see **LOS 32.s**).

LOS 32.s

We can decompose the manager's total active return into two parts: the true and misfit portions. The true active return is "true" in the sense that it measures what the manager earned relative to the correct, normal benchmark. The misfit active return is "misfit" in the sense that it measures that part of the manager's return from using a benchmark that is not suited to the manager's style. The decompositions are as follows:

true active return = manager's total return − manager's normal portfolio return

misfit active return = manager's normal portfolio return − investor's benchmark return

$$\text{total active risk} = \sqrt{(\text{true active risk})^2 + (\text{misfit active risk})^2}$$

The true and misfit decomposition allows a more accurate evaluation of the manager's performance by using the true information ratio:

$$\text{true information ratio} = \frac{\text{true active return}}{\text{true active risk}}$$

LOS 32.t

In an alpha and beta separation approach, the investor gains a systematic risk exposure (beta) through a low-cost index fund or ETF, while adding an alpha through a long-short strategy. This strategy may be particularly suitable for markets that are highly efficient and difficult to generate an alpha from.

For example, the investor may pick up a beta exposure in an S&P 500 index fund. The investor could pick up alpha by hiring a manager who specializes in long-short strategies in less efficient small-cap markets. If the manager decides to take a different index exposure, she could keep the small-cap alpha and pick up the beta exposure in some index (e.g., a MSCI World Index ETF). This strategy is an example of a portable alpha strategy.

LOS 32.u

Selecting investment managers involves both qualitative and quantitative considerations. **Qualitative considerations** are the strength of the firm's investment approach and research as well as the manager's personnel. **Quantitative considerations** include the manager's fees, performance, and style.

Though past performance is no guarantee of future performance, managers with poor performance are unlikely to be hired. A manager who achieves superior performance with a consistent staff and investment philosophy is more likely to be hired.

There are five sections of the **manager questionnaire**: staff and organizational structure, investment philosophy and procedures, resources and research utilization, performance, and fee schedule.

Fees can be charged on an *ad valorem basis* or *performance-based*. The former is straightforward and known in advance. Performance-based fees are more complicated but align the interests of the manager and investor.

LOS 32.v

In a **top-down approach**, investors begin their investment process by examining an economy to determine its future state. If, for example, the investor determines the economy is going to expand, cyclical stocks would be favored. Next, specific firms within cyclical industries are examined for attractiveness. Using a global perspective, the investor would also look at global economic factors and the projections for currencies.

In a **bottom-up approach**, the investor starts at the individual stock level. Stocks are chosen on the basis of their individual characteristics and valuation. For this type of investor, macroeconomic and industry conditions are not as important.

CONCEPT CHECKERS

1. Is there any historical evidence to suggest that bonds might be a better long-term investment than equities?

2. Many U.S. media outlets have recommended investing in global stocks because there may be more opportunities to exploit mispriced stocks. **Identify** the conditions under which this advice would be correct.

3. A market-value weighted index is considered the most representative of market conditions, especially when it is adjusted for free float. Some practitioners, however, have suggested moving away from this weighting scheme to one based on fundamentals such as the price-earnings ratio. **Explain** their reasoning.

4. Suppose a taxable investor has a large amount to invest and would like to invest long term. Would he be *more likely* to use an ETF or an index mutual fund?

5. A manager would like to create a fund that tracks the performance of a prominent developed and emerging country European index. There are 1,500 stocks in the index. The manager has $10 million initially to invest. Should the manager use replication, stratified sampling, or optimization?

6. Many researchers have found that value stocks have higher returns than growth stocks, on average over time. What would market efficiency proponents say about this performance differential?

7. An analyst wants to evaluate a manager who claims that she invests in mid-cap value stocks. The analyst uses both returns-based style analysis and holdings-based style analysis.

   Explain why the manager would pursue these stocks. **Describe** the indices the analyst should include in the returns-based style analysis. **Describe** the expected characteristics using the holdings-based style analysis.

8. A manager's portfolio has gradually shifted from high P/E, high P/B, and high earnings growth rate stocks into stocks with more moderate levels of the variables. **Discuss** the problem with this movement.

9. **Describe** the potential style bias in socially responsible portfolios.

10. **Explain** how a pair trade can go awry.

11. Why would an investor want to equitize a long-short portfolio?

12. Manager A has made independent forecasts for 450 stocks. Her IC is 0.03.

    Manager B has made independent forecasts for 200 stocks. His IC is 0.05.

    Which manager has the better performance as measured by the information ratio?

13. Are investors more risk averse when facing total risk or active risk? **Explain** why.

14. An investor uses a core-satellite approach to allocate funds amongst equity managers. The equity manager's active risk, active return, and allocations are shown as follows.

	Expected Active Return	*Expected Active Risk*	*Allocations*
Passive index	0.00%	0.00%	15%
Enhanced indexing	1.70%	2.50%	45%
Active Manager X	1.90%	3.00%	25%
Active Manager Y	3.30%	5.50%	10%
Active Manager Z	3.90%	7.20%	5%

Describe the investor's core. **Calculate** the investor's active return, active risk, and information ratio given the above allocations. Assume that the correlations between the equity managers' active returns are zero.

15.   Using the figures below, **evaluate** the manager's performance.

Manager return	15.0%
Investor's benchmark	11.0%
Normal portfolio return	8.0%
Total active risk	5.2%
Misfit active risk	3.8%

16.   An investor has a position with a successful small-cap growth manager. The investor would like to separate the alpha and beta and pick up the beta in less risky large-cap U.S. stocks. The investor is restricted from investing in long-short managers. **Explain** how the investor could separate the alpha and beta.

17.   **Describe** what a compensation schedule with high water marks does for investment manager motivation.

18.   Maria Castillo is an investment manager who is promoting the Japanese equity market to her investment management committee because she forecasts that the Japanese economy is finally rebounding from a decade long slump. She also thinks the Japanese yen will stay strong relative to other major currencies. What type of investment approach is Castillo using?

ANSWERS – CONCEPT CHECKERS

1. No. Using 106 years of data, equities have had higher returns than bonds in 17 countries. Equities have also had consistently positive real returns in 17 countries over 106 years. Bonds are poor inflation hedges.

2. This advice would be correct if the U.S. investor or her portfolio manager can gain access to the same information that investors have in the country they are considering. This may difficult to achieve. Additionally, smaller cap markets typically have higher transactions costs. The investor should be sure that the higher transactions costs in these markets do not offset the potentially higher returns.

   For these reasons, the U.S. investor may want to consider a passive indexing strategy in these markets.

3. A value-weighted index may overweight overvalued stocks because the overvalued stocks will have a higher market cap. By weighting by price-earnings ratio, these practitioners hope to avoid overweighting overvalued stocks. Stocks with high price-earnings ratios would have lower weights in such an index.

4. The large investor would be more likely to use an ETF because in a mutual fund, he would pay record-keeping costs for smaller investors. Given that the investor pays taxes, an ETF would be more appropriate because there are fewer taxes realized that are passed on to shareholders. If they are a long-term investor, they are more likely to use ETFs because in a mutual fund, they would pay for the costs of supplying liquidity to shorter-term investors.

5. Given that there are 1,500 stocks, the manager should consider a method other than replication. Furthermore, the manager has only $10 million to invest and many of the stocks, especially in the emerging countries, are likely to be illiquid.

   Optimization will provide lower tracking risk compared to stratified sampling, but it requires more frequent rebalancing. If tracking risk is not highly important, the manager may want to consider stratified sampling since the trading costs in some emerging countries can be particularly high. Stratified sampling also does not require or depend on the use of a model.

6. Market efficiency proponents would argue that these stocks have higher returns because investors expect their risk to be higher. As such, they have lower prices and the higher future returns (on average) are compensation for the increased risk.

   Indeed, the risk for value investors is that these stocks' low prices are justified (i.e., their weak earnings never recover). The value investor must have an expectation of how and when these stocks will recover before he invests in them.

7. The manager would pursue mid-cap stocks because mid-cap stocks may have less coverage than large-cap stocks but are less risky than small-cap stocks. Value stocks have excess returns on average over time, but the manager must understand that these stocks may be priced cheaply for a reason (i.e., they have higher risk).

   The analyst should include six indices for the returns-based style analysis: value and growth indices for small-, mid-, and large-cap stocks. This will help identify if the manager has any exposure to growth or to other capitalization stocks.

From the holdings-based style analysis for the mid-cap value manager, the manager should expect low P/E and P/B ratios, below average expected earnings growth, higher earnings volatility, and representation in the financial and utility industries. The manager should also find a market cap that reflects mid-cap.

8.   The manager's style is drifting. The portfolio is shifting from a growth orientation into a market orientation. When a manager's style drifts, the investor does not receive the intended exposure and the manager moves outside his area of expertise.

9.   Socially responsible portfolios have a potential bias towards growth stocks because they tend to shun basic industries and energy stocks, which are typically value stocks. Socially responsible portfolios also have a bias towards small-cap stocks.

10. A pair trade can go awry if the stock that was shorted rises in price and the stock that was bought decreases in price. The probability of a pair trade performing poorly increases if the investor uses leverage, receives a margin call, and has to liquidate the position early at adverse prices.

11. An investor would equitize a long-short portfolio if she thought the stock market was going to do well in the future. A market neutral strategy has no systematic risk, but a broad market exposure can be added by taking a long position in a futures contract, index fund, or an ETF. Note that exposures to other asset classes can also be added using an index security for them.

12. The approximate information ratio for each manager is:

$$IR_A = 0.03\sqrt{450} = 0.64$$
$$IR_B = 0.05\sqrt{200} = 0.71$$

Manager B's depth of knowledge is greater, which accounts for his greater information ratio.

13. Investors are more risk averse when facing active risk. To obtain an active return—a return higher than a passive benchmark—the investor must accept active risk. To believe that an active return is possible, the investor must believe that there are active managers who can produce it and that the investor will be able to pick those successful managers. Second, an active equity style will also be judged against a passive benchmark. It is difficult to generate alpha and those who don't face pressure from their superiors. Lastly, higher active returns mean that more is invested with the high return active manager, and this results in less diversification.

14. The investor has a core of 15% passive equity and 45% enhanced indexed funds for a total core of 60%. The satellites are 25%, 10%, and 5% around the core.

The investor's active return is calculated as a weighted average return:

expected active portfolio return
= (0.15 × 0%) + (0.45 × 1.7%) + (0.25 × 1.9%) + (0.10 × 3.3%) + (0.05 × 3.9%) = 1.77%

To calculate the portfolio active risk, we use the active risks and allocations:

portfolio active risk

$$= \sqrt{(0.15)^2(0)^2 + (0.45)^2(0.025)^2 + (0.25)^2(0.03)^2 + (0.10)^2(0.055)^2 + (0.05)^2(0.072)^2}$$

$$= \sqrt{0.000226} = 0.0150 = 1.50\%$$

The investor's information ratio is then: 1.77% / 1.50% = 1.18.

15.   The manager's style (as measured by the normal portfolio) underperformed the investor's benchmark by 3% (8% – 11%). But the manager outperformed the normal portfolio by 7% (15% – 8%). We use this true active return of 7% to more accurately evaluate the manager. More formally:

true active return = 15% – 8% = 7%

misfit active return = 8% – 11% = –3%

The true active risk is backed out of the total and misfit risk:

total active risk = $\sqrt{(\text{true active risk})^2 + (\text{misfit active risk})^2}$

5.2% = $\sqrt{(\text{true active risk})^2 + (3.8\%)^2}$

true active risk = 3.55%

The manager's performance generates a true information ratio of:

true information ratio $= \dfrac{7\%}{3.55\%} = 1.97$

16.   To separate the alpha and beta, the investor could pick up the desired beta by taking a long position in a large-cap U.S. equity index futures contract such as the S&P 500 contract. To create the market neutral alpha, the investor would then short a small-cap growth equity index futures contract.

17.   If a high water marks feature is in a compensation plan, the manager must make up poor past performance with superior performance before they receive performance-based compensation. This makes the compensation structure symmetric in that bad performance is penalized and good performance is rewarded. The symmetry of the compensation should motivate the manager to work harder on the investor's behalf.

18.   Castillo is using a top-down approach. She starts at the top of the economy to determine its prospects before moving down to the individual stock level.

CORPORATE GOVERNANCE

EXAM FOCUS

This topic review focuses on implementing an effective corporate governance system that will help align the interests of management and shareholders. For the exam, be familiar with the explicit and implicit incentives offered to managers that motivate them to act on the behalf of shareholders. Understand the role that the board of directors plays in corporate governance, the typical shortcomings of the board, and the suggested prescriptions for improving director oversight. Also, be able to identify and explain additional actions that can be taken to encourage an effective corporate governance system (e.g., active investors, increasing debt).

MANAGEMENT MALFEASANCE

LOS 33.a: Explain the ways in which management may act that are not in the best interest of the firm's owners (moral hazard) and illustrate how dysfunctional corporate governance can lead to moral hazard.

Recent scandals have increased the attention on corporate governance. Corporate governance is the means by which the corporation's capital providers assure a profit on their investment. Although some argue that the corporation has a responsibility to broad classes of stakeholders, the view here is narrower and is concerned with the firm's responsibility to shareholders.

There are two categories of deficiencies in management's responsibility to shareholders: (1) moral hazard problems and (2) dysfunctional responses to those problems by the corporate governance system.

Moral Hazard

A moral hazard can occur whenever there is the opportunity for someone to engage in wrongdoing. In the modern corporation, the owners of the firm often have a distant relationship with the firm's management. This provides managers with the opportunity to engage in self-serving or negligent acts that are contrary to the owners' interests. There are four moral hazard areas: (1) insufficient effort, (2) investment in extravagant projects, (3) entrenchment strategies, and (4) self-dealing.

The first moral hazard problem is that of **insufficient effort**. This does not just refer to the number of hours that management spends at work, but also their effort while they are at work. Managers may avoid unpleasant tasks such as firing labor or monitoring incompetent subordinates. Management negligence may occur because they overcommit to activities outside the firm, such as charities or board positions of other firms.

A second problem occurs when managers **invest in extravagant projects**. There is a great deal of empirical evidence that managers waste shareholder funds on pet projects or building empires. Oftentimes, a firm's stock price drops when an investment is announced, reflecting shareholder skepticism of management's actions. This is particularly a problem when management has excess cash to spend.

The third moral hazard problem concerns **entrenchment strategies** used by managers to keep their jobs. For example, a manager might invest in an industry or product line, which is at best a marginal investment but makes him look indispensable, because he is capable of running it well. The result is job security and added compensation from an investment that adds no value for shareholders. They might also resist hostile takeovers that would result in the loss of their job, even when the takeover would benefit shareholders. Cross-holding of shares in Asia (firms own the stock of other firms) and laws in Europe, for example, have enabled managers to more effectively thwart takeovers. Managers might also engage in activities to make themselves appear competent to shareholders. To do so, managers can manipulate accounting statements, engage in high-risk projects to recoup losses, or avoid taking enough risk when the firm is doing well so as to maintain the status quo.

Fourth, managers can engage in **self-dealing**, which refers to using the firm and its assets for their own purposes. Self-dealing can range from using the company jet for a personal vacation to outright theft of company funds. Other self-dealing activities include: engaging in nepotism; using company funds for a favored political party; leaking firm information for their own purposes; appointing their office with unnecessary luxuries; and consuming other perks at shareholder expense.

Recent scandals have focused mostly on self-dealing rather than the other behaviors, such as insufficient effort, because it is much more visible and easier to prove.

Inadequate Corporate Governance

As undesirable as managerial behavior sometimes is, it is worsened by the fact that corporate governance systems often fail to monitor or curb the behavior. There are four aspects of this problem.

First, there is a **lack of transparency** regarding management compensation. Compensation takes many forms, including salary, perks, and stock options.

Second, the **level of managerial compensation** has grown beyond what many consider reasonable. Others argue, however, that this growth is partly due to performance-based compensation that benefits shareholders.

Third, **managerial compensation is often independent of management performance**. This may be from a poorly designed compensation scheme, management selling their stock before bad news is announced, or because managers receive golden parachutes.

Professor's Note: A golden parachute is a lucrative "retirement package" for managers who are forced to retire or who leave the firm before being forced to do so through a restructuring by the board, takeover, etc. They are intended to reduce the tendency for a manager to "behave poorly" when faced with termination.

Fourth, **accounting manipulations benefit managers** at the expense of shareholders. Misleading financial statements and quarterly reports obscure poor managerial performance, inflate the value of managerial equity, and/or allow the firm to receive additional financing at a time when it should be denied.

MANAGERIAL PERFORMANCE INCENTIVES

LOS 33.b. Evaluate explicit and implicit incentives that can align management's interests with those of the firm's shareholders.

A manager's compensation, including salary, bonus, stock options, and other monetary incentives, creates *explicit incentives* that are designed to motivate the manager to act on behalf of the shareholders. The *implicit incentives* for managerial behavior are perhaps less obvious but no less real. Examples range from the threat of job loss, either at the hands of the board or through a hostile takeover, to losing control of the company in bankruptcy court.

Explicit Managerial Incentives

Executive compensation comes in three forms: base salary, bonus, and stock-based (e.g., stock options). The base salary is fixed for a period of time and is generally not considered an incentive component. The bonus and the stock-based portion are considered incentives, with the stock-based portion the larger of the two. The use of stock-based compensation has grown internationally.

For stock-based pay to remain an incentive, managers cannot be allowed to sell their positions in the firm's equity. Accordingly, managers are often required to hold a minimum amount of the firm's stock and are legally liable, if they use their private information when trading in the firm's stock. Some managers have gotten around these restrictions, though, through the use of equity swaps. The effectiveness of bonuses as an incentive is also limited by the fact that they are usually tied to accounting figures, which are subject to managerial manipulation.

Professor's Note: See Study Session 15 Topic Review 43 for a discussion of equity swaps.

Bonuses and stock-based compensation are complements to one another in the executive compensation package, but they serve different purposes. As mentioned previously, bonuses are based on accounting figures, which tend to reflect the executive's short-term success. Stock-based compensation, especially stock options, are affected more by the manager's longer-term successes.

Regarding the base salary, it is generally agreed that a manager's pay should not be affected by factors outside their control (i.e., external factors such as increases in input prices). To some degree, these shocks are immunized through the firm's risk management system. Some have proposed that external effects could be adjusted by paying a manager less when the firm's competitors do better, although this scheme has rarely been implemented. Other researchers have found that managers are rewarded for good external effects beyond their control but not penalized for bad external effects.

When designing a compensation package, the board must decide on whether stock or stock options should be paid. The advantage of using stock options is that their value depends on the stock price being greater than the exercise price. In contrast, shares of stock provide managers compensation even when the firm is performing poorly. Thus, stock options should provide a greater incentive.

The disadvantage of stock options is that when they are out of the money, managers have an incentive to take greater risks. Thus, managers may take on too much risk in the hope that the options come into the money. Alternatively, management may just leave the firm, if they believe that the chance of the options coming into the money is low.

On the other hand, if the option is currently in the money, it is similar to stock in terms of its incentive effect. The only difference is that the option will provide lower compensation (the stock price minus the exercise price) relative to the stock. Whether or not stock options or stock are the better compensation has not been answered. Some firms, such as Microsoft, pay only stock.

Implicit Managerial Incentives

Implicit incentives should also motivate managers to work on behalf of the shareholders. Implicit incentives include the possibility of:

- Being fired by the board.
- Losing the job due to hostile takeover, reorganization, or bankruptcy.
- Losing managerial freedom with the election of new, independent board members.
- Losing outside financing sources.

Implicit and explicit incentives are typically viewed as substitutes; the greater the implicit incentive, such as threat of firing, the less the need for explicit incentives, such as salary and bonus. There are times, however, when the two types of incentives can be viewed as complements, in that they move in the same direction (i.e., are positively correlated). For example, a confident manager would be willing to accept high performance-based pay (a strong explicit incentive) accompanied by an increased threat of job loss for poor performance (a strong explicit incentive).

Implicit incentives can also be viewed from a somewhat different perspective. A manager with less confidence would be willing to accept less performance compensation (reduced explicit incentive) for increased job security (increased explicit incentive). In this case we look at the promise of job security, rather than the treat of firing, as the explicit incentive and the two types of incentives are substitutes.

In addition to incentives, managers are also subject to monitoring. Large stockholders, such as venture capital firms, pension funds, and mutual funds, will monitor management to protect their investment. Institutions providing debt, such as banks and large creditors, also provide monitoring. Monitoring can be active—the monitor intervenes in the actual management of the firm; or it can be speculative—the monitor uses information about the firm to increase or decrease a position in the firm. By doing so, the speculative monitor (e.g., an institutional investor) can put pressure on the stock price, which can affect the value of managers' equity. Other monitors (e.g., stock analysts) may face conflicts of interest in their monitoring.

 Professor's Note: Conflict of interest is discussed at length in Standard VI: Conflicts of Interest in the Standards of Practice Handbook and in the Schweser Level 3 Study Notes, Book 1. You will also find Standard VI outlined in the Level 3 Standards Pack in Book 5.

A competitive product market will also motivate managerial performance. Not only is the firm compared against its competitors, but managers must also be on their toes to prevent the firm from slipping into financial distress and bankruptcy, where they might lose their jobs. Competition does not substitute for a good governance structure though, as recent firm failures (e.g., Enron) in competitive markets have demonstrated.

THE BOARD OF DIRECTORS

LOS 33.c: Explain the shortcomings of boards of directors as monitors of management and state and discuss prescriptions for improving board oversight.

The board of directors' purpose is to represent shareholders' best interests. They are involved in matters such as managerial compensation, reorganizations, new investments, acquisitions, tender offers for the firm, and audits of the firm. The primary complaint about boards is that they are too close to management to exercise effective oversight of management.

The Shortcomings of Boards

Boards are thought to be ineffective for several reasons. First, boards typically *lack independence*. A board member is referred to as independent if he is not in management or does not have a supplier relationship with the firm. However, many board members are managers, and the chairman is often the CEO. Even those board members that are not managers may owe their nomination to the board to management or have business dealings with the company. Some CEOs even sit on each other's boards, and directors often run in the same social circles as management.

Another problem with boards is that members pay *insufficient attention* to board matters. Many outsider directors are managers of other firms and are too busy to monitor the firm's managers and business. These board members have no time to prepare for board meetings and will often rubberstamp whatever management tells them.

A third problem is that *board compensation has traditionally not been connected to firm performance*. This is changing in the United States, though, as more board members are being paid with stock options. Although board members face a punishment for poor performance in the form of shareholder lawsuits, in reality this is not a strong incentive. Courts are reluctant to judge the fitness of business decisions, so shareholder lawsuits are difficult to win. Directors are also often indemnified from damages. Directors have liability insurance paid for by the firm, and damages not covered by the insurance are often picked up by the firm. The net result is that directors are rarely found liable for nonperformance and, even if they are, shareholder suits are effectively paid out of shareholders' pockets (i.e., by the firm).

Lastly, boards are often ineffective because board members prefer to *avoid conflict*. Even if board members are independent, they still have to depend on management for information and cooperation in future board meetings. Confrontation can create an unpleasant relationship that thwarts this sort of relationship with management.

Bebchuk and Fried (2004)[1] provide a dismal view of board effectiveness. They argue that the majority of boards collude with management rather than monitor them. In addition to the items mentioned earlier, they also discuss how board members receive perks from management. Management makes donations to board member charities, pays extra compensation to the directors, and/or sets up business deals with directors who were independent when brought on the board and remain classified as such. Bebchuk and Fried argue that directors often camouflage management compensation to prevent criticism from shareholders at large. Examples of camouflaged compensation include compensation when a takeover occurs and generous retirement benefits, including consulting contracts.

These problems with boards beg the question as to whether boards have any effectiveness. Boards do fire incompetent managers, as noted previously. They also may side with the bidder in a hostile takeover. Generally, boards become more active during periods of crisis or when the stock price declines. It is at these times when the personal relationship between managers and directors deteriorates, and board members find themselves in the spotlight.

Improving Director Oversight

Though the discussion of board effectiveness is quite dismal, the relationship between the board and management is not as simple as it seems, and the relationship changes over time. The directors depend on management to provide them with information, and they usually work toward the same goals. Asking directors to have a confrontational relationship with managers diverges from the cooperative relationship that is more frequently required. Additionally, paying directors with stock options might encourage them to monitor management more closely, but might also encourage them to take excessive risk, just as it does for management. Likewise, making directors legally liable for their decisions sounds good, but it might provide directors an incentive to behave too conservatively or even motivate quality directors to avoid board membership altogether.

---

1. Lucian Bebchuk and Jesse Fried, *Pay Without Performance: The Unfulfilled Promise of Executive Compensation.* (Cambridge: Harvard University Press, 2004).

In summary, although reform is certainly needed to improve the functioning of boards, the relationship between the board and management is complicated, so reform will not be easily implemented. The following prescriptions have been offered, however, for improving board effectiveness:

[This is a list of some of the prescriptions put forth by the Cadbury Report in the U.K. and by the California Public Employees' Retirement System (CalPERS) in the United States.]

- The board should have an independent chairman.
- The majority of the board should be independent.
- The audit, compensation, ethics, and nominating committees should be dominated by independent directors.
- Some board and/or committee meetings should be held without management present.
- The board should be able to seek outside advice at the firm's expense.
- Directors should be required to hold a minimum amount of equity.
- Director compensation should be equity-based.
- Directors should have a mandatory retirement age.
- Self-evaluations of boards should be done.

Additionally, some have suggested that whistleblowing be encouraged so that directors are better informed. However, employees with such a pattern are stigmatized and may find it difficult to remain employed. Encouraging whistleblowing may also stifle information flow within the firm. Thus, providing whistleblowers with access to the board is most likely to succeed when the whistleblower can maintain anonymity. This occurs when others besides the whistleblower can possess the information, and when the information can be verified by the board without contacting the whistleblower. The board must also be willing and able to follow up on the information.

 Professor's Note: You are probably aware of the Sarbanes-Oxley Act of 2002, which was instituted following the uncovering of various corporate abuses.

Increasingly, various entities (e.g., securities exchanges, regulators) throughout the world have developed professional codes regarding corporate governance. These codes are not binding but increase awareness on the importance of good corporate governance. In contrast, corporate laws concerning corporate charters are binding. There is some controversy, however, as to whether they should be binding since they effectively form a contract between the shareholders and the firm without giving shareholders the right to legal guidance.

ACTIVE MONITORING

LOS 33.d: Discuss why active monitoring by investors requires control, the various mechanisms by which control is exercised, and the limitations of active monitoring.

Active investors push for changes at corporations regarding takeover defenses, board structure, and in other areas. To effect change, however, the **active investor** must have control, and to have control, the shareholder must have either a majority of the firm's shares (*formal control*) or be able to persuade other minority shareholders of their position (*real control*). The latter type of control is influenced by the ability of the investor to communicate with other investors and by agreement of investor interests. Agreement of investor interests is influenced by the active investor's reputation, any conflicts of interest, and how much the active shareholder has invested in the firm. With respect to the last issue, active investors who are willing to buy stock with cash in a tender offer have more credibility than those who do not.

In a proxy fight, an active investor attempts to get herself or her representative elected to the board of directors, or an active investor may use a proxy fight to get a specific resolution adopted by the board. It is called a proxy fight because most shareholders do not attend shareholder meetings. Instead, they authorize another party to vote on their behalf (i.e., they vote by proxy).

Sometimes, just the threat of a proxy fight will cause change. As noted earlier for control, the success of a proxy fight depends on the ability of investors to communicate with one another, and on whether other shareholders trust the activist. It also depends on how costly it is, but recent reforms in the United States have reduced the cost of proxy contests.

The effectiveness of the active investor is influenced by stock ownership patterns, which vary internationally. Individual investors hold larger proportions of firm equity in the United States than do investors in France, Germany, or Japan. Pension funds own more stock in the United States than in France, Germany, Italy, and Japan. Comparing countries of Anglo-Saxon origin to other countries, share ownership is more diffuse, cross-holdings of shares (where firms own shares of other firms) is less frequent, stock market values are higher (relative to GDP), and trading is more frequent.

Takeovers and leveraged buyouts of firms represent another form of investor activism and are thought to increase corporate and macroeconomic efficiency. If managers underperform, they face the threat of firing once the new owners of the firm implement changes. A change of ownership is not always optimal, however, if the new owners operate the firm even more poorly than the previous owners. Additionally, the threat of a takeover may encourage managers to focus too much attention on short-term performance. Managers have been successful in convincing their firms to adopt a number of different takeover defenses.

The Limitations of Investor Activism

Although active investors can push for change, there are limits to their effectiveness. First, active investors themselves are often unmonitored. For example, institutional investors rarely face the same pressure that they apply to corporations. Their compensation is usually based on managed assets instead of performance, they are not subject to proxy fights, and they do not carry debt which, as discussed later, can force corporations to have leaner operations. Furthermore, corporate managers claim that institutional investors do not understand corporate management and that they are too focused on short-term returns.

Second, active investors do not always have the same goals as the rest of the shareholders and may not monitor effectively. The active investor may not wish to offend management when there is some side benefit for them remaining silent. Additionally, if the active investor only has a small portion of the firm's shares, they may not monitor to the extent needed because there is less incentive for them to do so.

Third, institutional investors can always sell their stock if they don't approve of the firm's management. Thus, because they need not be long-term investors, they don't have a strong incentive to push for change. Some argue that if institutional investors had limits placed on the liquidity of their positions, they would be forced to monitor more effectively. Such liquidity restrictions might consist of holdings of private equity, large blockholdings of stock, or resale-restricted stock.

Fourth, there may be negative side effects from monitoring if corporate managers become too focused on short-term performance. If managers become overly concerned with pleasing the monitor, they might lose their objectivity.

Last, there may be regulations discouraging large holdings of stock and, thus, active investors. As noted previously, directors (which large shareholders often are) are legally liable for the board's decisions and, as such, face restrictions on the trading of the firm's stock. They cannot hold more than 10% of the firm's stock without losing their tax advantage.

Professor's Note: Section 16(b) of the Securities and Exchange Act of 1934 requires that any insider, including stockholders with at least a 10% ownership in the company, must pay back to the company any gains on company shares bought or sold within six months of a sale or purchase, respectively, and any stockholder has the right to bring suit for recovery of such gains against any covered individual who does so. In addition, for a mutual fund, pension fund, endowment, foundation, etc., to retain favorable tax treatment, it must hold less than 10% of an individual firm's equity.

DEBT AND CORPORATE GOVERNANCE

LOS 33.e: Critique the effectiveness of debt as a corporate governance mechanism.

Debt as a Management Motivator

We have focused on the role that shareholders play in corporate governance, and we now turn our attention to debt. Although debt has tax advantages in some countries, it also acts as an incentive for management, especially in the case of short-term debt. We discuss four ways in which debt motivates management.

1. Debt takes excess cash out of management's hands. With the pressure to make periodic interest and principal payments, management does not have the luxury of spending cash on frivolous projects and perks.

2. To ensure that the firm has cash flow for future investments after repaying its debt, the managers must assure the firm's liquidity. This is also true if the firm wants to be able to issue debt in the future. The risk of insufficient liquidity provides an incentive effect for management. In a severe liquidity crisis where the firm cannot repay its debt, the firm could be liquidated in bankruptcy proceedings.

3. If the firm lacks liquidity to the degree where debtholders force the firm into bankruptcy, the managers lose control of the firm and possibly their jobs. This occurrence, and the threat of it occurring, provides the debtholders with some influence over manager behavior. Managers also don't want debtholders to gain control of the firm because debtholders seek to limit the firm's risk, which may not be in the shareholders' best interests. Managers will ensure the firm's financial health to limit this potential threat.

4. If managers hold the majority of the firm's equity, then the issuance of debt, rather than equity, means they don't have to share their residual claim on profits. If equity had been issued instead, the managers/owners would be sharing residual profits with other equity holders. By issuing debt, the manager/owners can more clearly see the end result of their efforts, and this will motivate them to better performance.

The Limitations of Debt

Although debt can help motivate management, it does have its drawbacks. First, the threat of illiquidity that motivates management can also deny the firm investment in new projects. The illiquidity may be due to circumstances beyond management's control. For example, a new competitor may enter the market and/or input prices may increase. These external shocks often cannot be anticipated by the firm. Though the firm could issue new securities to mitigate a liquidity crisis, it is at these times that investors will be most reluctant to provide the funds.

Secondly, if the firm is severely liquidity-constrained and cannot pay the interest on its debt, it might be forced into bankruptcy. Bankruptcy costs can be substantial and consist of two cost components, direct and indirect. Direct costs include the administrative and legal fees associated with bankruptcy. Indirect costs result from lost sales, management that is overly conservative, and other costs surrounding the bankruptcy process. Another problem concerning bankruptcy is that it does not actually discipline management to the extent expected. Managers are often able to retain their positions during the bankruptcy process.

STAKEHOLDERS VS. STOCKHOLDERS

LOS 33.f: <u>Explain</u> the social responsibilities of the corporation in a "stakeholder society" and <u>evaluate</u> the advantages and disadvantages of a corporate governance structure based on stakeholder rather than shareholder interests.

For the Exam: Your focus in this LOS should be on the ability to discuss and compare a stakeholder wealth maximization focus and a shareholder wealth maximization focus.

The current and long-standing goal of managing the modern corporation is the maximization of *shareholder wealth*. Shareholders in this case are narrowly defined as the firm's stockholders, so the goal translates into maximizing the firm's stock price. From a socially responsible view, however, proponents suggest the maximization of *stakeholder wealth*. The definition of "stakeholder" can be very loosely defined as anyone who in any way depends upon the firm, and includes employees, creditors, suppliers, and the surrounding communities.

Proponents of the stakeholder society claim that, by sacrificing some short-term profits, being socially conscious translates into increased wealth for shareholders in the long-run. For example, by treating employees fairly with respect to salaries, job security, training, child care, exercise facilities, special family time off, etc., the firm generates a feeling of community within its organization that makes employees feel secure. This community-building within the firm makes the firm part of the outside community and establishes a good reputation. Viewing the firm as a responsible member of the business community, local governments begin to extend tax breaks and other incentives to keep the firm in the area. Creditors are inclined to offer better financing terms, and suppliers are inclined to offer better input pricing and better credit terms.

To advance and secure the relationships among the stakeholder groups, contracts that define the goals and responsibilities of each are required. In addition, representatives of all classes of stakeholders should sit on the firms' boards. One problem with this is that government regulations frequently restrict the ability of the stakeholders to form contracts. Another is the need for each group to thoroughly understand its role as well as the contracts that define it. Frequent involvement of the courts in this process is interpreted as an argument for governmental regulations, which have become more common.

Stakeholder Structure: Disadvantages

There are four primary disadvantages to stakeholder maximization as the goal for the firm: (1) *limited ability to raise capital;* (2) *inefficient decision-making;* (3) *lack of managerial control;* and (4) *inefficient redistribution of taxes.*

1. *Limited ability to raise capital.* Giving operating control of the firm to all the firm's stakeholders could discourage investment. Stockholders (and creditors) may be hesitant to invest fearing that gains must be shared with other stakeholders. The result could be insufficient profits to repay the invested funds plus a reasonable return on investment.

   Due to the reluctance of the outside capital providers to provide the funds necessary to grow the firm, stakeholders should relinquish control of the firm to the investors. The result is shareholder wealth maximization. Under shareholder wealth maximization, investors (i.e., both equity investors and creditors) feel more certain that their interests will be protected and are more willing to invest.

2. *Inefficient decision-making.* Having all concerned parties provide input into decisions may lead to natural impasses. Due to the nature of factors that determine their payoffs, the goals of the stakeholders (e.g., stockholders, management, bond holders) can be at odds. The result is a natural tendency toward an ability to build consensus, which leads to slow, inefficient decision-making.

   Under shareholder wealth maximization decisions are made more easily because management has a single goal. Rather than receiving input from several diverse groups with differing goals, management can focus on maximizing share price and the most efficient way to operate the firm.

3. *Lack of managerial control.* A single goal, such as maximizing stock price, is fairly easily understood and monitored. The set of goals associated with stakeholder wealth maximization, however, is far less concrete (i.e., it can be quite vague) and very hard to monitor. The irony is that by attempting to protect the best interests of all stakeholders, managers are left largely unmonitored.

   The shareholder wealth maximization structure has built-in methods for monitoring management actions. For example, if a manager takes actions that depress the stock price, he is removed. If he violates the debt covenants, bond holders can apply severe penalties.

4. *Inefficient redistribution of taxes.* Taxes are by their very nature a means of redistributing wealth. To realize the best and most efficient redistribution, the funds are typically handled by elected officials who must answer to their constituents for their decision-making. Stakeholder wealth maximization imposes a de facto tax on investors. The proceeds are then redistributed by the firms' managements and boards to their constituents. The argument against this is a lack of evidence that they can do a better job than elected government officials (i.e., that this represents a more efficient redistribution of wealth).

Under shareholder wealth maximization, redistribution of taxes (i.e., redistribution of wealth) is done by elected government officials.

Shareholder Wealth Maximization

- Proponents of shareholder wealth maximization do not necessarily disagree with advocates of stakeholder wealth maximization. Rather they tend to feel that the rights of the stakeholders are better managed through regulations and contracts than through the actions of management. For example, unions are formed to protect employees' interests. Also, rather than rely on management to protect them against actions that would jeopardize their interests, creditors insist on covenants in debt contracts.
- In order to insulate themselves against potentially adverse shareholder actions, creditors usually structure contracts with *flat claims* and *exit options*. Flat claim refers to the fixed amount of the creditor's claim, which is often supported through a claim on collateral. Exit options provide creditors with exit strategies. By utilizing short term debt, for example, the lender has the repeating option to renew the loan or not (i.e., exit). Convertible bonds provide another exit option. If shareholders take actions that generate wealth at the expense of the bondholders, the bondholders become shareholders by exercising the convertibility option.

For the Exam: This material on *stakeholder* wealth maximization was added to Level 3 in 2009. I would not expect significant coverage on the exam, but I would expect a question or two worth three to six points total. One possible form of question is a short essay asking you to describe the difference in focus of the two structures. Another is a question asking you to list and discuss disadvantages of a stakeholder system compared to a shareholder wealth maximization structure. CFA Institute has been trying for years to incorporate material into the Level 3 curriculum on aligning corporate interests and effectively structuring a board of directors. I would, therefore, fully expect that you will see questions on this material as well as the material in LOS 33.g.

THE CADBURY REPORT[2]

LOS 33.g: Discuss the Cadbury Report recommendations for best practice in maintaining an effective board of directors whose interests are aligned with those of shareholders.

The Cadbury Report was prepared by the Committee on the Financial Aspects of Corporate Governance. The committee was established in the U.K. in 1991 by the Financial Reporting Council, the London Stock Exchange (LSE), and the Accountancy profession. The report includes recommendations as well as a Code of Best Practices with accompanying notes.

---

2. From a summary of the Cadbury Report as found in the 2011 Level 3 Curriculum, Appendix 33A, Vol. 4, pp. 353–357.

The Code of Best Practices

1. The board should meet regularly and have complete control of the company and monitor executive management.

2. Top management should be separated so that no one individual has total control. When one person is both president and chairman of the board, the board should be as strong and independent as possible, and the independent element of the board should contain at least one senior member.

3. The board should contain a sufficient number of non-executive members to provide significant influence.

    Discussion. The notes specify that this stipulation can be satisfied with at least three non-executive members. The chairman of the board can be considered among the non-executive members as long as she does not hold an executive position in the firm, but two of the three members should be totally independent. A non-executive board member is expected to provide independent judgment. Independence in this case is interpreted as meaning the individual's decisions are not influenced by the management of the firm or by excess remuneration received for board participation. Because of the unique nature of the chair position (i.e., access to management), it is not considered truly independent of management, even if filled by someone from outside the firm.

4. The board should maintain a regular schedule containing a list of regular matters, such that control of the company is maintained.

    Discussion. Regularly discussed topics should include the acquisition of material assets, investments, risk management policies, authority levels, et cetera. Policies relative to expenditure size should be established to determine when more than one signature is required for authorization.

5. Directors should be able at the company's expense to seek outside professional guidance.

    Discussion. The procedure for doing so should be clearly laid out in the articles of incorporation or in the letter of appointment to the board.

6. The company secretary should be responsible for assuring that board procedures are followed. All directors should have necessary access to the secretary, and the secretary should be removed only by a vote of the board.

Non-Executive Directors

1. Non-executive directors should apply independent judgment.

2. The majority of non-executive directors should be independent from management's influence and have no conflicts of interest.

    Discussion. The board should decide the definition of independence. To maintain the independence of non-executive directors, they shouldn't be paid using performance options and should not be eligible for a pension.

3. Appointment should be for a specified term without automatic renewal.

   Discussion. The letter of appointment should clearly specify the non-executive director's duties and remuneration.

4. The full board should follow a formal policy when appointing non-executive directors.

   Discussion. A nomination committee composed of a majority of non-executive directors should make recommendations to the board.

Executive Directors

1. The shareholders must approve any executive director's contracts in excess of three years.

   Discussion. At the implementation of the Code, this will be enforced upon renewal of existing contracts.

2. Total remuneration, including a breakdown of the types of remuneration, should be disclosed for every executive director.

3. Remuneration should be recommended by a remuneration committee comprised mainly of non-executive directors.

   Discussion. The committee and its chair should be identified in the Directors' Report.

Reporting and Controls

1. The board is to provide a full and understandable assessment of the company.

   Discussion. The wording used is as important as the figures presented, and both positive and negative events should be discussed.

2. An objective and professional relationship with the auditors is to be maintained.

3. An audit committee consisting of *at least three non-executive directors* should be formed, and its authority and duties should be clearly written.

   Discussion.

   - The audit committee should be a sub-committee of the board and should meet at least twice per year.
   - The head of the internal audit committee, the external auditor, and the director of finance should attend committee meetings. Any board member has the right to attend, also.
   - The audit committee should meet at least once per year with the external auditor without any executive board members.
   - The committee should have full authority to investigate matters that fall under its authority. It should have access to any necessary information and the right to hire outside consultants as well as invite outsiders (i.e., individuals not associated with the firm) with relevant expertise.

- A list of the members of the committee should be available in the annual report, and the committee chair should be available to answer questions at the annual general meeting.

4. Directors should explain their responsibilities immediately before the auditor's statement in the annual report.

   Discussion. The directors' statement should state the following:

   - The directors' legal requirement to prepare complete, fair, and accurate annual statements reflecting the firm's condition.
   - The directors' responsibilities to maintain accurate accounting records, safeguard the firm's assets, and prevent fraud or other injuries to the firm.
   - That relevant accounting standards have been followed consistently and reports prepared with reasonable prudence and judgment using fair estimates.
   - Any material departures from applicable accounting standards are disclosed and explained.

5. The directors should file a report on the effectiveness of the internal control system.

6. The directors should file a report that the firm is a going concern and any expectations for change.

   Discussion. The fact that the Committee on the Financial Aspects of Corporate Governance has not provided guidance for 5 or 6 should be stated in the Directors' Report.

Recommendations

- All companies should follow the Code.
- Any listed company registered in the U.K. *must* follow it.
- Reviewed compliance statements are necessary for continued listing on the London Stock Exchange.
- In annual reports after June 1993, listed companies should provide a discussion of how they have complied with the Code as well as cases where they did not.
- Auditors should verify the compliance statements.
- The Code is to be followed by individuals and boards who should ensure that actions meet the spirit of the Code.
- Smaller companies without the necessary resources for immediate compliance may list reasons for that non-compliance, but are encouraged to appoint non-executive board members as soon as is feasible.

For the Exam: You probably have noticed the similarities in the structure of this Code to that of the CFA Institute Code of Ethics and Professional Standards. Since the latter has been tested in item set format for as long as I can remember, I would expect this material to be tested that way, also. As mentioned in a previous "For the Exam" note, CFA Institute has been searching for source materials to include in the Level 3 curriculum for several years that provide a good coverage of the possible shortcomings of corporate governance systems and how to achieve a better alignment of shareholder and board goals. I completely expect that you will see this material on the exam.

KEY CONCEPTS

LOS 33.a

Two categories of deficiencies in management's responsibility to shareholders relate to moral hazard problems and inadequate corporate governance problems.

A **moral hazard** can occur whenever there is the opportunity for someone to engage in wrongdoing. There are four moral hazard areas: (1) insufficient management effort, (2) management investing in extravagant projects that waste shareholder funds, (3) management using entrenchment strategies to keep their jobs, and (4) management engaging in self-dealing—refers to using the firm and its assets for their own purposes.

As undesirable as managerial behavior sometimes is, it is worsened by **inadequate corporate governance**. There are four aspects of this problem: (1) lack of transparency regarding management compensation in the form of salary, perks, and stock options, (2) the level of managerial compensation has grown beyond what many consider reasonable, (3) managerial compensation is often independent of management performance, and (4) accounting manipulations benefit managers at the expense of shareholders.

LOS 33.b

Explicit managerial incentives come in three forms. The base salary is generally not considered an incentive component. The bonus and the stock-based portion are considered incentives. Bonuses and stock-based compensation are complements because bonuses reflect the executive's short-term success whereas stock-based compensation reflects the manager's longer-term successes. Shares of stock provide managers compensation even when the firm is performing poorly. The disadvantage of stock options is that when they are out of the money, managers have an incentive to take greater risks or leave the firm.

Implicit managerial incentives include: the manager may be fired by the board, in a takeover, or in a bankruptcy; new independent board members may be elected that limit managerial freedom; and the firm may lose financing from outside sources. Implicit incentives are usually substitutes for explicit incentives because the stronger the implicit incentive, the lower the need is for explicit incentives. Managers are also subject to monitoring by large stockholders, creditors, and other market participants. A competitive product market will also motivate managers.

LOS 33.c

The shortcomings of boards:
* Boards typically lack independence.
* Members pay insufficient attention to board matters.
* Board compensation is not connected to firm performance.
* Board members want to avoid conflict and thus are ineffective.

Prescriptions for improving director behavior:
- The board should have an independent chairman.
- The majority of the board should be independent.
- Some board meetings should be held without management present.
- The firm should pay for the board if they seek outside advice.
- Directors should hold a minimum amount of equity.
- Director compensation should be equity-based.
- Directors should have a mandatory retirement age.
- Self-evaluations of boards should be done.

LOS 33.d

Active investors push for changes at corporations regarding takeover defenses, board structure, and in other areas by having control either through a majority of the firm's shares (*formal control*) or the ability to persuade other minority shareholders of their position (*real control*).

The limitations of investor activism:
- Active investors themselves are often unmonitored in the case of institutional investors which rarely face the same pressure that they apply to corporations and are too focused on short-term results.
- Active investors do not always have the same goals as the rest of the shareholders and may not monitor effectively.
- Institutional investors can sell their stock if they don't approve of the firm's management, thus there is not a strong incentive to push for change.
- There may be negative side effects from monitoring if corporate managers become too focused on short-term performance.
- There may be regulations discouraging large holdings of stock, thus discouraging active investors.

LOS 33.e

Debt as a management motivator:
- Debt takes excess cash out of management's hands with the pressure to make periodic interest and principal payments.
- To ensure that the firm has cash flow for future investments after repaying its debt, the managers must assure the firm's liquidity.
- If the firm lacks liquidity to the degree where debtholders force the firm into bankruptcy, the managers lose control of the firm and possibly their jobs.
- If managers hold the majority of the firm's equity, then the issuance of debt (rather than equity) means they don't have to share their residual claim on profits.

The limitations of debt:
- The threat of illiquidity that motivates management can also deny the firm investment in new projects.
- If the firm is severely liquidity-constrained and cannot pay the interest on its debt, it might be forced into bankruptcy.

LOS 33.f

The definition of "stakeholder" can be very loosely defined as anyone who in any way depends on the firm, and includes employees, creditors, suppliers, and the surrounding communities. Proponents of the stakeholder society claim that, by sacrificing some short-term profits, being socially conscious translates into increased wealth for shareholders in the long-run. There are four primary disadvantages to stakeholder maximization as the goal for the firm:

1. *Limited ability to raise capital.* Giving operating control of the firm to all the firm's stakeholders could discourage investment.

2. *Inefficient decision-making.* Having all concerned parties provide input into decisions may lead to natural impasses.

3. *Lack of managerial control.* The set of goals associated with stakeholder wealth maximization can be quite vague and very hard to monitor.

4. *Inefficient redistribution of taxes.* In stakeholder wealth maximization, the proceeds are redistributed by the firms' managements and boards to their constituents. The argument against this is a lack of evidence that they can do a better job than elected government officials. Under shareholder wealth maximization, redistribution of taxes is done by elected government officials.

Proponents of shareholder wealth maximization feel that the rights of the stakeholders are better managed through regulations and contracts than through the actions of management.

LOS 33.g

The Code of Best Practices

1. The board should meet regularly and have complete control of the company and monitor executive management.

2. Top management should be separated so that no one individual has total control.

3. The board should contain a sufficient number of non-executive members to provide significant influence.

4. The board should maintain a regular schedule containing a list of regular matters, such that control of the company is maintained.

5. Directors should be able at the company's expense to seek outside professional guidance.

6. The company secretary should be responsible for assuring that board procedures are followed.

Non-Executive Directors

1. Non-executive directors should apply independent judgment.

2. The majority of non-executive directors should be independent from management's influence and have no conflicts of interest.

3. Appointment should be for a specified term without automatic renewal.

4. The full board should follow a formal policy when appointing non-executive directors.

Executive Directors

1. The shareholders must approve any executive director's contracts in excess of three years.

2. Total remuneration, including a breakdown of the types of remuneration, should be disclosed for every executive director.

3. Remuneration should be recommended by a remuneration committee comprised mainly of non-executive directors.

Reporting and Controls

1. The board is to provide a full and understandable assessment of the company.

2. An objective and professional relationship with the auditors is to be maintained.

3. An audit committee consisting of at least three non-executive directors should be formed, and its authority and duties should be clearly written.

4. Directors should explain their responsibilities immediately before the auditor's statement in the annual report.

5. The directors should file a report on the effectiveness of the internal control system.

6. The directors should file a report that the firm is a going concern and any expectations for change.

CONCEPT CHECKERS

1. An analyst is valuing a firm with a great deal of cash on its balance sheet. Management has just announced plans to use the cash for a major project. Why might this firm not be a good investment?

2. U.S. corporate managers are accused of having too strong of a short-term focus. If this is true, what will constitute the largest portion of their explicit incentives?

3. Many regulations are said to have unintended consequences. What would the unintended consequences be if board directors were held legally liable for their decisions? What would the unintended consequences be if managers and board directors were paid in stock options?

4.   All else equal, institutional investors prefer more liquid investments to less liquid investments. Yet a shareholder who holds the same stock as an institution might actually prefer that an institution's holdings are illiquid. **Explain** why.

5.   Debt can limit a firm's liquidity. This has advantages and disadvantages for the firm. **Discuss** them both.

ANSWERS – CONCEPT CHECKERS

1. It is sometimes the case that when management has cash at their disposal, they are tempted to use the cash for purposes that do not enhance shareholder wealth. Management might spend the cash on pet projects or building empires, or they may invest in weak businesses that they are good at, just to make themselves indispensable.

2. Assuming that managers respond to the compensation incentives provided to them, the largest part of their compensation will be that of the bonus if their orientation is primarily short-term. A manager's bonus is based on accounting figures, which may encourage a focus on shorter-term results. In contrast, a manager's base salary is thought to not have an incentive component. Stock-based compensation should provide a longer-term focus and incentive.

3. If board directors were held legally liable for their decisions, they would be more careful about the board decisions they make. However, the unintended consequence would be that the directors might act too conservatively, or quality directors might avoid board membership altogether.

   If managers and board directors were paid in stock options, they would be motivated to work harder for the shareholders. However, the unintended consequence would be that they would be encouraged to take excessive risk. If the options are worthless because they are out of the money, the managers and directors have nothing to lose (as far as the option payoff goes) by taking excessive risk so that the stock price goes up and the options have value.

4. If an institution's holdings were illiquid, then the institutional investor would not be able to sell the stock as easily if they were dissatisfied with firm management. As a result, the institutional investor would be more likely to become active and push for change, thereby increasing the value of the stock.

5. Debt limits a firm's liquidity because the firm must make periodic interest and principal payments. By limiting liquidity, management will not have excess cash to invest in frivolous pet projects or perks. It also forces management to run lean operations so that the firm does not have a liquidity crisis in the future. If the liquidity crisis is severe enough, the managers face the threat of losing their job in a bankruptcy process.

   The disadvantage of insufficient liquidity is that the firm may not have the cash necessary for profitable projects. The illiquidity may be due to circumstances beyond management's control. Although the firm could issue new securities to mitigate a liquidity crisis, it is at these times that investors will be most reluctant to provide the firm with funds.

The following is a review of the Equity Portfolio Management principles designed to address the learning outcome statements set forth by CFA Institute®. This topic is also covered in:

INTERNATIONAL EQUITY BENCHMARKS

EXAM FOCUS

The composition and tracking of international equity benchmarks are discussed in this review. International equity indices have unique characteristics that make tracking them a challenge. For the exam, be able to explain why float, liquidity, reconstitution, crossing, objectivity, and transparency are all critical measures for the portfolio manager to consider. As you read this material, think about how the concepts relate to the emerging markets material in the Level 3 curriculum.

FLOAT ADJUSTMENT

LOS 34.a: Discuss the need for float adjustment in the construction of international equity benchmarks.

> **For the Exam:** Benchmarks continue to be emphasized in the Level 3 curriculum. Questions relating to this material could show up in an equity item set in the afternoon or an equity essay question in the morning. Alternatively, it could show up as an item set or an essay dedicated to benchmarking that includes fixed income and equity indices, both from a domestic and an international perspective.

A problem with equity benchmarks (international or domestic) is determining the capitalized weight of included firms. Oftentimes, the cap weight overstates the true, tradable value of the firm. For example, a corporation might hold a controlling interest in another firm, or a portion of that other firm's shares are closely held. This means that not all the firm's shares are available for trade among investors (portfolio managers). Another example is including two firms in an index, when each holds shares in the other. This "cross-holding" creates double counting when the total values of both firms are considered.

The portion of the outstanding shares of a firm that are actually available for purchase is known as the *float* or *free float*. When calculating the capitalization of the firm in a market cap-weighted index, only those shares that are freely traded should be included. In this fashion, the index reflects the market capitalization that more closely reflects the tradable value of the firm.

 Professor's Note: Float adjustment is important for any international equity index, but even more so in emerging or developing markets. Float percentages, however, are not always easily determined for emerging market companies.

INTERNATIONAL INDICES: TRADE-OFFS

LOS 34.b: Discuss the trade-offs involved in constructing international indices, including 1) breadth versus investability, 2) liquidity and crossing opportunities versus index reconstitution effects, 3) precise float adjustment versus transactions costs from rebalancing, and 4) objectivity and transparency versus judgment.

Breadth vs. Investability

The **breadth** of an index is a measure of its coverage (i.e., the percentage of all firms in the market or sector that are included in the index). Managers prefer greater breadth because the greater the breadth, the better the index represents the market.

Investability is a liquidity measure (i.e., how easy it is for the manager to move in and out of the index components). Managers also prefer greater liquidity due to the costs associated with trading to construct and rebalance a portfolio.

With international indices, liquidity can be a concern because the shares of small-cap firms and firms with a large proportion of closely held shares can be illiquid (i.e., they have very low float). This means international indices face a trade-off; they can increase breadth only by reducing investability.

Liquidity and Crossing Opportunities vs. Reconstitution Effects

Index reconstitution refers to the process of adding and deleting securities from an index. Popular indices (those that are followed widely) are most liquid and generate correspondingly lower transaction costs for portfolio managers following them. **Crossing** refers to the process where a money manager matches buy and sell orders of different customers without using a broker and without incurring the resulting transaction cost.

Liquidity is critical for both program traders and portfolio managers following indices. Program trading (i.e., buying and selling entire portfolios) is performed at lower costs with more liquid index portfolios. Also, portfolios tracking popular indices tend to have lower transaction costs due to the speed and lower transaction costs associated with buying and selling securities in the index.

When indices add a security, they generate upward price pressure on that security. Similarly, deleted securities suffer from downward price pressure. Both of these actions result in a real cost (**reconstitution effect**) for portfolios tracking the indices, as they have to sell deleted securities at reduced prices and buy added securities at increased prices. The price pressure from index reconstitution is lower for less popular indices, but such indices have lower liquidity and lower crossing opportunities.

Precise Float Adjustment vs. Transactions Costs From Rebalancing

Some *index managers* continually adjust the float and resulting market cap of firms in their indices. This "precise float adjustment" results in frequent rebalancing with accompanying high transactions costs for portfolios tracking those indices. Instead of

©2010 Kaplan, Inc.

making precise float adjustments, other indices use a band adjustment. The managers of the index create ranges that they feel capture the true percentage of the firm's market cap that is free floating (e.g., 65% to 85%). As long as the firm's estimated free float stays within that band, they do not adjust the firm's weight in the index.

Objectivity and Transparency vs. Judgment

Objectivity refers to the use of a fixed set of criteria to determine what securities should be included in an index. **Transparency** refers to the availability of those criteria to interested portfolio managers. Objectively (and transparently) constructing an index makes predicting the contents of the index easier and allows for more efficient trading, with lower associated costs.

Using subjective judgment for deciding on index composition (such as a committee for S&P 500), makes the index construction process less transparent. Due to the resulting tendency toward frequent index reconstitution, this imposes additional transactions costs on those who track the index. Note that if the index is popular enough (highly liquid), the additional liquidity tends to offset the lack of objectivity.

COUNTRY CLASSIFICATION: EMERGING VS. DEVELOPED

LOS 34.c: <u>Discuss</u> the effect that a country's classification as either a developed or an emerging market can have on market indices and on investment in the country's capital markets.

For a country "at the margin," classification as *emerging* or *developed* can have significant consequences for both the country and the index of which it is a member. When an emerging country (economy) has reached a considerable size, for example, it becomes a major component in the emerging markets index (i.e., a large frog in a small pond). The overall index, therefore, is unduly affected by this country. That is, due to its size and out-performance relative to other countries in the index, it comprises a considerable proportion of the index, which affects the average size of the countries in the index as well as the average performance. In other words, inclusion of the country in an emerging market index can cause distorted (i.e., upward biased) results.

When the country is moved to a developed market index, it becomes a "small frog in a large pond." Its effect on the index is more in keeping with its economic size and growth and, since developed countries' equities are more widely traded, its stock becomes more readily available for international trading. Thus, the move to a developed index can actually mean the inflow of more international currency, which in turn helps the country develop further.

 Professor's Note: An emerging market index denoted as Free *(i.e., EMF Index) is one in which international investors are not hindered. That is, they do not experience the restrictions (particularly those that apply to currency exchange and movement) that are placed on foreign investors by some developing countries.*

KEY CONCEPTS

LOS 34.a

Float refers to the portion of a company's outstanding shares that is freely traded. International equity markets have large cross-holdings between companies, and many shares are restricted for a variety of reasons. Both of these characteristics cause a reduction in the float. Float adjustment is the downward adjustment of the capitalized weight of companies in an index to reflect the reduced number of shares that are freely traded.

LOS 34.b

Managers tracking international indices need to be aware of four trade-offs:

- Large coverage (breadth of the index) versus the costs of investing in a large number of securities, some of which may be illiquid.
- Liquidity of popular indices versus the cost of altering a portfolio tracking a popular index every time the index is reconstituted.
- Making a precise float adjustment versus the cost of reconstituting a portfolio that is tracking an index that makes precise float adjustments.
- Investing in a popular index, which offers the highest liquidity versus the cost of lack of objectivity in construction of the index.

LOS 34.c

If an emerging country has become too large for an emerging markets index, it will artificially inflate both the average performance and size of countries in the index. When an emerging country is reclassified as developed, the country's equities become more widely traded, which can help increase the rate of development.

CONCEPT CHECKERS

1. Float adjustment is required because of all of the following except:
    A. shares of some companies are closely held.
    B. some markets have a large proportion of cross-holdings of stock.
    C. the breadth of some international equity markets can be extensive.

2. Rob Schweigert is the portfolio manager for an emerging market international portfolio. His benchmark index is MQM emerging markets index. MQM is a relatively new index and has not yet gained wide acceptance. MQM is marketed as a very broad index with 95% coverage of the market. If Rob tries to track the index completely, his portfolio will *most likely* have which of the following characteristics?
    A. Good breadth, good liquidity.
    B. Poor breadth, poor liquidity.
    C. Good breadth, poor liquidity.

3. Allied Metals, Inc.'s defined benefit plan trustees are in the process of selecting managers for the international equity component of the pension fund assets. They hired Excel Advisors, Inc. as consultants to screen all the potential money managers specializing in international equity. The search process yielded Arthur Green and Associates as desirable money managers. Arthur Green, a principal of the firm, made a presentation for the trustees suggesting that the fund try to follow passive investing with broad diversification and low transaction costs and management fees. During the presentation, Green suggested the benchmark for the fund should be the ABT EAE index. ABT EAE index is a broad international equity index with coverage of 65% of the European, Asian, and Emerging markets. This index is very popular and is widely followed. ABT EAE makes precise float adjustments. Other international indices are available that cover 90% of the markets but are not as widely followed and only have broad bands for float adjustments. ABT EAE also selects the constituent securities very carefully utilizing an advanced proprietary model. Other competing indices utilize only publicized market capitalization cutoff rules for selection of the constituent securities.

    In his recommendation of ABT EAE, Green makes two statements that are questioned by the trustees:

    Statement 1: Because ABT EAE makes precise float adjustment, transaction costs will be lower in tracking it.

    Statement 2: The transparency of the ABT EAE is lower, resulting in lower transaction costs due to rebalancing.

    Regarding Green's statements:
    A. only one statement is correct.
    B. both statements are correct.
    C. neither statement is correct.

4.   Sharon Higgins, CFA, manages a GDP-weighted emerging markets index that is used as a benchmark by many portfolio managers. Continually increasing trade in stocks of one of the countries in the benchmark has led her to analyze that country's economy. She has decided to reconstruct the index, including removal of any stocks issued by firms in that country. **Explain** how the performance of a country in an emerging market index can lead to its reclassification and removal from the index.

ANSWERS – CONCEPT CHECKERS

1. **C** Float adjustment is required because of the large number of securities that are closely held and because of cross-holdings of securities. The breadth of the market refers to the number of different firms, not their cap weights, and is irrelevant to float adjustment.

2. **C** Because MQM is a new index and has not yet gained wide acceptance, it probably has poor liquidity. The coverage of 95% means that it has good breadth (high coverage).

3. **C** Both statements are incorrect. Precise float adjustment results in frequent rebalancing and hence *increases* transaction costs. Because the index construction model is proprietary, the index's transparency is low. This actually *increases* the transaction costs because managers are unable to predict index reconstitution.

4. When an emerging economy increases in size to the point where it can be reclassified as developed, leaving it in an emerging markets index can lead to distorted index construction and misleading risk-adjusted performance measures. The now developed economy becomes very large compared to the other economies in the index, which places over-emphasis on the developed economy (i.e., the country becomes a very large component of GDP-weighted indices and portfolios using them as benchmarks).

   At this point, the index can no longer be considered a pure emerging markets index. The average size of the economies in the index is increased, and performance results are not purely those of emerging markets. Whether the nominal performance of the index is positively or negatively biased will depend upon the performance of the other economies in the index relative to the performance of this larger economy.

   The smaller, truly emerging economies in the index should be more volatile than the larger, misclassified economy. Then, since the misclassified economy is considerably larger than the others, the volatility of the index could be negatively biased (reduced) compared to other emerging markets indices.

EMERGING MARKETS FINANCE

EXAM FOCUS

You should know that as a segmented market transitions to an integrated market, developing country equities increase in price and decrease in expected return. An economy can be liberalized but not fully integrated with the rest of the world. The changes that accompany liberalization and the issues unique to investing in emerging markets are also important for the exam.

MARKET INTEGRATION

LOS 35.a: <u>Discuss</u> the process of financial liberalization and <u>explain</u> the expected impact on pricing and expected returns as a segmented market evolves into an integrated market.

Professor's Note: When considering integrated versus segmented, think in terms of the degree to which the individual market is part of and interacts fully with the global market. A completely segmented market could be viewed as standing alone and not interacting with other countries. A fully integrated market would interact freely with global trading partners. There would be absolutely no barriers of any kind that would inhibit free trade. It is clear, then, that few if any countries would be classified as completely segmented or fully integrated.

Financial and Economic Market Integration

In the developmental economics literature, financial liberalization refers primarily to domestic liberalization, which is often characterized by the privatization of firms and bank reform.

In the context of the discussion here, effective financial liberalization and complete market integration occurs when there is unrestricted free flow of capital so that domestic investors can invest in foreign markets and foreign investors can invest in domestic markets. From a finance perspective, markets are completely integrated when assets of the same risk offer the same expected return.

Changes Resulting from Market Integration

The opposite of an integrated market is a segmented market. A market is segmented when capital does not flow freely into or out of it, and foreign investors face restrictions on investing in the country's equities. Segmented markets are more common in developing countries, whereas most developed markets are integrated.

If a market is segmented, its valuation depends on investor risk aversion and the market's expected payoff and *variance*. If instead the market is integrated, its prices depend on its *covariance* with the world market. This is because investors are now able to include the country's equities in a global portfolio, and in a well-diversified portfolio, covariance risk (measured by beta) is the only priced risk.

Professor's Note: When a developing market becomes integrated, its equity prices increase because its covariance with world markets is lower than its stand-alone variance. In other words, holding the country's stocks in a diversified portfolio of global stocks entails less risk than holding the stocks by themselves. There is evidence that emerging markets are at least partially segmented with low correlations with developed markets. Thus, their contribution to portfolio risk is not as great as would be expected from a stand-alone basis.

Equity prices and liquidity increase when the government announces a *liberalization* policy and the greater the credibility of the announcement, the greater the price increases. That is, when the announcement is made, investors analyze both the impact of the liberalization policy and the probability that it will be fully implemented. Initial price increases will benefit local investors only, since foreign investors will only be allowed in the market after liberalization has taken place.

As mentioned above, the expected return for the newly liberalized market should decline due to its covariance being less than its variance. This implies that the *cost of capital* for local firms should *decrease*, which should result in increased economic activity and increased initial public offerings. As a result, competition in the market should increase.

In summary, as a segmented market evolves into an integrated market, equities increase in price as expected returns decrease.

Professor's Note: The comparison of variance and covariance indicates the way the asset is priced by the global market. The more segmented a market, the more it is viewed, and priced, in a stand-alone framework. In that case, the market's required return will be based on its total risk (i.e., variance). Its covariance with the global market (i.e., its beta with the global market) will be low. As the market becomes more and more integrated with the global market, it begins to be valued from (its risk assessed from) more of a global portfolio perspective. Its covariance with the global market increases, evidenced by the increase in its global beta, but its risk is less than when measured stand-alone. Think in terms of measuring required return using σ (CML) and using β (SML). When σ represents total risk, systematic, and unsystematic, the required return using the CML is greater than the required return using the SML.

> **For the Exam:** This material on changes resulting from moving from a segmented to an integrated market is important for the exam. Just remember that the resulting low risk (from a diversification standpoint) is the cause of higher prices and increased economic activity.

MARKET LIBERALIZATION

LOS 35.b: <u>Explain</u> the benefits that may accrue to an emerging market economy as a result of financial liberalization.

Market Liberalization vs. Market Integration

The difference between market liberalization and market integration is that an economy can be liberalized but not fully integrated with the rest of the world due to various impediments. In other words, the two concepts are related but not necessarily the same in the real world. The presence of one does not guarantee the presence of the other. Liberalization is a slow and intricate process. Integration is difficult to measure, and there are various degrees of integration.

For example, a market can be accessible through American Depository Receipts (ADRs) or through closed-end country mutual funds before the government begins the liberalization process. In this case, the market is partially integrated.

Alternatively, the government can begin the liberalization process when the country is not fully integrated. Legal barriers to investment, such as taxes and restrictions on the amount of foreign owned stock, can prevent a market from becoming integrated. Other barriers are less obvious but still prevent foreign investment. These include deficiencies in information, investor protection, and accounting standards. There are also risks specific to emerging markets, such as political risk and liquidity risk, that prevent foreign investment. Research has verified the importance of these barriers and risks to investors, which demonstrates that governmental efforts at liberalization do not ensure market integration.

In addition, although a government may have stated intentions to liberalize a market, their efforts do not immediately become credible with investors. So investors might not immediately invest in the emerging market. Investors might also shun the emerging market because they have a home country bias, where they invest a disproportionate amount in their home market and less in foreign markets.

Financial Effects of Liberalization

The financial changes due to liberalization are reflected in the country's financial markets in the form of its *stock market performance*, *capital flows*, *political risk*, and *diversification benefits*.

Stock market performance. When a country's financial markets are liberalized, global investors bid up the prices of equities previously unavailable to them. After liberalization, stock returns decline, due to reduced capital costs (required returns). These country level results are also confirmed by examining ADR returns, assuming that the ADR listing is liberalization on a small scale.

Liberalization can increase return variability if greater information flow results in greater return reactivity or if speculative capital flows increase. On the other hand, there should not be as much deviation from fundamental value, so return variability may decline. The empirical evidence, however, demonstrates that liberalization does not affect the volatility of returns. Over the long run, return variability should decline as the economy matures.

As the market becomes more integrated, liberalization leads to higher correlations with world markets and higher global betas. The results for volatility, correlations, and beta hold even after controlling for other country events.

Capital flows. Liberalization results initially in increased capital flows into a country and higher stock prices. This can produce lower costs of capital for the country's firms, but it is disputed as to whether the price increases are permanent or temporary. Nonetheless, the presence of reduced dividend yields in developing countries after liberalization suggests that the reduction in the cost of capital is permanent.

 Professor's Note: Assuming aggregate dividend payouts remain about the same, reduced dividend yields would indicate increased prices. This is seen as an indication of permanent reductions in capital costs.

The capital flows themselves first increase sharply with liberalization as foreign investors add the market to their portfolios and then decline (see For the Exam below). Foreign capital is not found to destabilize a country's capital markets. Although the volatility of capital flows tends to increase with liberalization, it is perhaps not surprising given the absence of capital flows before liberalization. Furthermore, capital flow volatility is actually higher in developed countries, relative to developing countries.

For the Exam: Topic Review 24 discusses how macroeconomic stability is important for economic growth, which can result in a favorable investment environment. You should be able to integrate topic reviews 24 and 35 and recognize that capital flows do not become more volatile post-liberalization, even though it is commonly thought that they do. Liberalization can therefore be favorable for emerging market investors.

Political risk. Political risk declines with liberalization. Lower political risk results in higher stock prices because political risk is priced by investors (i.e., a political risk premium is included in firms' required returns). Lower political risk is reflected in part by a government's willingness to open its markets and pursue market-oriented changes such as the privatization of state-owned industries.

Diversification benefits. Despite their higher stand-alone risk, emerging markets offer diversification benefits because of their low correlations with the developed world. These benefits can be obtained by investing in ADRs and open-end mutual funds, and to a lesser extent from investing in closed-end funds. However, there is disagreement among academicians as to whether the benefits still exist after controlling for transactions costs and short-sale constraints.

Liberalization should reduce the diversification benefits from emerging markets, because the markets become more integrated with the rest of the world. However, research has found that the increase in correlations after liberalization is small.

Economic Effects of Liberalization

Liberalization has also been found to have beneficial effects for the economy at large in the form of improved *firm efficiency*, *GDP growth*, and *other macroeconomic changes*.

Firm efficiency. As discussed previously, liberalization should result in lower cost of capital for developing country firms. As more capital is invested in an economy, economic growth should increase. Although some have argued that foreign capital is squandered, it has been found that investment increases after liberalization while consumption stays constant. Furthermore, it has been found that liberalization increases firm efficiency, perhaps due to the improved corporate governance demanded by foreign investors.

Growth in GDP. It has also been found that financial liberalization increases GDP, even after controlling for other factors that could affect growth such as macroeconomic reforms. The relationship between liberalization and growth also holds after controlling for financial market reforms such as the increased enforcement of insider trading laws.

Other macroeconomic effects. Some postulate that the increased capital flows following liberalization results in a "bubble" economy. Contrary to this belief, however, volatility in economic growth and consumption does not increase post-liberalization. In fact, it is found that the volatility of consumption actually decreases post-liberalization.

It has also been found that liberalization is followed by an expansion of trade, less country debt, decreased inflation, and decreased currency volatility.

ISSUES FOR EMERGING MARKET INVESTORS

LOS 35.c: <u>Discuss</u> the major issues confronting emerging market investors, including excess correlations during times of crisis (contagion), corporate governance, price discovery, and liquidity.

It has been found that the actual portfolio allocations of U.S. investors in emerging markets outperform several typical benchmarks. However, investing in emerging markets entails many issues and associated risks that are not present in the developed world. These include *contagion, returns that are not normally distributed, less efficient markets, changes in the cost of capital*, and *weaker corporate governance*.

©2010 Kaplan, Inc.

Contagion. If a country tries to maintain its currency value to a peg while at the same time engaging in lax fiscal and monetary policies, its currency can come under speculative attack. The result is that the currency value declines and foreign investors suffer as the values of their investments decline. Unfortunately, however, it does not appear that currency crises are predictable enough for investors to avoid them.

Contagion occurs when a crisis spreads to other countries. Contagion in currencies may occur for one of five reasons:

1. A country might devalue its currency to keep its exports competitive with another country who devalued.

2. A country might see its exports decline to countries in crisis.

3. The initial devaluation might serve as a "wake-up call" to investors that other countries' currencies have weaknesses.

4. A crisis in one country creates a credit crunch in others.

5. The initial crisis causes investors to liquidate their investments in other countries.

Of these explanations, the first two (trade-based) explanations have the most empirical support.

Although there is disagreement on what constitutes contagion in equity markets, there is evidence that extreme negative movements in one market coincide with the same in others. Note that the mere presence of increased correlations between markets during crisis periods does not suffice as evidence of contagion because correlations increase as volatility increases due simply to the statistical properties of the correlation measure.

Indeed, research has shown that once these properties are controlled for, there was no contagion during recent crises. Other research shows that the July 1997 Asian crisis resulted in contagion, but the December 1994 Mexican crisis did not.

> **For the Exam:** In Study Session 8 Topic Review 27, LOS 27.g, we discussed how correlations between markets can increase during periods of crisis. Be ready to discuss how contagion is possible in emerging markets and how this would weaken the benefit from diversifying into emerging markets. This would most likely appear as a short constructed response question on the morning section of the exam.

Non-Normal Return Distributions

It is well documented that returns are not normally distributed in emerging markets. Furthermore, historical data often contain structural breaks. For example, when liberalizations occur, the pattern of stock returns dramatically changes. If a country is expected to undergo a structural change in the future, then historical data are not very useful for prediction.

Professor's Note: The standard mean-variance analysis, where we find the portfolios with the lowest risk for a given amount of return, assumes that asset returns are distributed normally. The distributions of emerging market stock returns actually have fat tails (leptokurtic distributions), and large negative returns are more frequent (negative skew) than under a normal distribution. This can weaken the case for investing in emerging markets.

Market Efficiency and Market Microstructure

The microstructure of a market affects its efficiency because a condition of efficient markets is that information is quickly reflected in security prices. A microstructure that facilitates efficient markets is one in which transactions costs are low, liquidity is high, and transactions are executed quickly. These conditions should facilitate security prices that reflect the fundamental value of the security and are immune to manipulation by a large trader.

It is usually the case that market reforms will result in a better microstructure. For example, the Moroccan stock market was once state owned. Once the economy was liberalized and the exchange was privatized, liquidity and volume increased. However, this does not mean that bid-ask spreads decrease. In fact, it has been found that spreads actually increase post-liberalization, possibly because new, less experienced foreign investors are exploited by the local dealers.

Market Efficiency and Price Discovery

The efficiency of a market can also be evaluated using the pricing of individual securities. If a market is efficient, information should be reflected quickly in security prices, and differences in expected returns should be solely attributable to risk. In inefficient markets, however, investor reactions to information can seem irrational.

It has been found that security prices do not fully react to publicly released information in Mexico, for example, because there is leakage of information and that information is already partially reflected in security prices when the announcement is made. Furthermore, it appears that foreign investors trade on the information later than local investors, indicating that foreigners are at an informational disadvantage.

Some of the security return patterns found in developed markets have also been documented in emerging markets. The value effect, where stocks with low price multiples (value stocks) outperform high valuation stocks (growth stocks), has been documented in emerging markets. The small firm effect (higher returns for small-cap stocks) and the momentum effect (persistence in returns over time) have also been documented. These return differences are not attributable to differences in risk and exist even after considering transactions costs.

Privatizations and the Cost of Capital

As noted earlier, the cost of capital in emerging markets decreases post-liberalization because security prices increase and expected returns decrease. Likewise, when firms that were formerly government owned are privatized, the government signals its intent to reduce its interference in the economy and investors become more willing to invest in risky assets. Hence expected returns and cost of capital fall in the economy.

Privatizations also increase investment opportunities which allows for better performing portfolios. This also increases investors' willingness to hold risky assets and reduces the cost of capital.

Potentially offsetting these effects, some investors in the developed world exhibit a home country bias where they shun foreign securities, especially emerging markets securities. In this case, the cost of capital will not be reduced as much because the demand for emerging securities will not be as great.

> **For the Exam:** As a Level 3 portfolio manager, you should recognize that a lower cost of capital can result in lower financing costs for firms, greater economic growth, and higher long-run stock returns in an economy. The link between economic growth and stock returns is more fully explored in Topic Review 24.

Corporate Governance

Corporate governance practices vary widely in emerging markets. In most emerging countries, however, corporate governance practices and the enforcement of shareholder rights have traditionally been weak. Although corporate governance practices are improving as more emerging firms seek cheaper foreign capital, the following are some of the negative attributes of corporate governance in emerging countries:

- Management often has greater voting power, and this results in the firm's shares selling at a greater discount.
- The frequency of takeovers that could discipline poor management is negligible.
- Firm shares may be owned by another firm that concentrates control of the firm.
- The government may impose capital controls that benefit favored firms.
- Some countries have strong creditor rights that result in a greater frequency of bankruptcy filings.
- Firms with weaker corporate governance are more likely to suffer during emerging market crises.
- Firms with high degrees of insider control have less CEO turnover after poor performance, so poor management is left in place.

Corporate governance in emerging countries can be improved, however, with the following mechanisms:

- Outside shareholders with a large degree of control who have a strong incentive to monitor management.
- A higher level of debt issued by the firm, especially when it is issued internationally, because debt holders can help monitor management.
- The firm lists its stock as an ADR, which requires stricter adherence to corporate governance standards. This improves firm valuation especially when the firm is domiciled in a country with weak shareholder rights.

- The firm's analyst coverage increases, which improves firm valuation, especially when the firm is controlled by family and management and when the firm is from a country with poor shareholder rights.
- Greater press coverage.

 Professor's Note: Shareholder rights are generally stronger in countries with a legal system established under English common law [this occurs most frequently in countries that were once a British colony (e.g., the United States)].

For the Exam: Be ready to integrate your knowledge of Topic Review 33 on corporate governance with the information presented here, perhaps as part of a short constructed response question. You should be able to distinguish between good and bad corporate governance practices, how some emerging firms are deficient in this area, and how practices can be improved.

Emerging Market Bonds

Emerging market *bond investors* should be aware that defaults are not uncommon. Higher credit risk in an emerging country is associated with lower GDP and higher population growth. Additionally, the correlation between emerging market equities and emerging market bonds is quite high, perhaps because higher credit risk bonds frequently behave similarly to equity.

KEY CONCEPTS

LOS 35.a
Effective **financial liberalization** and complete market integration occur when there is unrestricted free flow of capital so that domestic investors can invest in foreign markets and foreign investors can invest in domestic markets. From a finance perspective, markets are completely integrated when assets of the same risk offer the same expected return.

A market is segmented when capital does not flow freely in or out of it and foreign investors face restrictions on investing in the country's equities. A segmented market's valuation depends on investor risk aversion and the market's expected payoff and *variance*. If instead the market is integrated, its prices depend on its *covariance* with the world market.

Equity prices and liquidity increase when the government announces a *liberalization* policy. Any increase in prices will initially benefit local investors only since foreign investors will not be allowed in the market until liberalization has taken place. The expected return for the newly liberalized market should decline due to its covariance being less than its variance. As a segmented market evolves into an integrated market, equities increase in price as expected returns decrease.

LOS 35.b
The difference between market liberalization and market integration is that an economy can be liberalized, but not fully integrated with the rest of the world due to various impediments. In other words, the two concepts are related, but not necessarily the same in the real world. The presence of one does not guarantee the presence of the other. Liberalization is a slow and intricate process. Integration is difficult to measure and there are various degrees of integration. For example, a market can be accessible through American Depository Receipts (ADRs) or closed-end country mutual funds before the government begins the liberalization process. In this case, the market is partially integrated. Or the government can begin the liberalization process, but the country is not fully integrated.

The financial changes due to liberalization are reflected in the country's financial markets in the form of its *stock market performance*, *capital flows*, *political risk*, and *diversification benefits*. Liberalization has also been found to have beneficial effects for the economy at large in the form of improved *firm efficiency*, *GDP growth*, and other *macroeconomic changes*. Liberalization is followed by an expansion of trade, less country debt, decreased inflation, and decreased currency volatility.

LOS 35.c

Contagion occurs when a crisis spreads to other countries. There is evidence that extreme negative movements in one market coincide with the same in others. The mere presence of increased correlations between markets during crisis periods does not suffice as evidence of contagion because correlations increase as volatility increases due simply to the statistical properties of the correlation measure.

In most emerging countries corporate governance practices and the enforcement of shareholder rights have traditionally been weak. Corporate governance practices are improving as more emerging firms seek cheaper foreign capital.

The efficiency of a market can also be evaluated using the pricing of individual securities. If a market is efficient, information should be reflected quickly in security prices and differences in expected returns should be solely attributable to risk. In inefficient markets, however, investor reactions to information can seem irrational.

A microstructure that facilitates efficient markets is one in which transactions costs are low, liquidity is high, and transactions are executed quickly. These conditions should facilitate security prices that reflect the fundamental value of the security and are immune to manipulation by a large trader.

CONCEPT CHECKERS

1. **Explain** the link between liberalization and a reduced cost of capital in emerging countries.

2. **Discuss** the effect of liberalization on the diversification benefit of emerging markets.

3. **Discuss** the problem to investors of contagion and excess correlation during contagion.

ANSWERS – CONCEPT CHECKERS

1. In a newly liberalized market, the emerging market will be priced according to its covariance risk instead of its variance risk because investors will now be able to include the country's equities in a portfolio. The expected return for the emerging market should decline due to its covariance being less than the variance. This implies that the cost of capital for local firms should decrease, which should result in increased economic activity.

    Expected returns and the cost of capital also decline in newly liberalized countries because political risk declines. When firms that were formerly government owned are privatized, the government signals its intent to reduce its interference in the economy and investors become more willing to invest in risky assets. Privatizations also increase investment opportunities, which allows for better performing portfolios. This also increases investors' willingness to hold risky assets in the country and reduces the cost of capital.

    The presence of reduced dividend yields in developing countries after liberalization suggests that the reduction in the cost of capital is permanent.

2. Liberalization may reduce diversification benefits from emerging markets because the markets become more integrated with the rest of the world and their correlations and betas should increase. However, research has found that the increase in correlations after liberalization is very small.

3. Investing in emerging markets offers diversification benefits due to the lower correlation between developed and emerging markets. During times of crisis in an emerging country a contagion can occur in which the crisis spreads to other emerging countries and neighboring developed countries. During these economic crises the correlation of stock market returns of the countries involved tend to increase at the precise moment when investors need diversification the most (uncorrelated investments). A contagion can take several different forms in which it may or may not spread to other emerging countries or developed countries. Due to a statistical property of correlation as volatility increases correlation will also increase appearing as though the correlation between countries has increased when in fact the true correlation has not increased.

Use the following information for Questions 1 through 6.

Kathy Berg is the private wealth adviser to Caroline Corbin, a woman in her 40s who has recently come into a large inheritance. Corbin feels her age enables her to take on significant risk, so Berg has suggested a fairly substantial equity allocation to the portfolio.

Berg and Corbin have assessed a variety of approaches to equity investing, both passive and active. They have now reached the point of beginning to identify, assess, select, and contract with the appropriate equity managers to implement their strategic asset allocation.

Berg explains to Corbin that she investigated a variety of managers for potential addition to the portfolio stable of managers. She explains, "Managers should be considered on both qualitative and quantitative considerations. Qualitative considerations include the strength of the firm's investment approach and research, the manager's personnel, and the firm's investment style. Quantitative considerations include the manager's fees and performance record."

Berg elaborates that she also considers it important that the manager's style not conflict with her own analytic views. "Since I start my asset allocation process by assessing the overall economy, I don't want our asset managers to make their own economic decisions. I want asset managers who focus on individual securities and don't use overall macroeconomic analysis. I want them to ignore the big picture and start with the top line for the individual company. For that reason, I only considered managers who use a top-down approach to research."

Berg informed Corbin that she initially investigated a wide range of managers and narrowed the field by assessing them with a Manager Questionnaire. Berg provided Corbin with the following list of topics included in the manager questionnaire:

Topic 1:   Staff and organizational structure, including staff resumes and how long the staff has worked together as a team.

Topic 2:   Investment philosophy and procedures, including how it intends to capture alpha, how risk is managed and monitored, and how portfolios are composed.

Topic 3:   Manager performance, including benchmark, expected alpha, and portfolio holdings.

Topic 4:   Competitive position in the investment management industry, including comparative analysis of firm performance against leading competitive firms, decomposed into alpha and beta.

Topic 5:   Fees, including performance-based components, with fee caps and high water marks, if any.

Corbin specifies, "I want to make sure that any manager we consider has a strong performance history. Even though we all know that past performance is no guarantee of future results, statistics show that the managers with the best recent performance are most likely to outperform going forward." She also adds, "We should only hire managers who charge fees on an ad-valorem basis. I prefer to pay for performance and not merely for the value of assets under management."

Corbin asks Berg about implementing an alpha and beta separation in the portfolio. She says, "I want to have exposure to large-cap U.S. equities, like the S&P 500, but I am unconvinced that a manager will be able to add alpha to such an efficient market. Instead, I'd prefer to have the beta of the S&P 500 through a passive index and pick up alpha by hiring a manager who specializes in long-short strategies in a less efficient sector of the market, such as micro-cap equities."

Berg argues against such an approach, pointing out, "The risks in an alpha and beta separation approach are less clearly defined than the risks in a long-only active strategy." She recommends instead that Corbin consider equitizing a long-short portfolio.

1. Is Berg correct in her description of a top-down research approach and of the quantitative/qualitative considerations in hiring an investment manager?
    A. Berg is incorrect regarding only one of the statements.
    B. Berg is incorrect regarding both statements.
    C. Berg is correct regarding both statements.

2. Of the topics in Berg's manager questionnaire, the topic that is *least likely* to be found in a typical manager questionnaire is:
    A. Topic 1, staff and organizational structure.
    B. Topic 2, investment philosophy.
    C. Topic 4, competitive position.

3. Which of the following statements about manager fee schedules is *least accurate*?
    A. A principal advantage of performance-based fees is that they help managers retain staff since they reward good performance.
    B. The principal purpose of a fee cap is to prevent managers from taking unnecessary risk in order to enhance fees.
    C. The principal disadvantage of ad-valorem fees is that they do not effectively align the interests of managers and investors.

4. Is Corbin correct in her descriptions of manager fees and the likelihood that managers who performed best recently will perform best going forward?
    A. Corbin is incorrect regarding only one of the statements.
    B. Corbin is correct regarding both statements.
    C. Corbin is incorrect regarding both statements.

5. Are Corbin and Berg correct in their description of an alpha and beta separation approach?
    A. Both Berg and Corbin are incorrect.
    B. Both Berg and Corbin are correct.
    C. Only one is correct.

6.   Which of the following statements about equitizing a long-short portfolio is *least accurate?*

A. It can be accomplished by taking a long position in an equity futures contract with a notional principal equal to the cash from the short sales.

B. The investor's total return equals the net profit or loss from the long/short position plus the profit or loss from the futures contract, all divided by the equity the investor put up for the transaction.

C. The benchmark for the equitized strategy should be the index underlying the futures contract or ETF.

SELF-TEST ANSWERS: EQUITY PORTFOLIO MANAGEMENT

1. **B** Berg is incorrect about both. A top-down approach to research begins with economic analysis. A manager who considers only the individual securities and not the overall economy is using a bottom-up approach. Qualitative considerations are strength of the firm's investment approach and research and the manager's personnel. Quantitative considerations are the manager's fees, performance record, and style.

2. **C** Topic 4, competitive position, is not typically included in a manager questionnaire. The section not listed in Berg's questionnaire that would usually be listed is resources and research.

3. **A** A principal disadvantage of performance-based fees is that the increased volatility of a manager's compensation can create problems with retaining staff. The other statements are accurate.

4. **C** Corbin is incorrect on both points. A contrarian strategy (e.g., investing in recent losers) often works as well with managers as it does with stocks. Ad-valorem fees are also referred to as asset under management (AUM) fees and depend on asset value managed, not manager performance.

5. **C** Berg is incorrect because the risks are more clearly defined in an alpha and beta separation approach than in a long-only strategy. Corbin is correct that an alpha and beta separation strategy could be implemented by taking a long passive position in an index such as the S&P 500 for beta and picking up alpha in a long-short active strategy in a less efficient market.

6. **B** An investor's total return equals the net profit or loss from the long/short position plus the profit or loss from the futures contract, plus the interest earned on the cash from the short sale, all divided by the equity the investor put up for the transaction. The other statements are accurate.

FORMULAS

portfolio effective duration: $D_p = \sum_{i=1}^{n} w_i D_i = w_1 D_1 + w_2 D_2 + w_3 D_3 + \ldots + w_n D_n$

dollar duration of a bond or portfolio:

$DD = -(\text{modified or effective duration})(\text{decimal change in interest rates})(\text{price})$

portfolio dollar duration: $DD_P = \sum_{i=1}^{n} DD_i = DD_1 + DD_2 + DD_3 + \ldots + DD_n$

rebalancing ratio $= \dfrac{\text{old DD}}{\text{new DD}}$

$R_p = R_i + [(B / E) \times (R_i - c)]$

leveraged portfolio duration: $D_p = \dfrac{D_i I - D_B B}{E}$

target dollar duration: $DD_T = DD_P + DD_{\text{Futures}}$

dollar interest on a repo $= (\text{loan amount})(\text{repo rate})\left(\dfrac{\text{repo term}}{360}\right)$

dollar duration of a futures contract $\left(DD_f\right) = \dfrac{DD_{CTD}}{\text{conversion factor}}$

number of contracts to adjust portfolio $DD = \dfrac{DD_T - DD_P}{DD_f}$

number of contracts for complete hedge $= \dfrac{-DD_P}{DD_f}$

hedge ratio $= \dfrac{DD_P}{DD_{CTD}} \times \text{conversion factor for the CTD} \times \text{yield beta}$

$$OV = \max[(strike - value), 0]$$

$$OV = \max[(actual\ spread - strike\ spread) \times notional \times risk\ factor, 0]$$

payoff to a credit spread forward:

$$FV = (spread\ at\ maturity - contract\ spread) \times notional \times risk\ factor$$

approximate forward premium or discount: $f_{d,f} = \dfrac{(F - S_0)}{S_0} \approx c_d - c_f$

breakeven yield change: $\dfrac{\%\Delta price}{-duration} \times 100 = \Delta y$ in basis points

INDEX

A

active investors 187
active management 12
active management by larger risk factor
    mismatches 12
active return 155
active risk 155
adjusting dollar duration 28
adjustments to the immunized portfolio 22
ad valorem fees 163
advantages of interest rate futures 76
aligning risk exposures 15
alpha and beta separation approach 161
alpha correlations 99, 104
assessing relative value methodologies 59
average absolute price change 118

B

barbell strategy 37
basis risk 79
bond index as a benchmark 9
bond indexing strategies 10
bond portfolio benchmarks 9
bond risk measures 73
bond structures 61
bottom-up approach 55, 164
breadth 204
breakeven spread analysis 96
buffering 147
bullet strategy 37
bullet structures 61
buy and hold 60
buy-side analyst 164

C

Cadbury Report 186, 192
callable bonds 61
call risk 36
cap risk 36
caps 82
cash flow matching 38, 40
cash flow reinvestment trades 58
cell-matching 15
cheapest to deliver (CTD) 75
classical immunization 20
classical single-period immunization 21
combination matching 41
completeness fund 158

conditions for cash flow matching 38
contagion 215
contingent claim risk 36
contingent immunization 33
conversion factor 75
convexity 113
core-satellite approach 156
corporate governance 217
covered call 82
covered interest arbitrage 92
credit analysis 62, 87, 103
credit default swaps 85, 102
credit-defense trades 58
credit derivative instruments 84
credit forwards 85
credit options 84
credit risk 14
credit spread options 84
credit spread risk 83
credit swaps 85
credit-upside trades 57
cross hedging 79, 92
crossing 204
currency selection 87, 103
cyclical changes 56, 64

D

default risk 83
developed market 205
dollar duration 26, 76
dollar duration of a futures contract 78
downgrade risk 83
duration 16
duration contribution 25, 89
duration management 87, 103

E

early retirement provisions 61
economic effects of liberalization 214
effective duration 24
effect of leverage on duration 70
emerging market 205
emerging market debt 97
enhanced indexing 153
enhanced indexing by matching primary risk
    factors 11
enhanced indexing by small risk factor
    mismatches 12
equal-weighted index 132

Notes

Notes

Notes

Notes

Notes

Notes

Notes

Notes